I0005275

Structure and Inference in Classical Planning

Nir Lipovetzky
University of Pompeu Fabra

Published by

AI Access

AI Access is a not-for-profit publisher with a strong scientific board that publishes open access monographs and collected works. Our text are available electronically for free and in hard copy at close to cost. We welcome proposals for new texts.

©Nir Lipovetzky 2014

ISBN 978-1-312-46621-0

AI Access
Managing editor: Toby Walsh
Monograph editor: Kristian Kersting
Collected works editor: Pascal Poupart
URL: aiaccess.org

To my family

Acknowledgements

This thesis is only possible thanks to the contributions and support of many people. First I would like to express my gratitude to my PhD advisor Hector Geffner, whom with endless patience guided me into this work, always inspiring and encouraging me. I'm forever in debt with him. As a fellow PhD student said, nothing could be more inspiring than taking a short walk to Hector's office. He went far beyond my expectations, both as a researcher and as a person, I could not have wished a better supervisor, I feel privileged to have been his student for the past five years.

The endless nights before conference deadlines could not have been tolerable without the support of my office mates and friends Alexandre Albore, Emil Keyder, Miquel Ramirez and Hector Palacios.

The planning community is remarkable. I had the pleasure to meet, share thoughts and learn through various summer schools from Carmel Domshlak, Jörg Hoffmann, Blai Bonet and Malte Helmert. I had fruitful discussions with many other researchers throughout the conferences, and shared a wonderful time with many people. I should also say, that not a single planner I programmed would have been possible without the kindness of Miquel Ramirez, Malte Helmert, and Jörg Hoffmann, who shared their codes and thoughts on the practical issues of planning.

Of course, life is much better with all the friends that make you feel home, everybody with something unique. Melbourne it is especially beautiful thanks to Tanita's love, the purest human being, and the warmest and most generous soul.

A truly thank goes to my parents and sister, what can I say about them without falling short. Since I have memories they always gave me everything they had, and I can tell I have a surplus of affection by now. My parents have led the way to most of the pleasures of life I enjoy, their kindness, their righteous attitude, their support, everything has been an example for me.

Abstract

Classical planning is the problem of finding a sequence of actions for achieving a goal from an initial state assuming that actions have deterministic effects. The most effective approach for finding such plans is based on heuristic search guided by heuristics extracted automatically from the problem representation. In this thesis, we introduce alternative approaches for performing inference over the structure of planning problems that do not appeal to heuristic functions, nor to reductions to other formalisms such as SAT or CSP. We show that many of the standard benchmark domains can be solved with almost no search or a polynomially bounded amount of search, once the structure of planning problems is taken into account. In certain cases we can characterize this structure in terms of a novel width parameter for classical planning.

Preface

The classical planning problem consists of finding a sequence of actions, a plan, that maps a given initial state of the world into a goal situation. The problem can be cast as a path finding problem in an implicitly defined directed graph, whose nodes represent states, and whose edges represent the state transitions made possible by the actions. A domain-independent planner searches for a path in the graph connecting the initial state to a state satisfying the goal condition, given a compact representation of the planning problem.

Heuristic Search is the dominant approach in classical planning. In order to guide the search for a solution, heuristic search planners use a heuristic function that estimates the cost of reaching the goal of the problem from any given state. Heuristic functions derived from a simplified (relaxed) version of the original problem, introduced by McDermott (1996); Bonet et al. (1997), improved significantly the scalability of domain-independent planners. State-of-the-art heuristic search planners such as FF (Hoffmann and Nebel, 2001) and LAMA (Richter and Westphal, 2010), go beyond the choice of the search algorithm and the heuristic function, and incorporate a variety of search enhancements such as helpful actions, landmarks and multiple queues for combining various heuristic functions.

Satisficing classical planning in the worst case is PSPACE-complete, even when no guarantee on the optimality of the solution is given. Still as Bylander (1994) said:

> If the relationship between intelligence and computation is taken seriously, then intelligence cannot be explained by intractable theories because no intelligent creature has the time to perform intractable computations. Nor can intractable theories provide any guarantees about the performance of engineering systems.

Current planners solve most existing benchmark domains in a few seconds (Hoffmann and Nebel, 2001; Richter and Westphal, 2010), after *quickly exploring many of the states in the problem*. Their performance has been improved by devising new search algorithms, and new heuristic estimators. On the other hand, *simple* problems that should be solved with almost no search, still require the planners to perform extensive search before finding a solution. Consider for example a known variation of the Blocks World domain, Tower-n, where n blocks on the table must be arranged in a single tower with block i on top of block $i + 1$. The actions available are to pick up and put down one block at a time. This problem does not feature a complex combinatorial structure such as

Rubik's cube or the 15-puzzle; a simple solution consists of stacking first block $n-1$ on top of block n, then the block $n-2$ on top of block $n-1$, etc. In such problems, planners should be able to find a solution without extensive search. In contrast, a state-of-the-art planner like FF (Hoffmann and Nebel, 2001), still needs to explore a significant part of the state space before finding a solution. Moreover, a slight variation of the same problem, where initially all blocks are on the table but block n, which is on top of block 1, may cause the planner even to fail. Instead of improving performance of planners in such problems using better heuristic estimators, in this thesis we explore alternative approaches to perform inference over the *structure of planning problems* along with novel search algorithms that exploit such structure. We show that problems like Tower-n can be solved with no search, by means of cost effective domain independent inferences.

In the first part of the dissertation we review the classical planning model and the main computational approach to classical planning. In the second part, we develop an inference scheme, in the context of forward-state search, that does not appeal to a heuristic function but to the notion of *causal links*, originally used in the context of partial order planning (Tate, 1977; McAllester and Rosenblitt, 1991). We show that by exploiting the semantics of causal links, we are able to propagate information along sequences of causal links $a_0, p_1, a_1, p_2, a_2, \ldots, p_n, a_n$ and show that some of such sequences are impossible to hold in any valid plan. The information encoded by such sequences is exploited in different ways, resulting in a planner that solves most of the benchmarks with almost no search.

To explore the synergy between different type of inferences, we also formulate and test a new dual search architecture for planning based on the idea of *probes*: single action sequences computed without search from a given state that can quickly go deep into the state space, terminating either in the goal or in a failure. We show experimentally that by designing these probes carefully using a number of existing and new polynomial inference techniques, most of the benchmarks can be solved with a single probe from the initial state, with no search. Moreover, by using one probe as a lookahead mechanism from each expanded state in a standard greedy best-first search, we show that we can solve as many problems as state-of-the-art planners. The resulting planner PROBE, presented in the International Planning Competition 2011 (IPC-7), was the second best planner in terms of the quality of the first solution found.

In the third part of the dissertation, we present a new type of parameter that bounds the complexity of a planning domain. Through this new parameter, we develop an approach to recognize and exploit the *structure of planning problems*. Specifically, we present two *blind search algorithms* that by only exploiting the structure of the problem, with no heuristic estimator at all, perform as well as baseline heuristic search planners. Finally, we show how the key ideas for exploiting this new parameter can be integrated in a standard best-first search algorithm along with other inferences such as helpful actions and landmarks, yielding a new state-of-the-art planner.

The work presented in this thesis has been published in the following articles:

- Nir Lipovetzky and Hector Geffner. *Inference and Decomposition in Planning*

Using Causal Consistent Chains. In *Proceedings of the 19th International Conference on Planning and Scheduling (ICAPS-09)*, pages 159–166. AAAI Press, 2009. [Chapter 3 and 2]

- Nir Lipovetzky and Hector Geffner. *Path-Based Heuristic (Preliminary Version).* In *Proceedings of the ICAPS-09 Workshop on Heuristics for Domain-Independent Planning (HDIP-09)*, 2009. [Section 3.3]

- Nir Lipovetzky and Hector Geffner. *Searching for Plans with Carefully Designed Probes.* In *Proceedings of the 21st International Conference on Planning and Scheduling (ICAPS-11)*, pages 154–161. AAAI Press, 2011. [Chapter 4]

- Nir Lipovetzky and Hector Geffner. *Searching with Probes: The Classical Planner PROBE.* In *Proceedings of the 7th International Planning Competition (IPC-7)*, pages 71–74, 2011. [Chapter 5]

- Nir Lipovetzky and Hector Geffner. *Width and Serialization of Classical Planning Problems.* In *Proceedings of the 20st European Conference on Artificial Intelligence (ECAI 12)*, pages 540 545, 2012. [Chapter 6 to 9]

This monograph of my PhD thesis is published by AI Access

Contents

Part I

Background

Chapter 1

Classical Planning

Había aprendido sin esfuerzo el inglés, el francés, el portugués, el latín. Sospecho, sin embargo, que no era muy capaz de pensar. Pensar es olvidar diferencias, es generalizar, abstraer. En el abarrotado mundo de Funes no había sino detalles, casi inmediatos.

Without effort, he had learned English, French, Portuguese, Latin. I suspect, nevertheless, that he was not very capable of thought. To think is to forget a difference, to generalize, to abstract. In the overly replete world of Funes there were nothing but details, almost contiguous details.

Funes el Memorioso.
Jorge Luis Borges

In this chapter we review the classical planning model and the STRIPS factored representation. We then review the main computational approach to classical planning, and present its standard algorithms, heuristics and other techniques.

1.1 Introduction

Classical planning is the problem of finding a sequence of actions that maps a given initial state to a goal state, where the environment and the actions are deterministic. The computational challenge is to devise effective methods to obtain such action sequences called plans. The last two decades have brought significant advances in classical planning (Kautz and Selman, 1996; Blum and Furst, 1995; Bonet and Geffner, 2001) with the heuristic search approach begin the most successful (i.e. using heuristic search algorithms on the underlying state model guided by heuristic estimators extracted automatically from the classical problem).

1.2 Model and Factored Representation

A classical planning problem can be understood as a path-finding problem in a directed graph whose nodes represent states, and whose edges represent actions that change the state represented by the source node of the edge, to the state represented by the target node. A plan, the sequence of actions that transform the initial state into a goal state, can be understood as a path from the initial node in the graph to a node whose state is one of the goal states of the problem. The formal model underlying a classical planning problem can be described as follows:

Definition 1.1 (Classical Planning Model). *A planning model* $\Pi = \langle S, s_0, S_G, A, f \rangle$ *consists of:*

- *A finite and discrete set of states S, i.e., the state space,*

- *An initial state $s_0 \in S$,*

- *A set of goal states $S_G \in S$,*

- *A set of actions A,*

- *The actions applicable $A(s) \subseteq A$ in each state $s \in S$, and*

- *The deterministic transition function $s' = f(s, a)$ for $a \in A(s)$.*

The state resulting from an action a applied in a state s is $f(s,a)$, also denoted as $s[a]$. The application of a sequence of actions to a state can be defined recursively as

$$
\begin{aligned}
s[\epsilon] &= s \\
s[a_0, \ldots, a_n] &= (s[a_0, \ldots, a_{n-1}])[a_n]
\end{aligned}
$$

A classical plan π is a sequence of actions $\pi = a_0, \ldots, a_n$ that generates a sequence of states $s_0, \ldots, s_{n+1}$, such that $a_i \in A(s_i)$ is applicable in s_i, results in state $s_{i+1} = f(s_i, a_i)$, and $s_{n+1} \in S_G$ is a goal state. That is, the sequence of actions π is a plan if $s_0[\pi] \in S_G$.

In the presence of a cost function that maps each action in the model to a non-negative cost, plans with lower cost are preferred, where the cost of a plan π is defined as the sum of the cost of its actions:

$$
cost(\pi) = \sum_{i=1}^{n} c(a_i)
$$

A plan is said to be *optimal* if it has minimum cost among all possible plans achieving a goal state. If a cost function is not defined, actions are assumed to have uniform cost, i.e. each action is assumed to have a cost of 1, and plans of lower length are preferred to those with higher length.

In large problems, explicitly enumerating the state space is not feasible. In this case, *factored* representations are used in which states are complete assignments to a set of variables whose domains are finite and discrete. The conditions and effects of actions, the applicability function, and the transition function are also defined in terms of these variables.

The most common representation in planning appeals to boolean variables known as *fluents*, *facts* or *atoms*, whose domain are the values *true* or *false*, stating whether a proposition about the world holds in a given state. This representation is known as STRIPS (Fikes and Nilsson, 1971).

Definition 1.2 (STRIPS). *A planning problem in* STRIPS, $\Pi = \langle F, O, I, G \rangle$ *consists of:*

- *A set of boolean variables (fluents, facts or atoms) F,*

- *A set of tuples O representing operators, each having the form $\langle Pre(o), Add(o),$ $Del(o)\rangle$, where $Pre(o)$, $Add(o)$, $Del(o) \subseteq F$*

- *A set $I \subseteq F$, describing the initial state*

- *A set $G \subseteq F$, describing the set of goal states.*

The state space model underlying the classical planning problem is implicitly described by the STRIPS factored representation. Each state $s \in S$ is a subset $s \subseteq F$ of the set of fluents in which the facts $p \in s$ have the value *true*, while the facts $p' \in F \setminus s$ are assumed to be *false* [1]. Then, I describes the initial state s_0, and G describes the set of goal states $S_G = \{s \mid G \subseteq s\}$. The applicable actions in a given state s are $A(s) = \{o \mid Pre(o) \subseteq s\}$ the actions whose preconditions are true in s, and the transition function $f(s, o) = (s \cup Add(o)) \setminus Del(o)$ progress a state s with operator o by setting the propositions in $Add(o)$ to *true* and the propositions in $Del(o)$ to false, which corresponds to adding the propositions $Add(o)$ to s and subtracting the ones in $Del(o)$.

An action sequence $\pi = a_0, \ldots, a_n$ is a classical plan if each action a_i is applicable in s_i, i.e., $Pre(a_i) \subseteq s_i$, and the state resulting from the application of the plan from the initial state $s_o = I$ contains the goal fluents $G \subseteq s[\pi] \in S_G$.

Most work in classical planning has been done for problems expressed in STRIPS. More recently, however, the Planning Domain Definition Language, PDDL (McDermott et al., 1998), has become a standard, as it is the language for the International Planning Competitions (IPC) (McDermott, 2000; Bacchus, 2001; Fox and Long, 2003; Hoffmann and Edelkamp, 2005; Gerevini et al., 2009; Helmert et al., 2008; Olaya et al., 2011). PDDL represents STRIPS problems as well as extensions to STRIPSin a first-order language with a finite number of predicates, variables and constants. Classical planners (systems that solve the planning problem) *ground* the actions defined in PDDL, i.e. they transform predicates, variables, and constants into a propositional representation like STRIPS.

Other factored representations have been proposed, such as SAS^+ (Bäckström and Nebel, 1995), which describes the planning problem in terms of variables

---

[1] It corresponds to the *closed world assumption*, in which any fact not mentioned in the initial state is assumed to be false

with domains of finite size, known as multivalued variables. Only STRIPS representation is used in this dissertation and we do not discuss further representations.

Blocks World Domain To illustrate the PDDL language, consider the *Blocks World* domain. Blocks World is a planning domain that consists of stacking towers made of a finite number of blocks, from one initial situation into a desired one. All blocks are either on the table, held by a single arm, or on top of another block. The actions available for the single arm are to pick up a block from the table, to unstack and hold a block that is on top of another block, to put down on the table the block the arm is holding, and to stack the block held by the arm on top of another block. A description in PDDL of the Blocks Word domain is shown in Figure 1.1.

Many examples in this thesis will make use of simple Blocks World instances to illustrate and help elucidate the ideas that will be presented. Though it has little practical significance, this domain has been widely used in AI planning over the last 30 years. Moreover, domain-independent planners until the late 90's could not solve problems even with very few blocks. This domain offers a crisp, clear and simple setting in which to understand the techniques that planning systems employ. A thorough analysis of Blocks World has been carried out by Slaney and Thiébaux (2001), where they enhance the understanding of the complexity of Blocks World problems.

1.2.1 Complexity

Given a classical planning problem Π in its factored representation, the decision problem PlanExt(Π) is defined by the question: *does a plan π for Π exist?* and the decision problem PlanCost(Π, k), given a positive real constant value k, is defined by the question: *does a plan π for Π with $cost(\pi) < k$ exist?* Both decision problems are PSPACE-complete (Bylander, 1994), and since theoretically in the worst-case planning problems are intractable, planning approaches are generally assessed in terms of their practical performance on a set of benchmarks, regardless of their worst-case guarantees.

Computational approaches to classical planning differ if a guarantee on the optimality of the solution is needed (PlanCost(Π, k)). If the algorithm is concerned instead with finding a plan without an optimality guarantee, trading plan quality for speed, the problem is known as *satisficing classical planning* (PlanExt(Π)).

1.3 Planning as Heuristic Search

Given that the state space S of classical planning problems Π can be understood as directed graphs whose nodes represent states, and whose edges represent actions, any graph-search algorithm can be used in order to find a plan, a path from the initial state to a goal state in the graph. Yet, blind search algorithms such as Dijkstra (Cormen et al., 2001) do not scale up due to the size of the

```
(define (domain BLOCKS)
  (:requirements :strips :typing :equality)
  (:types block)
  (:predicates (on ?x ?y - block) (ontable ?x - block) (clear ?x - block)
               (handempty) (holding ?x -block))

  (:action pick-up
     :parameters (?x - block)
     :precondition(and (clear ?x) (ontable ?x) (handempty))
     :effect (and (not (ontable ?x)) (not (clear ?x)) (not (handempty))
     (holding ?x))
  )

  (:action put-down
     :parameters (?x - block)
     :precondition (holding ?x)
     :effect (and (not (holding ?x)) (clear ?x) (handempty) (ontable ?x))
  )

  (:action stack
     :parameters (?x ?y - block)
     :precondition (and (holding ?x) (clear ?y) (not (= ?x ?y)))
     :effect (and (not (holding ?x)) (not (clear ?y)) (clear ?x) (handempty)
                  (on ?x ?y))
  )

  (:action unstack
     :parameters (?x ?y - block)
     :precondition (and (on ?x ?y) (clear ?x) (handempty) (not (= ?x ?y)))
     :effect (and (holding ?x) (clear ?y) (not (clear ?x)) (not (handempty))
   (not (on ?x ?y)))
  )
)
...
(define (problem blocks-sussman)
(:domain BLOCKS)
(:objects A B C - block)
   (:init (clear C) (clear B) (ontable B) (ontable A) (on C A) (handempty))
   (:goal (and (on A B) (on B C)))
)
```

Figure 1.1: PDDL encoding of the famous Sussman anomaly instance of the Blocks World domain.

state space S, which can be exponential to the number of fluents of the problem Π. On the other hand, heuristic search algorithms have been proven to perform effectively, provided they use a heuristic function sufficiently informed to guide the search.

Indeed, the most successful planners from previous International Planning Competitions use this approach (Bonet and Geffner, 2001; Hoffmann and Nebel, 2001; Helmert, 2006; Richter and Westphal, 2010). Since the first heuristic search planner HSP (Bonet and Geffner, 1999) appeared, many heuristic functions have been proposed that improve their accuracy. The gap on performance with present planners, however, seems to be more related to search enhancements included in later systems. In the remainder of the section, we briefly review heuristics and search algorithms, along with the search enhancements that state-of-the-art systems use.

1.3.1 Heuristic Search Algorithms

Heuristic search algorithms use a heuristic estimator to guide the search in a graph for a path from the initial node to a goal node. Given a classical planning problem $\Pi = \langle F, I, O, G \rangle$, the path takes the form of a sequence of actions that reach a goal node from the initial situation. The state space of the problem explored by the algorithm is represented by nodes n, which are structures that contain the state $s \subseteq F$ description along useful information, such as the action used to reach the state in order to recover recursively the path up to the initial state, the cost of the complete path leading to s, and the value of the evaluation function used to ranks nodes. For simplicity we hereafter refer to nodes and states indistinctly.

The algorithms we discuss next perform forward search in the state space induced by the planning problem Π. We discuss two of the most successful algorithms in *satisficing classical planning*, used by most of the high performance planners, and with which we compare in the experiments shown throughout the thesis. The first one is the family of search algorithms known as *best-first search* and the second is *enforced hill-climbing*.

Best-First Search

Best-first search (BFS) algorithms use two distinct sets of nodes for storing search nodes, the *closed list* and the *open list*, where nodes are sorted according to the evaluation function. Nodes that have not yet been expanded, i.e., those whose successors have not yet been generated, are placed in the open list. Nodes which have been already expanded are placed in the closed list. Intuitively, the state space explored so far by the algorithm can be understood as a tree whose leaf nodes (search frontier) are in the open list, and the inner nodes are in the closed list. Thus, the choices of the algorithm are to select iteratively which node in the open list (frontier) to expand next. Once a node from the open list is selected, the node is moved to the closed list (inner nodes) and its successors are generated. The successors are then evaluated through the heuristic estimator and inserted into the open list, as all these nodes belong to the search frontier. If a node n

from the open list is selected for expansion and the goal G is true in n, the path is retrieved up to the initial node and the solution is returned. The algorithms below differ in how they select the next node to be expanded, and how they treat duplicated states. Best-first search algorithms rank all nodes in the open list according to some evaluation function $f(n) = z \cdot g(n) + w \cdot h(n)$, which is typically a linear combination of the accumulated cost $g(n)$ up to node n, and the estimated cost of reaching the goal from n according to the heuristic estimator $h(n)$ used by the algorithm (Pearl, 1983). The node to expand next is the one with minimum $f(n)$. The following algorithms differ in the value they assign to the constant values z and w, changing the properties of the search. In the simplest case where $z = 1, w = 0$, the resulting search algorithm is the blind (uninformed) uniform-cost search [1] or breadth-first search if costs are uniform, where the current shortest path in the search is always expanded first without taking into account the heuristic value. As the search space induced by classical planning problems is finite, best-first search algorithms are complete since eventually they will exhaust the search space.

Greedy Best-First Search. The first variant heuristic search algorithm is greedy best-first search (GBFS), using the constants $z = 0, w = 1$ rendering the evaluation function to be $f(n) = h(n)$ (Pearl, 1983). It always expands first the node with the lowest heuristic value in the open list, the one whose estimated cost to the goal is lower according to the heuristic estimator. Greedy best-first search is called greedy, because it only pays attention to getting closer to the goal, no matter how expensive the paths to the goal are. Therefore, when a duplicated node is generated, i.e., the node resulting from an expansion is already in the closed or open list, it is simply deleted. GBFS does not take into account path length $g(n)$ in $f(n)$, and a shorter path is considered to be the same as a longer one. GBFS is widely used in *satisficing classical planners*, also throughout this thesis, as GBFS trades solution quality for speed, generally finding solutions faster than other variants of BFS.

A^* **and Weighted** A^* The A^* algorithm uses the constants $z = w = 1$, expanding first the node in the open list that minimizes the evaluation function $f(n) = g(n) + h(n)$. If more than one node has the same $f(n)$ value, it prefers the one with the lowest distance to the goal $h(n)$ (Hart et al., 1968). A^* is typically used in optimal classical planning along heuristic estimators that satisfy some properties. Given a *consistent* and *admissible* heuristic estimator that satisfies $h(n) \leq cost(a_{n'}) + h(n')$ for all n and n', where $cost(a_{n'})$ is the cost of the action leading to n' from n; the algorithm does not ever need to *re-expand* a node to guarantee *optimality*, and therefore duplicate nodes are deleted directly. When an *inconsistent* but *admissible* heuristic estimator is used, where previous inequality does not hold but still $h(n) \leq h^*(n)$ [2] for all nodes n, the algorithm still can guarantee optimal solutions. If a previously expanded node is reached through a different path with lower accumulated cost $g(n)$, the new value $g(n)$ is propagated to the successors

---

[1] Uniform cost is a variant of Dijkstra where only the shortest paths up to a goal node are expanded instead of the shortest paths to all nodes   [2] h^* maps any state to the optimal solution from that state.

already generated in the search tree. A deeper discussion about A^* optimality can be found in Dechter and Pearl (1985).

An alternative to A^* is WA^*, that trades solution quality for speed by weighting the heuristic value $h(n)$ with a factor $w > 1$ (Pohl, 1970). As $z = 1$, the evaluation function becomes $f(n) = g(n) + w \cdot h(n)$. The larger the value of w is, the more greedily the search algorithm acts, and pays more attention to minimizing the distance to the goal $h(n)$ than the distance up to the node $g(n)$. The use of a large w factor generally results in a speed up, finding solutions faster but without any optimal guarantee, as $w > 1$ makes the heuristic estimator inadmissible. Nevertheless, the ratio between the solution cost found by WA^* and the optimal solution is bounded by w. This property is exploited by *anytime planners* that do not stop after the first solution. They search initially with a high value of w, and once a solution is found and time is still left, the search is started again but with lower w values until $w = 1$, using previous solutions to bound the depth of subsequent searches (Richter et al., 2010). Anytime planners have become common in the last two International Planning Competitions (2008 and 2011 IPC) where a window of 30 minutes is given to each planner to give the best possible solution. One planner proposed in this thesis uses this approach as well.

Enforced Hill-Climbing

Enforced hill-climbing (EHC) is a *local* search algorithm that keeps track only of its current node n and the path from the initial node up to n. It iteratively searches for a successor state with lower heuristic value $h(n)$, and once it is found, EHC commits to setting the current state to this node. Each iteration is a *breadth-first* search from the current node until a better state is found. Recall that breadth first search is equivalent to a best-first search with the evaluation function $f(n) = g(n)$ assuming all action costs to be 1. If the planning problem contains non-uniform costs, they are ignored, and EHC always first expands the nodes closer to the current state (Hoffmann and Nebel, 2001). While scaling up effectively by avoiding many oscillations in the search, the algorithm is incomplete as it can get trapped in dead-ends: states from which there is no solution. Moreover, the actions considered in every state are only a subset of the applicable actions, known as helpful actions (Hoffmann and Nebel, 2001). EHC is used by the FF planner, which has represented the state-of-the-art from 2000 until 2008. EHC is used in the experiments of the first chapter of this thesis.

1.3.2   Model-Based Heuristics

Heuristic functions $h : S \mapsto \mathbb{R}_0^+$ are estimators that compute from a given state the cost of reaching the goal. Although being impractical, the perfect heuristic estimator h^* maps any state to the optimal solution from that state. *Admissible* heuristic estimators never overestimate the cost of the optimal solution from any state s, i.e., $h(s) \leq h^*(s)$ for all states $s \in S$. For example, the euclidean distance between two cities in a map that contains roads linking cities, is guaranteed to be a lower bound on the real minimum distance that must be driven. Admissible heuristics have an important property when used with search algorithms that always explore first the paths with lowest cost: they are guaranteed to find an optimal solution. On the other hand, non-admissible heuristics may lead to suboptimal solutions. Generally, both admissible and non-admissible heuristics are defined over a simplified version of the original problem. These simpler instances of the original problem Π are known as relaxations, as they abstract away some properties from Π (Pearl, 1983). When any solution of the original problem is also a solution to the relaxed one, the cost of the optimal solution of the relaxed problem is an admissible estimator. We omit the discussion of important approaches to derive heuristics in classical planning such as the causal graph (Helmert, 2004; Helmert and Geffner, 2008), pattern databases (Edelkamp, 2001; Haslum et al., 2005, 2007), merge-and-shrink (Helmert et al., 2007) and structural patterns (Katz and Domshlak, 2008). We focus only on the heuristics that are mostly used in *satisficing classical planning* and throughout this thesis, either as building blocks for new ideas or taking part of state-of-the-art planners that we compare with.

Delete-Relaxation Based Heuristics

The most used relaxation is the delete-relaxation Π^+ (Bonet and Geffner, 2001), where the delete effects of actions are ignored, i.e. $Del(o) = \emptyset$ for all $o \in O$; and actions can only *add* fluents increasing monotonically the set of true facts from a given state.

Definition 1.3 (Delete relaxation). *Given a* STRIPS *problem* $\Pi = \langle F, O, I, G \rangle$, *its* delete relaxation Π^+ *is described by the tuple* $\Pi^+ = \langle F, O^+, I, G \rangle$, *where*

$$O^+ = \{\langle Pre(o), Add(o), \emptyset \rangle \mid o \in O\}$$

A relaxed plan for Π is a sequence of actions that form a plan for its relaxed version Π^+.

The $cost(\pi^+)$ of the optimal plan π^+ for Π^+ yields an admissible heuristic, and is known as h^+, although its computation is NP-hard (Bylander, 1994). Instead, the plan existence in the delete free problem is in P. As the set of fluents achieved in a relaxed plan increases monotonically and no operator needs to be applied more than once; a set of goals can be achieved with at most $|O|$ actions. Thus, generally delete relaxation based heuristics seek to approximate h^+ in polynomial time.

The Max and Additive Heuristic. h_{max} and h_{add}, approximate both h^+, the first being admissible and the second not. Both heuristics estimate the cost of a set of atoms, h_{max} estimate it as the *maximum* cost of an atom in the set, while h_{add} heuristic as the *sum* of the costs of the atoms in the set. The cost of an atom depends on the cost of its *best supporter*, i.e., the action that makes the fact true with minimal estimated cost. The estimated cost of an action is determined by the cost of the atoms in its precondition (Bonet and Geffner, 2001). Below we give a formal definition first of h_{add} and then of h_{max}:

$$h_{\text{add}}(p; s) \stackrel{\text{def}}{=} \begin{cases} 0 & \text{if } p \in s \\ \min_{a \in O(p)} h_{\text{add}}(a; s) & \text{otherwise} \end{cases} \tag{1.1}$$

where $O(p)$ range over the actions adding p, and

$$h_{\text{add}}(a; s) \stackrel{\text{def}}{=} cost(a) + h_{\text{add}}(\textbf{Pre}(a); s) \tag{1.2}$$

$$h_{\text{add}}(Q; s) \stackrel{\text{def}}{=} \sum_{q \in Q} h_{\text{add}}(q; s) \tag{1.3}$$

$$h_{\text{add}}(s) \stackrel{\text{def}}{=} \sum_{q \in G} h_{\text{add}}(q; s) \tag{1.4}$$

$$best\_supp(p; s) \stackrel{\text{def}}{=} \text{argmin}_{a \in O(p)} h_{\text{add}}(a; s) \tag{1.5}$$

The additive heuristic is pessimistic, as it assumes that achieving one fluent in a set does not make any progress towards achieving other fluents in the set. Thus, $h_{add} \geq h^+$ is an upper bound on the optimal cost of the delete relaxation problem. Alternatively, the max heuristic is optimistic, assuming that achieving the most expensive fluent of a set will be enough for achieving the other fluents in the same set as a side-effect. It defines the cost of a set of fluents to be the cost of the most expensive fluent as follows:

$$h_{\max}(p; s) \stackrel{\text{def}}{=} \begin{cases} 0 & \text{if } p \in s \\ \min_{a \in O(p)} h_{\max}(a; s) & \text{otherwise} \end{cases} \tag{1.6}$$

where

$$h_{\max}(a; s) \stackrel{\text{def}}{=} cost(a) + h_{\max}(\textbf{Pre}(a); s) \tag{1.7}$$

$$h_{\max}(Q; s) \stackrel{\text{def}}{=} \max_{q \in Q} h_{\max}(q; s) \tag{1.8}$$

$$h_{\max}(s) \stackrel{\text{def}}{=} \max_{q \in G} h_{\max}(q; s) \tag{1.9}$$

$$best\_supp(p; s) \stackrel{\text{def}}{=} \text{argmin}_{a \in O(p)} h_{\max}(a; s) \tag{1.10}$$

The only difference between the additive and the max heuristic is their definition of the cost of a set of atoms. Indeed, this small change yields the max heuristic $h_{\max}$ to be admissible, and can be used along some search algorithms such as A^* for optimal planning. On the other hand, the additive heuristic is more adequate in terms of practical performance for *satisficing planning*, trading optimality for solution time.

The FF Heuristic. h_{FF} estimates the distance to a goal G from a given state s to be the length of a suboptimal relaxed plan, extracted from the *relaxed planning graph* (Hoffmann and Nebel, 2001). Thus, the FF heuristic is computed in two phases, the first one builds the graph (forward), and the second extracts a relaxed plan from it (backwards). The relaxed planning graph is a directed layered graph with two types of layers (nodes), the fluent layer F_i and the action layer O_i. The first fluent layer F_0 contains all facts true in a given state s, and the action layer O_i contains all actions whose preconditions are in F_i, e.g., the first action layer O_0 contains all actions applicable in state s. Layer F_{i+1} is then the fluents added by actions in O_i along with fluents contained previously in F_i, without ever taking into account the delete effects (Blum and Furst, 1995). Therefore, in a parallel relaxed plan where more than one action can be applied in the same time step, fluents in F_i are the reachable fluents in i-steps. Analogously, actions in O_i are all actions that could be applied in the ith step of a parallel relaxed plan. Extra *no-op* actions [1] for each fluent $p \in F$ are added to the graph to denote the propagation of facts that have been added at some time step into later time steps. Each action $o \in O_i$ has incident edges from its preconditions at F_i and outgoing edges to its add effects at F_{i+1}. The graph can be computed in polynomial time reaching a fixed point when it is not possible to add any new fact to a layer. Formally, given a planning task $\Pi = \langle F, O, I, G \rangle$ and a state s, the layers of its relaxed planning graph are defined as:

$$F_i \stackrel{\text{def}}{=} \begin{cases} s & \text{if } i = 0 \\ F_i \cup_{\bigcup_{a \in O_{i-1}}} Add(a) & \text{if } i > 0 \end{cases} \tag{1.11}$$

$$O_i \stackrel{\text{def}}{=} \{a \in O \mid Pre(a) \in F_i\} \tag{1.12}$$

Both sets grow monotonically until reaching a fixed point. No-ops are not considered in the equations for simplicity. Once the forward phase is finished and the relaxed planning graph obtained, the second phase begins extracting a relaxed plan π^+ from the graph. Starting from the goals $g \in G$ of the problem, the actions adding each goal g are included to the relaxed plan π^+. Then, actions are added to π^+ until all preconditions of actions in the relaxed plan are supported by some action or they belong to F_0. The FF heuristic then estimates the distance to the goal as

$$h_{\text{FF}}(s) \stackrel{\text{def}}{=} |\pi^+|$$

If the cost of the actions is taken to be the first i layer in which they appear, there is a correspondence with the $h_{\max}(a; s)$ estimate. Alternatively, the relaxed plan π^+ can be defined recursively in terms of the best h_{max} supporters of the fluents p: namely, π^+ contains the best supporter a_g of g, and for each action a in π^+, a best supporter for each precondition p of a not in s. The relaxed plan can also be extracted following the best supporters according to h_{add}, which has been proven experimentally to scale better in non-uniform cost planning problems (Keyder, 2010).

The original definition in Hoffmann and Nebel (2001) uses the relaxed planning graph and no-ops, along with a preference for no-op supporters which amounts to a preference for best (h_{max}) supports.

Heuristic Family h^m A generalization of h_{max} is obtained through the family of admissible heuristic estimators h^m for $m > 1$; where as a special case $h^m = h_{max}$ for $m = 1$, and for a sufficiently large m, $h^m = h^*$ is the optimal heuristic.[2]

---

[1]   A no-op action for fluent p, contains p in its precondition and in its add effect.   [2] The value of m in order to converge into the optimal heuristic h^* is at most the number of fluents in the problem.

Intuitively, when $m = 1$ the heuristic h^m estimates the cost of a set of atoms as the cost of the most expensive *single atom* in the set. When $m = 2$, it estimates the cost of a set of atoms as the cost of the *atom pair* most expensive in the set, and so on. The h^m family can be computed in polynomial time $O(F^m)$ where F is the number of fluents of the problem. Formally, h^m is defined as:

$$h^m(C; s) \stackrel{\text{def}}{=} \begin{cases} 0 & \text{if } C \in s \\ \min_{\langle B,a \rangle \in R(C)}[cost(a) + h^m(B; s)] & \text{if } |C| \leq m \\ \max_{D \in C, |D|=m} h^m(D; s) & \text{if } |C| > m \end{cases} \qquad (1.13)$$

where $R(C)$ refers to the set of pairs $\langle B, a \rangle$ such that B is the result of regressing the set C through action a, a adds an atom in C, $Add(a) \cap C \neq \emptyset$, a does not delete any atom in C, $Del(a) \cap C = \emptyset$, and $B = (C \setminus Add(a)) \cup Pre(a)$ (Haslum and Geffner, 2000). If $m = |F|$, the last condition of the definition never applies. Note that the last condition is the one that approximates the cost of large sets of fluents C as the cost of its most expensive subset of size m. In practice, h^2 is too expensive to be computed in every state visited by any search algorithm. But if it is computed just once from the initial state, it can be used in a form of regression search for optimal planning (Haslum and Geffner, 2000). h^2 can be used also to capture the notion of *(structural) mutexes*: pairs of atoms that cannot be both true in any reachable state and which can be computed in polynomial time (Blum and Furst, 1995). More precisely, pairs $\langle p, q \rangle$ are mutex if the heuristic $h^2(\langle p, q \rangle)$, closely related to the heuristic underlying Graphplan, is infinite (Haslum and Geffner, 2000). Mutexes can be computed more effectively by setting the costs of all actions to 0.

Landmark Heuristic. The landmarks of a problem Π are necessary features of any possible solution (Porteous et al., 2001). Among these features, *Fluent landmarks* are formulas over the set of fluents F that must be satisfied by some state along any valid plan. *Fluent Landmark* formulas are typically used in the form of atomic single fluents, although disjunction and conjunction of fluents have also been proposed and used in different settings (Karpas and Domshlak, 2009; Richter et al., 2008; Keyder et al., 2010). Instead *Action landmarks* are formulas over the set of actions O that must be included in any valid plan. Their use in the disjunctive form has been successfully used in optimal planning (Helmert and Domshlak, 2009). Different landmark orderings can be defined and exploited during the planning phase. Orderings over fluent landmarks are statements about the order in which they must be made true.

The landmark heuristic is computed in two phases, the first one computed only once from the initial state. The landmark heuristic extracts in polynomial time an incomplete set of single fluent and disjunctive fluent landmarks, along with their orderings; from which the landmark graph is built (Hoffmann et al., 2004). Then, for every state s, the landmark heuristic approximates the distance to the goal as the number of landmarks that still need to be achieved from s. Given a partial plan π from the initial state s_0 up to s, the set of landmarks to achieve is defined as:

$$L(s, \pi) \stackrel{\text{def}}{=} (L \setminus Accepted(s, \pi)) \cup ReqAgain(s, \pi) \qquad (1.14)$$

where L is the set of all landmarks discovered, $Accepted(s, \pi)$ is the set of landmarks achieved along π up to s, and $ReqAgain(s, \pi)$ is the set of *accepted* landmarks that are required again. A landmark $l \in L$ is accepted if it is true in s and all landmarks ordered before l are accepted in the state preceding s along π. An *accepted* landmark l is *required again* if it is not true in s and either $l \in G$ is a goal or is ordered to be true strictly before some other landmark l' that is not accepted yet. The landmark heuristic is then defined as the size of $L(s, \pi)$:

$$h_L(s, \pi) \stackrel{\text{def}}{=} |L(s, \pi)| \qquad (1.15)$$

Note that the landmark heuristic is not a state heuristic like the ones presented before, as its definition does not only depends on the state s, but on the way s has been achieved. As a single action can achieve more than one landmark, the landmark heuristic is not admissible.

1.3.3 Search Enhancements

A number of improvements to search algorithms have been proposed in the context of planning. Successful *satisficing planners* use a variety of search enhancements, being less monolithic than the first plain heuristic search planner HSP (Bonet and Geffner, 2001). One such enhancement is *helpful actions* [1] (Hoffmann and Nebel, 2001), a subset of the applicable actions that are *heuristically* goal oriented. *Delayed evaluation* is another technique that reduces the computational cost derived from the use of heuristics (Helmert, 2006), and *multiple queues* proposes an approach to combine several heuristics in the same search algorithm (Helmert, 2006). We now briefly review these three search enhancements that are used in some experimental results presented in this thesis.

Helpful Actions

Helpful Actions is a technique that allows planners to reduce the branching factor, avoiding the generation of all successors but those considered to be helpful, and therefore allowing such planners to scale up to larger problems (Hoffmann and Nebel, 2001). Heuristics, rather than estimating only the distance to the goal from a given state, also estimate a subset of the applicable actions considered to be promisingly *goal oriented*.

Relaxation-based heuristics typically estimate as helpful the actions from the relaxed solution that are applicable in the current state. For example, h_{FF} does not only return the estimated distance to the goal as the size of the relaxed solution it finds, but also the actions from that solution applicable in the current state. Various approaches have been proposed for incorporating helpful actions into search algorithms. The most common ones, either generate only successors from the set of helpful actions, or give a preference to expand first successors that come from helpful actions on top of the ones that come from non-helpful actions. The first planner to propose such actions and include a search approach to exploit them is FF, reducing the state space through sacrificing completeness,

---
[1] Helpful actions are also known as *preferred operators*.

it initially considers only helpful actions, and resorts to a normal search if this failed. Recently, the approach used by most planners is to alternate between exploring states resulting from helpful actions and those resulting from all others (Helmert, 2006). This approach gives the ability to search algorithms to take advantage of the information encoded by such actions without loosing completeness. From an algorithmic point of view, it is implemented through the use of multiple open lists in the best-first search algorithms.

As helpful actions depend on the solutions of the relaxed problem, which typically include random tie-breaking of actions to be included, the set of helpful actions is not well defined where the same state can include different sets of helpful actions depending on the order in which actions are considered. In Chapter 2, we propose an alternative characterization of helpful actions, and in Chapter 9, we lay an alternative method to include such actions into the search algorithm through the evaluation function $f(n)$.

Multiple Queues

Multiple queues (open lists) is an enhancement that has two proposes: first to enable the incorporation of multiple heuristic estimators in an orthogonal way under a single search algorithm, and second to incorporate helpful actions without loosing completeness. If more than one heuristic estimator is used, the algorithm employs one queue for each heuristic alternating between them for choosing which state to expand next. Numerical priorities can be assigned to expand nodes more often from one queue than another. When a state is chosen for expansion, its successors are evaluated with every heuristic and introduced to their respective queue. When a heuristic estimator also returns a set of helpful actions, an extra queue is used, e.g., the search uses four queues if the algorithm employs two heuristics that each return a set of helpful actions. When a state is selected for expansion, the successors that result from helpful actions are placed in one queue and the non-helpful in the other. As the number of helpful actions tend to be much smaller than the number of applicable actions, the helpful actions queue explores deep into the search space faster. Note that states chosen for expansion from the non-helpful queue can generate successors that are helpful, and vice versa. Eventually, the search evaluates the states from each queue, being less sensible to poorly informed heuristics that return shallow sets of helpful actions, and being able to guarantee completeness (Helmert, 2006).

Delayed Evaluation

Most of the computational effort of heuristic search planners is spent in the computation of the heuristic estimator $h(n)$, up to 80% of the time in some instances according to Bonet and Geffner (1999). Moreover, most of the states placed in the open list are never expanded, using the heuristic estimation of each state just to disqualify it from immediate expansion. The Fast Downward planner proposed a technique to include a variation known as *delayed evaluation*, where states are not evaluated before being introduced into the open list but just after they are selected for expansion (Helmert, 2006). When a state is expanded the heuristic is computed and its successors are assigned the value of the parent. This technique reduces the number of heuristic evaluations at the cost of a less informative evaluation function $f(n)$, which in turn is compensated by the ability of the algorithm to explore a larger portion of the state space. A deep analysis of the interaction between helpful actions and delayed evaluation has been done by Richter and Helmert (2009).

1.3.4 State-of-the-art Heuristic Search Planners

Heuristic Search Planners that combined the techniques explained above represent the state-of-the-art in *satisficing classical planning* since 1998, when the first International Planning Competition took place (IPC). Since then, the competition has been held roughly every two years. Typically, each competition tested planners with a new set of benchmark domains. A variety of performance criteria have been considered, from the number of solved problems, to the amount of time needed, etc. up to current criteria that takes into account the best possible solution a planner can find in 30 minutes.

The first high performance heuristic search planner was introduced by Bonet and Geffner (1999). The first version of *HSP* used h_{add} heuristic estimator along a variation of *hill-climbing*,[1] a local search algorithm that proceeds the search until a fix number of impasses occurs, restarting the search if necessary. *HSP2.0* instead implemented *greedy best-first search* and WA^* using the additive heuristic as forward search, and h^2 computed once and searched backwards from the goal, alternating the time window for each approach (Bonet and Geffner, 2001).

The *FF* planner, which in large extent represented the state-of the art since 2000 up to 2008, has been shown to scale up much better than HSP, with the heuristic h_{FF} used in FF, however, playing a relatively small role. In addition to the heuristic, FF introduced two ideas that account to a large extent for its remarkable speed: *helpful action pruning (HA)* and *enforced hill-climbing search (EHC)*. The EHC search, looks iteratively for a state s' that improves the heuristic of the current state s by carrying a breadth-first search from s, while pruning actions that are not helpful. Recall that helpful action pruning is not sound (it may render problems unsolvable) and the EHC search is not complete (it can miss the goal), yet together with the h_{FF} heuristic it can yield a powerful planner that constitutes the "basic architecture" of FF (Hoffmann and Nebel, 2001). When this basic architecture fails, FF switches to a slower but complete search mode: a best-first search from the initial state where no actions are pruned guided by h_{FF} heuristic.

The *LAMA* planner represents nowadays the state-of-the-art in *satisficing classical planning*. It was first introduced in 2008 and a second version was implemented in 2011, winning the last two international planning competitions. LAMA is based on several ideas introduced by *FD* and is built on top of this planner. FD uses a multivalued variable representation instead of STRIPS, and introduces the ideas of delayed evaluation, multiple open lists and helpful actions used as a preferential option. LAMA combines all these ideas in a greedy best-first search

---

[1] Hill-climbing is similar to enforced hill-climbing but without the breadth-first search procedure triggered to lower the heuristic value of the state. Instead, it just selects a successor and commits to it.

with four queues, one for the landmark heuristic h_L, another for the FF heuristic h_{FF}, and one queue for each set of helpful actions returned by each heuristic. In addition LAMA does not stop after the first solution is found, instead it continues searching for better solutions until the search space is exhausted or the time limit is reached. After finding the first solution with greedy best-first search, it switches to WA^* with decreasing weights, restarting the search from scratch every time an improved solution is found (Richter and Westphal, 2010).

1.4   Thesis Outline

All inference schemes for planning in this thesis are used in the context of forward-state search. The first one proposed in Chapters 2 and 3 does not appeal to a heuristic function but to the notion of *causal links* developed in the context of partial order planning (Tate, 1977; McAllester and Rosenblitt, 1991). A causal link a, p, b is a triple that states that action a provides the support for precondition p of b. This is taken as a *constraint* that implies that a must precede b in the plan and that no other action that adds or deletes p can appear between them. We show that by exploiting the semantics of causal links, we are able to propagate information along sequences of causal links $a_0, p_1, a_1, p_2, a_2, \ldots, p_n, a_n$ and show that some of such sequences are impossible to hold in any valid plan. Actions a_0 that cannot start any consistent causal chain can then be pruned. We then present an algorithm that uses such *paths as decomposition backbones* and a *heuristic estimate* of the cost of achieving the goal *along these paths*. This results in a planner that solves most of the benchmarks with almost no search, and suggests that planning with paths may be a meaningful idea both cognitively and computationally. As a result, a planner called c3 participated in the International Planning Competition 2008 (IPC-6) getting the 'jury award'.

In Chapters 4 and 5, we explore further the synergy between different type of inferences, by formulating and testing a new dual search architecture for planning that is based on the idea of *probes*: single action sequences computed without search from a given state that can quickly go deep into the state space, terminating either in the goal or in failure. We show experimentally that by designing these probes carefully using a number of existing and new polynomial inference techniques, most of the benchmarks can be solved with a single probe from the initial state, with no search. Moreover, by using one probe as a lookahead mechanism from each expanded state in a standard greedy best-first search, the number of problems solved increases and compares well to state-of-the-art planners. The resulting planner PROBE, presented in the International Planning competition 2011 (IPC-7), was the second best planner in terms of the quality of the first solution found. The success of probes suggests that many domains can be solved easily once a suitable serialization of the subgoals is found.

On the other hand, various approaches have been developed for explaining the gap between the complexity of planning mentioned before, and the ability of current planners to solve most existing benchmarks in a few seconds. Existing proposals, however, do not appear to explain the apparent simplicity of the standard domains. In Chapters 6 to 8, we introduce a new type of width parameter for planning that bounds the complexity of a planning domain in terms of the *goal structure* of the problem, which opens a new approach to understanding the complexity of classical domains. We then present a blind search algorithm that runs in both time and space exponential in the problem width, showing experimentally that many standard domain benchmarks have low width provided that goals are restricted to single atoms. As most benchmark goals are not expressed as single atoms, we explore a method to deal with problems that feature conjunctive goals by using the same blind search algorithm for generating a serialization of these goals while solving the induced subproblems.

Finally, in Chapter 9 we show how key ideas from the blind search algorithm presented in Chapter 8, novelty based pruning and goal decomposition, can be integrated into a standard best-first search algorithm; along with other inferences that have proven to be crucial for high performance planners. We then evaluate the resulting best-first search planner which performs as well as other state-of-the-art planners.

Part II

Inference

Chapter 2

Causal Chains (Paths)

Ahí estaban las causas y los efectos y me
bastaba ver esa Rueda para entenderlo todo,
sin fin. AąOh dicha de entender, mayor que
la de imaginar o la de sentir!

There they were the causes and the effects
and I only had to look at that Wheel to
understand it all, endlessly. Oh, the
happiness of understanding, greater than the
one of imagining or the one of feeling!

La escritura del dios.
Jorge Luis Borges

In this chapter we introduce a different approach to the problem of inference in planning that is not based on either the extraction and use of heuristic functions or reductions into SAT or CSPs. The proposed approach is based on a new notion of *consistent causal chains:* sequences of causal links a_i, p_{i+1}, a_{i+1} starting with an action a_0 applicable in the current state s and finishing in the goal, where p_{i+1} is an effect of action a_i and a precondition of action a_{i+1}. We first show that by enforcing the semantics of causal links, it is possible to propagate side effects along such chains and detect that some of these chains cannot be part of any plan. Actions a_0 that cannot start any consistent causal chain can then be pruned. We then show that while simple, this pruning rule is quite powerful: a plain backtracking forward-state search planner with a version of this pruning rule solves more problems than a plain heuristic search planner, and as many as the effective Enforced Hill Climbing search of FF that uses both helpful actions and h_{FF} heuristic. Moreover, many problems are solved backtrack-free.

2.1 Introduction

Current state-of-the-art planners solve problems, easy and hard alike, by search, expanding hundreds or thousands of nodes. Yet, given the ability of people to solve easy problems and to explain their solutions, it seems that an essential inferential component may be missing. The LAMA and FF planners (Richter et al., 2008; Hoffmann and Nebel, 2001) represent the best examples of such systems, being the best performers in many benchmarks for the last years. In spite of its success, the approach lacks transparency. It is not clear why it works, it is not easy to understand why some actions are chosen and others discarded, and most importantly, it is hard to explain each decision made by the system.

There is no question that more extensive search techniques and better heuristics are necessary for solving hard combinatorial problems, yet problems such as Tower-n in Vidal and Geffner (2005), are not hard, and the same can be said of many of the benchmarks in planning. This does not mean that 'easy' problems are easy for a domain-independent planner; the challenge is to recognize and exploit the structure that makes those problems easy by domain-independent methods, something that does not appear to be simple at all. Yet people appear to do that, and are able to explain their solutions, even if they are not particularly good at solving hard problems. In a problem such as Tower-n, where n blocks 1, 2, ..., n on the table must be arranged into a single tower with block i on block $i + 1$ for all $i < n$, they can immediately see that picking up a block other than $n-1$ is a wasted move. The reason for this, indeed, is not *heuristic* but *structural*: picking up a block m other than n-1 appears relevant to the goal through the 'path'

$$pick(m) \rightarrow hold(m) \rightarrow stack(m, m + 1) \rightarrow on(m, m + 1)$$

yet it can be formally proven that if this path is understood as a *sequence of causal links* (Tate, 1977), no plan for achieving the goal can comply with it.

The key notion is the *consistent causal chain*: a sequence of causal links a_i, p_{i+1}, a_{i+1} starting with an action a_0 applicable in the current state s and finishing with the *End* action a_n, where p_{i+1} is an effect of action a_i and a precondition of action a_{i+1}. We show that by exploiting the causal relations and the semantics of the actions, we are able to propagate side effects along these chains recognizing those that can not be a part of any plan. In other words, all a_0 that cannot start any consistent causal chain to the *End* action, can be pruned from the search space in this state. We demonstrate with a simple backtrack forward-state search planner the power of this pruning rule, with which we are able to solve as many benchmark problems as the Enforced Hill Climbing (EHC) search of FF, in most cases backtrack-free[1]. While we are able to work with this simple rule, in contrast, FF's EHC requires not only the helpful actions pruning rule, but also a heuristic estimator for measuring progress towards the goal.

The problem of determining whether there is a consistent causal chain a_0, $p_1, a_1,$ $p_2, a_2,$ ..., p_n, a_n ending in the goal turns out to be intractable, as there are an exponential number of causal chains. For this reason we try to obtain a subset of those: only the causal chains that do not contain irrelevant actions,

---

[1] FF(EHC), dominates FF(BFS) and each queue of LAMA independently

considering as relevant those actions that 'best help' the planner to reach the goal. Thus, we focus on the computation of the consistent causal chains where for each atom p_{i+1}, the action a_i is a *best supporter* of p_{i+1}. The notion of best supporters is obtained from a simple reachability analysis from the goal to the current state. By focusing on only a subset of possible consistent causal chains, the method is still sound but not complete, since a consistent causal chain might exist that does not belong to the subset we consider. We show empirically that the computation of these 'minimal' consistent causal chains, in every state s expanded in the search, can be carried out efficiently, resulting in solution times that are similar to and sometimes better than FF's EHC.

Another system called CPT has reported interesting backtrack-free behavior (Vidal and Geffner, 2005), approaching the problem using structural inferences and constraint propagation with a complex formulation of *partial-order causal-link* planning (Weld, 1994).

In the following sections we introduce the notions of relevant, minimal, and consistent paths. We explain then the basic formal properties of consistent paths, discussing their semantics and complexity, and show how to carry out the computation of minimal paths that are consistent. Building on these notions, we consider a simple forward-state planner that relies on a backtracking search and consistency-based pruning criteria, and report empirical results.

2.1.1 Basic Concepts

The inference scheme for planning below is used in the context of a forward-state search that does not appeal to a heuristic function, but to the notion of *causal links* developed in the context of partial order planning (Tate, 1977; McAllester and Rosenblitt, 1991). A causal link a, p, b is a triple that states that action a provides the support for precondition p of b. Semantically, this is taken as a *constraint* that implies that a must precede b in the plan and that no other action that adds or deletes p can appear between them. We will show below that by exploiting causal links as constraints, we will be able to propagate information along sequences of causal links $a_0, p_1, a_1, p_2, a_2, \ldots, p_n, a_n$ and show that some of such sequences are impossible. For this, we will make use of the notion of *(structural) mutexes*: pairs of atoms that cannot be both true in any reachable state and which can be computed in polynomial time (Blum and Furst, 1995). More precisely, pairs $\langle p, q \rangle$ are mutex if the heuristic $h^2(\langle p, q \rangle)$, closely related to the heuristic underlying Graphplan, is infinite (Haslum and Geffner, 2000), and can be computed even more effectively by setting the costs of all actions to 0. Provided with mutexes, it is simple to show that a causal link a, p, b must rule out from the interval between a and b not only the actions that delete p but also the actions c that do not add p and have a precondition q that is mutex with p. We say in these cases that c *e-deletes* p (Nguyen and Kambhampati, 2001; Vidal and Geffner, 2006).

In this chapter, given a STRIPS planning problem $P = \langle F, I, O, G \rangle$, without loss of generality, we assume as in partial order planning that O contains an *End* action whose preconditions are the real goals of the problem and whose only effect is a dummy goal G_d so that $G = \{G_d\}$. Thus all plans for P must include the action

End.

2.2   Minimal Paths

We are interested in the conditions under which an applicable action in an arbitrary state s can be pruned. helpful action pruning (Section 1.3.3) provides one such criterion but its justification is empirical; from a theoretical point of view sometimes it is too strong (rendering a problem unsolvable) and sometimes too weak (failing to prune actions that cannot help, as we will see). So we start with the more basic notion of *relevance* as captured by sequences of causal links a_i, p_{i+1}, a_{i+1} that we refer to as *causal chains*.

Definition 2.1 (Causal Chains). *A sequence $a_0, p_1, a_1, p_2, a_2, \ldots, p_n, a_n$ of actions a_i and fluents p_i is a causal chain in a state s if action a_0 is applicable in s, and fluent p_{i+1} is a precondition of action a_{i+1} and a positive effect (add) of a_i.*

A Causal chain defines a subset of plans for which the causal chain is a subsequence. We say then that an action a_0 is *relevant to the goal* if there is a causal chain that starts with a_0 and leads to the goal. We will actually refer to such complete causal chains simply as *paths*:

Definition 2.2 (Paths). *A path in a state s is a causal chain $a_0, p_1, a_1, p_2, a_2, \ldots p_n, a_n$ where a_n is the End action.*

This notion of relevance, considered already in Nebel et al. (1997), has a problem that is immediately apparent: a path may connect an applicable action a_0 to the goal, and yet fail to be goal-oriented in a meaningful sense.

For illustrating this and related definitions, we will appeal to a simple class of Block-World problems, where n blocks $1, 2, \ldots, n$ on the table must be arranged into a single tower with block i on block $i + 1$ for all $i < n$. This so-called Tower-n domain is considered in Vidal and Geffner (2005), where it is shown that most planners have to search in this domain in spite of its simplicity. Actually, the FF planner fails to solve a slight variation of the problem where block n is initially on top of block 1.[1]

The paths generated in the initial state of Tower-n include reasonable causal chains such as

$$t_1 : pick(i), hold(i), stack(i, i+1), on(i, i+1), End$$

for every i other than n, where a block i is picked up and stacked on its target destination, but also less reasonable ones such as:

$$t_2 : pick(i), hold(i), stack(i, j), on(i, j), unstack(i, j),$$
$$hold(i), stack(i, i+1), on(i, i+1), End$$

where, after block i is picked up, it is placed on top of another block $j \neq i+1$ along the way, for no apparent reason. Yet intuitively the irrelevant action $stack(i, j)$ is

---

[1] In our experiments, FF fails to solve such variation for $n > 20$, with a timeout of 30 minutes.

in this path for a 'reason': it supports the fluent $on(i, j)$ which is a precondition of the following $unstack(i, j)$ action that undoes the effect of the spurious action. Therefore, any applicable action can be relevant in Tower-n, e.g., in the state s' that results from picking up block 1, all actions $stack(1, i)$, and even the action $putdown(1)$, are deemed as relevant.

A simple way to prune such spurious paths from consideration is by requiring that the action a_i that supports (adds) the fluent p_{i+1} is not any supporter of p_{i+1}, but a reasonable one; i.e., a *best supporter* action a that adds p_{i+1} and has min $h_{max}(a; s)$ over the actions adding p_{i+1}. We call the resulting paths minimal paths:

Definition 2.3 (Minimal Paths). *A minimal path in state s is a path $a_0, p_1, a_1, p_2, a_2,$ ..., p_n, a_n where each action a_i, for $i = 0, \ldots, n - 1$, is a best supporter of fluent p_{i+1} in the state s.*

For example, while the path t_1 above is minimal, the path t_2 is not, as $pick(i)$ is the only best supporter of $hold(i)$ and not $unstack(i, j)$.

Minimal paths do not only exclude spurious actions from getting in but have a convenient monotonicity property: if action a_i precedes a_{i+1} in the path, then $h_{max}(a_i; s) < h_{max}(a_{i+1}; s)$. This follows because a_i being a best supporter of p_{i+1} implies $h_{max}(p_{i+1}; s) = 1 + h_{max}(a_i; s)$, and since p_{i+1} is a precondition of a_{i+1}, $h_{max}(p_{i+1}; s) \leq h_{max}(a_{i+1}; s)$.

Minimal paths do not refer to paths with the shortest length; indeed minimal paths come in different lengths. Yet if we define the *length of a path* as *the number of actions in the path*, we can establish a relation between the length of the longest minimal paths in s and the value of the h_{max} heuristic in the same state:

Proposition 2.4 (Path Length and h_{max} Heuristic). *The length of the longest minimal paths t in s is equal to $h_{max}(s)$.*

Proof sketch: Given $\Pi = \langle F, I, O, G \rangle$ and a state $s \subset F$, $h_{max}(s)$ can be defined inductively in terms of the following sets:

- $P_0 = s$

- $A_i = \{a \in O \mid pre(a) \subseteq P_i\}$

- $P_{i+1} = P_i \cup \{p \in add(a) \mid a \in A_i\}$

where the value of $h_{max}(s)$ is the index k of the first propositional set P_k that contains the Goals' set G. The indexes i of each action a_i and fluent p_i of a minimal path $t : a_0, p_1, a_1, p_2, a_2, \ldots, p_n, a_n$ correspond to the indexes of the sets P_i and A_i, i.e., $a_0 \in A_o, p_1 \in P_1, \ldots, a_n \in A_n$. Given that a_n is the *End* action, whose preconditions are the goals $g \in G$, and P_k the first set P that contains the goal set G; the longest minimal path t is then the path where the last atom of the path $p_n \in G$ is a goal atom and $p_n \in P_k$. As the value of $h_{max}(s)$ is the highest index k of P_k, $h_{max}(s)$ is equal to the longest minimal path t in s plus the *End* action. $\square$

Indeed, $h_{max}(s)$ represents the length of all the minimal paths $a_0, p_1, a_1, \ldots p_n, a_n$ where p_i, for every $i = 1, \ldots, n$, is a 'critical' precondition of the action a_i (i.e., a precondition with highest h_{max} value). The length of the minimal paths where at least one of the atoms p_i is not a critical precondition of a_i will be necessarily smaller than $h_{max}(s)$.

Minimal paths are implicit in the definition of helpful actions in FF. If we say that an action a is *minimal* in state s when there is a *minimal path* starting with $a_0 = a$, then we obtain the following:

Proposition 2.5 (Helpful and Minimal Actions). *If an action a is helpful in the state s according to FF, then a is minimal in s.*

Proof sketch: Assume that $a \notin Minimal$ and $a \in HA$. If a is not in a minimal path in state s, a does not start a path $a_0, p_1, a_1, p_2, a_2, \ldots, p_n, a_n$ where each action a_i, for $i = 0, \ldots, n-1$, is a *best supporter* of fluent p_{i+1}. The set of helpful actions (HA) is built by doing a regression from the goal set up to layer P_0 through the relaxed planning graph. The process starts by propagating alternately the preconditions of the best-supporters that add each goal, and then the best-supporters of these preconditions until reaching applicable actions in state s. Therefore, if a is not *minimal*, it can not be a best-supporter of any atom p propagated backward from the goal. The set of helpful actions only contains actions that are best-supporters, if a is not minimal, a can not be in HA.   □

In other words, actions that are not minimal are never helpful. On the other hand, FF may declare actions that are minimal as unhelpful. This is actually because FF selects as helpful *only* the minimal actions that occur in the *selected relaxed plan* contained in the relaxed planning graph. Note that more than one relaxed plan can be extracted from the relaxed planning graph. Minimal and helpful actions thus coincide when a single relaxed plan (taken as a set of actions) complies with h_{FF} heuristic (Section 1.3.2). Otherwise, the minimal actions correspond to the applicable actions that occur in *some* relaxed plan; where different relaxed plans are obtained according to the way ties among best h_{max} supporters are broken.

In Tower-n, there is a single relaxed plan for the initial state s_0 that includes the actions $pick(i)$ and $stack(i, i+1)$ for $i = 0, \ldots, n-1$. Thus, the minimal and helpful actions in s_0 coincide and correspond to the $pick(i)$ actions, which in turn represent the set of all the actions that are applicable in s_0. This is reasonable, as indeed, all these actions are necessary for solving the problem. Yet only the action $pick(n-1)$ makes sense in s_0; all the other pickup actions do not help in s_0 as blocks i cannot be placed on top of block $i+1$ until block $i+1$ is well-placed. Heuristic search planners evaluate the heuristic $h(s_a)$ of the states that result from executing the applicable action a in s, with the hope that the action that is best leads to a state with a lower heuristic value. Yet, this does not always happen; in this case, actually, FF assigns the heuristic value of $2n$ to s_0 and the value $2n - 1$ to **all** its possible sons s_a. FF ends up solving these problems anyway, but not due to its heuristic, that fails to distinguish the action that makes sense from all the others, but due to an extra device that finds orderings among subgoals.

We want to argue that the 'wrong' actions can be ruled out in this and many other cases, not on *heuristic* grounds – namely, because they lead to states that appear to be farther away from the goal – but on *logical* or *structural* grounds –

namely, because they can be shown not to 'lead' to the goal in a precise sense that we define below.

2.3 Consistency

The key idea is to show that certain causal chains and paths cannot be part of any 'reasonable' plan. We will articulate this idea in two parts. First we will show that side effects can be propagated along causal chains $a_0, p_1, a_1, \ldots, p_n, a_n$, provided that each segment a_i, p_{i+1}, a_{i+1} in the chain for $i < n$ is regarded as a *causal link*. Second, we will show that if an action a cannot start a causal chain ending in the goal (a path), then the action a cannot appear as the first action of any plan that is not redundant; i.e., where every action supports the precondition of a later action or is the *End* action.

Recall that a causal link a_i, p_{i+1}, a_{i+1} states that action a_i supports the pre-condition p_{i+1} of action a_{i+1} and implies that no other action that either adds or deletes p_{i+1} can occur between a_i and a_{i+1}. A causal link u_i, p_{i+1}, u_{i+1} thus ensures that the fact p_{i+1} is preserved in a given interval, and yet by preserving p_{i+1} it may preserve other facts as well. For example, if q is true after the action a_i, and all actions that delete q either add or (e-)delete p as well, then due to the semantics of the causal link a_i, p_{i+1}, a_{i+1}, q must remain true until the action a_{i+1} is applied.

We formalize the notion of side-effects along causal chains using the following definition of *labels*:

Definition 2.6 (Labels). *For a causal chain* $t : a_0, p_1, a_1, \ldots, p_n, a_n$ *in a state* s, $Label_t^-(a_i)$ *and* $Label_t^+(a_i)$ *for* $i = 0, \ldots, n$ *are sets of fluents defined recursively as:*

- $Label_t^-(a_0) = s$

- $Label_t^+(a_i) = Update(a_i; Label_t^-(a_i))$

- $Label_t^-(a_{i+1}) = Persist(p_{i+1}; Label_t^+(a_i))$

where $Update(a; s)$ is the set of facts

$$(s \cup Pre(a) \cup Add(a)) \setminus Del(a)$$

and $Persist(p; s)$ is the set

$$\{q \in s \mid \forall_{a \in D(q)} (p \in Add(a) \vee p \in eDel(a))\}$$

Where $D(q)$ stands for the actions of the problem that delete q. Taking the causal chain $a_0, p_1, a_1, \ldots, p_n, a_n$ as a sequence of causal links that starts in the state s, $Label_t^-(a_i)$ $(Label_t^+(a_i))$ captures what can be inferred to be true right before (respectively right after) action a_i is executed in *any plan* that makes the causal chain t true (more about this below). Thus, since a_0 is applied in s, s must be trivially true right before a_0 is applied, and $Update(a_0, s)$ must be true right after. The definition of the $Update(a_{i+1}; s)$ operator is standard as it says that right after a_{i+1} whatever was true before the action a_{i+1} is applied that is not deleted, must be true after the action, along with the positive effects of the action. The operator $Persist(p_{i+1}, Label_t^+(a_i))$ is used in turn to infer that if q was true right after action a_i, then it will remain true at least until the action a_{i+1} is applied, if every action that deletes q violates p_{i+1}. Namely, These actions are ruled out by the causal link a_i, p_{i+1}, a_{i+1} and q persists.[1]

By propagating the side effects along causal chains, we easily can detect that certain causal chains are impossible. We say then that such causal chains are *inconsistent*:

Definition 2.7 (Inconsistent Chains). *A causal chain a_0, p_1, a_1, ..., p_n, a_n is inconsistent if for some action a_i, $i = 1, \ldots, n$, $Label_t^-(a_i)$ is mutex with $Pre(a_i)$.*

Consider for example the minimal path

$$t : pick(k), hold(k), stack(k, k+1), on(k, k+1), End$$

in the initial state s_0 of Tower-n. We show that this path is inconsistent for any block $k < n - 1$, meaning that all such paths provide no 'evidence' that the action $pick(k)$ is relevant to the goal in s_0. For this, we show that the atom $ontable(k + 1)$ which is true in s_0, gets propagated until the end of the path, thus being part of $Label_t^-(End)$. Then since $ontable(k + 1)$ for $k < n - 1$ is mutex with the real goal $on(k + 1, k + 2)$, which is a precondition of the action End, the path t must be inconsistent. Notice that $ontable(k + 1)$ is true right after the action $pick(k)$ in s_0. Moreover, the only action that deletes $ontable(k + 1)$ is $pick(k + 1)$ which e-deletes the condition $hold(k)$ in the first causal link of t (this is because $hold(k)$ is mutex with the precondition $handfree$ of $pick(k + 1)$ and is not added by the action). This means that $ontable(k + 1)$ must be true right before, and also right after the action $stack(k, k+1)$ in t. Finally, since the only action that deletes $ontable(k + 1)$ is $pick(k+1)$ which also e-deletes $on(k, k+1)$ (the action has a precondition $clear(k+1)$ mutex with the atom $on(k, k + 1)$), then we obtain that the atom $ontable(k, k + 1)$ must be true right before the action End. Indeed, the labels that are obtained for the path t above for any block $k < n - 1$, that we abbreviate as $L_t^-(a_i)$ and $L_t^+(a_i)$ for each of the 3 actions a_i in t (pick,stack,End) are:

- $L_t^-(a_1) = \{ontable(j), clear(j), handfree\}$
- $L_t^+(a_1) = \{ontable(i), clear(i), hold(k)\}$
- $L_t^-(a_2) = \{ontable(i), clear(i), hold(k)\}$
- $L_t^+(a_2) = \{ontable(i), on(k, k+1), clear(z), handfree\}$
- $L_t^-(a_3) = \{on(k, k+1), ontable(k +1)\}$

where i, j and z range over $[1..n]$ with $i \neq k$ and $z \neq k + 1$.

Before describing the formal properties of consistent paths, let us define the *consistent actions* in s as follows:

---

[1] The use of the notion of e-deletes in the set $Persist(p; s)$, that appeals to the notion of mutexes, arises because a causal link that preserves a condition p does not only rule out the actions that explicitly delete p but also those that presume that p is false. On the other hand, for removing an atom q from the label, q must be explicitly deleted by an action; the actions that presume q to be false do not need to be taken into account.

Definition 2.8 (Consistent Actions). *An action a is consistent in s when it is the first action in a consistent path in s.*

2.3.1 Formal Properties

There is a positive and a negative aspect about consistent paths: the positive one is that inconsistent paths and actions can be safely ignored; the negative one is that determining whether there is a consistent path is computationally intractable. Our strategy will be to keep the positive part and avoid the negative part by considering later only the *minimal* paths that are consistent.

Soundness

Causal links have been used in the context of partial order planning (Tate, 1977; McAllester and Rosenblitt, 1991), where search branches on the flaws in the current partial plan (open supports and causal link threats) and the possible ways to fix these. We can interpret the semantics of causal chains and paths in the context of partial order planning, but we do not need to. Since we aim to use these notions in the context of a forward-state planner, we can rather talk about the implicit causal structure of standard, sequential STRIPS plans, and state the conditions under which a causal chain is true in a plan. For this, we need to map actions in the chain to actions in the plan, as the same action can appear multiple times in the plan. We use the notation $\pi(k)$ to refer to the k-th action in the plan π.

Definition 2.9. *A causal chain $a_0, p_1, a_1, \ldots, p_n, a_n$ is true in a plan $\pi = \langle b_0, \ldots, b_m \rangle$ for the mapping $f(i)$, $i = 0, \ldots, n$, $0 \le f(i) < f(i+1) \le m$, if the following three conditions hold:*

1. $f(0) = 0$

2. $a_i = \pi(f(i))$ *for $i = 0, \ldots, n$*

3. $\pi(f(i))$ *adds the precondition p_{i+1} of $\pi(f(i+1))$ for $i = 0, \ldots, n-1$ and no action b_k in the plan , $f(i) < k < f(i+1)$, adds or deletes p_{i+1}.*

The definition says that the actions in the chain occur in the right order in the plan, that the first action in the chain and in the plan coincide, and that the causal links in the chain are all true in the plan. The side effects captured in the *Label* function can then be shown to be sound in the following sense:

Proposition 2.10. *If the causal chain $t . a_0, p_1, a_1, \ldots, p_n, a_n$ is true in the plan $\pi = \langle b_0, \ldots, b_m \rangle$ for the mapping $f(i)$, then the atoms in $Label_t^-(a_i)$ ($Label^+(a_i)$) are true in the plan right before (resp. right after) the action $\pi(f(i))$ is executed in the plan π .*

Proof sketch: We first introduce some notation: given a chain $t : a_0, p_1, a_1, \ldots, p_n, a_n$, true in a plan $\pi = \langle b_0, \ldots, b_m \rangle$ and applicable in state s; the state resulting from applying the sequence of actions $\langle b_0, \ldots, b_j \rangle$ from plan π for $j \le m$ in s, is denoted by $s[b_0, \ldots, b_j]$.

Proof by Induction on the value of i. For $i = 0$, $Label_t^-(a_0) = s$ is the initial state and $Label^+(a_0) = Update(a_0; s) = s[a_0]$ is the state $s[a_0]$ that results from progressing s through the applicable action $a_0 = \pi(f(0))$.

By inductive hypothesis and for $0 < i < n$, following Definition 2.6:

1. the set $Label_t^-(a_{i-1}) \subset s[b_0, \ldots, b_{f(i-1)-1}]$ ($Label^+(a_{i-1}) \subset s[b_0, \ldots, b_{f(i-1)}]$) contains atoms that are true in the plan right before (resp. right after) $a_{i-1} = \pi(f(i-1))$ is applied;

2. and no action b_k adds or deletes p_i in the chain, for $f(i-1) < k < f(i)$.

For $a_i = \pi(f(i))$,

- Because of (2) above, the set of atoms true right before a_i is $Label_t^-(a_i) = Persist(p_i; Label^+(a_{i-1})) \subset s[b_0, \ldots, b_{f(i)-1}]$, as no action that adds or deletes p_i is applied since a_{i-1}.

- The atoms right after applying the action $a_i = \pi(f(i))$ are obtained from the previous state $s' = s[b_0, \ldots, b_{f(i)-1}]$ plus the preconditions $Pre(a_i)$, which are guaranteed to hold as the action a_i is applicable in the state. To this set of atoms, the effects $Add(a_i)$ and $Del(a_i)$ of the action are applied, ending up in a state s'' given by

$$s'' = \big(s' \cup Pre(a_i) \cup Add(a_i)\big) \setminus Del(a_i) \tag{2.1}$$

The new state s'' corresponds to the definition of $Label_t^+(a_i) = Update(a_i; Label_t^-(a_i))$, thus $Label_t^+(a_i) \subset s[b_0, \ldots, b_{f(i)}]$.

□

Proposition 2.11. *If a mapping $f(i)$ exists for which the path $a_0, p_1, a_1, \ldots, p_n, a_n$ is true in some plan π, then the path is consistent.*

Proof sketch: In contradiction, assume that there is an inconsistent path $t : a_0, p_1, a_1, \ldots, p_n, a_n$, true in a plan π. From the Definition 2.7, there is some action a_i ($i = 1, \ldots, n$) for which $Label_t^-(a_i)$ is mutex with $Pre(a_i)$[1]. This brings a contradiction, as by Proposition 2.10, for a true path in π, every $Label_t^-(a_i) \subset s[b_0, \ldots, b_{f(i)}]$ and therefore $Label_t^-(a_i)$ cannot be mutex with $Pre(a_i)$.   □

A direct consequence is that inconsistent paths cannot be true in any plan for any mapping. We then say that a plan $\pi = b_0, \ldots, b_m$ is *irredundant* if every action $b_i \neq End$ is the support of a precondition p of action b_j, for $i = 0, \ldots, m$, and $0 \leq i < j \leq m$, i.e., there is a true causal link b_i, p, b_j in π for every action b_i in π other than the End action.

Proposition 2.12. *If the action a is inconsistent in s, then a cannot be the first action of any irredundant plan from s.*

---

[1] For the index $i = 0$, $Label_t^-(a_0)$ is mutex with $Pre(a_0)$, therefore a_0 is not applicable and according to Definition 2.1, t is not a causal chain.

Proof sketch: In contradiction, assume that an inconsistent action a is the first action of an irredundant plan π from s. If a is in π, a mapping $f(i)$ exists that makes the chain $t : a, p_1, a_1, \ldots, p_n, a_n$ true. From Definition 2.8, if action a is inconsistent then all the paths starting with a are inconsistent in s. However, the Proposition 2.11 states that if there is a mapping that makes t true in a plan, then the path t is consistent, which brings the contradiction. $\square$

The results above show that a path $t : a_0, p_1, a_1, \ldots, p_n, a_n$ can be taken as evidence of the relevance of the action a_0 to the goal, except when the path t is inconsistent, and hence impossible to belong in any (irredundant) plan. Inconsistency pruning is thus *sound* but it is *not complete*; i.e., an action a may be consistent in s and yet not head any (irredundant) plan. Indeed, later we will consider another definition of path consistency that is stronger, sound, and polynomial, but hence incomplete as well.

Complexity

Determining whether a given path is consistent can be done in polynomial time, but the problem of determining whether there is a consistent path is intractable.

Proposition 2.13. *Determining whether there is a consistent path from a state s is NP-Complete.*

Proof sketch: The result follows from a reduction from the NP-Complete problem 'Paths with Forbidden Pairs' (PFP): this is the problem of determining whether there is a path in a directed graph from a given source node n_0 to a given target node n_m that contains at most one node from each pair of nodes in a 'forbidden pairs list' (Garey and Johnson, 1990). It suffices to create for each node n_i two fluents p_i and q_i, and for each directed edge $n_i \to n_j$ in the graph, an action with preconditions p_i and q_i, positive effect p_j, and negative effects q_k for each node n_k in a forbidden pair (n_j, n_k). In the initial state all fluents q_i must be true for all i along with the fluent p_0. The goal is p_m. There is then a 1-to-1 correspondence between the causal chains that terminate in the goal and the directed paths in the graph that connect n_0 to n_m (no action adds fluents q_i, hence all causal chains can mention only the fluents p_i), and also a 1-to-1 correspondence between the directed paths connecting n_0 and n_m with no forbidden pairs and the consistent causal chains ending in the goal. $\square$

2.4 Minimal Consistent Paths: Computation

We seem to have arrived nowhere: the computation of consistent paths is computationally hard. Yet, a simple refinement will solve this problem: rather than considering the paths that are consistent, we will consider only the *minimal paths* that are so. We call these the *minimal consistent paths*: these are the paths $a_0, p_1, a_1, \ldots, p_n, a_n$ that are consistent and where each action a_i is a *best supporter* of fluent p_{i+1} (actions a that add p_{i+1} and have min $h_{max}(a; s)$ from a given state s).

Rather than pruning an action a in state s when it is not the first action in a consistent path, we will prune it when it is not the first action in a *minimal consistent path*. The resulting pruning criterion, that we refer to as *minimal consistency*, is neither sound nor complete, but it seems adequate from a heuristic point of view: it tends to be correct (pruning actions that are not good), powerful (pruning many actions), and efficient (as it can be computed sufficiently fast, even if it is also intractable in the worst case).

We focus now on the computation of all the minimal consistent paths. The algorithm computes the labels $Label_t^-(a_i)$ and $Label_t^+(a_i)$, for all *minimal paths* t, while pruning the minimal paths that are not consistent. Recall that a path $t = a_0, p_1, a_1, \ldots, p_n, a_n$ is not consistent if for some action a_i in the path, $Label_t^-(a_i)$ is mutex with $Pre(a_i)$.

While $Label_t^-(a_i)$ and $Label_t^+(a_i)$ were used before to carry the side effects that are true before and after the action a_i, $LBS^-(a_i)$ and $LBS^+(a_i)$ below will capture the *collection of labels* that express the true conditions in a plan that complies with *some minimal consistent causal chain up to* a_i. In other words, the set of fluents L (a single label) will be in the set of labels $LBS^-(a_i)$ ($LBS^+(a_i)$) if and only if $L = Label_t^-(a_i)$ (resp. $L = Label_t^+(a_i)$) for some consistent minimal causal chain $t : a_0, p_1, \ldots, a_i$.

Input: A planning problem $P = \langle F, I, O, G \rangle$
Output: The set of consistent minimal paths

1. Compute h_{max} for all p and a

2. Determine the minimal paths

3. Propagate labels along minimal paths keeping pointers

$$LBS^-(a_0) = \{s\}$$
$$LBS^+(a_i) = \{Update(a_i; s') \mid s' \in LBS^-(a_i)\}$$
$$LBS^-(a_{i+1}) = \{P(p_{i+1}; s') \mid p_{i+1} \in Pre(a_{i+1}),$$
$$s' \in LBS^+(a_j), a_j \in O^*(p_{i+1}) \text{ s.t.}$$
$$Pre(a_{i+1}) \textbf{ not mutex with } P(p_{i+1}, s')\}$$

4. Read off and return the consistent minimal paths

Figure 2.1: Computation of *minimal consistent paths*

We use some abbreviations in the algorithm: $O^*(p)$ stands for the best supporters of fluent p, $P(p_{i+1}; s')$ refers to $Persist(p_{i+1}; s')$, and actions a_i stand for actions in minimal paths with $h_{max}(a_i; s) = i$. Algorithm 1 then proceeds in four steps:

Step 1 and 3 involve forward passes from the initial situation: the first to compute the heuristic h_{max} and the third to propagate the labels. Steps 2 and 4, on the other hand, involve backward passes from the goal (*End* action): the second to determine the minimal paths, the fourth, to determine the minimal paths that are consistent. Step 3 takes advantage of the fact that the propagation of labels along a given path is markovian (only the last label matters), and prunes a path as soon it is found to be inconsistent (this is the role of the mutex condition). The consistent minimal paths are retrieved in Step 4 following stored pointers; namely, using the precondition p_{i+1}, label s', action a_j responsible for the inclusion of a label in $LBS^-(a_{i+1})$, Step 3.

In the worst case, this computation grows with the number of minimal paths, which can be exponential although seldom is. A tighter measure of the complexity of the computation is obtained by assessing the size of the collections of labels $|LBS^-(a_i)|$ and $|LBS^+(a_i)|$ that measure the number of minimal paths up to the action a_i that are consistent, which in most of the benchmarks appears to be small.

2.5 Experimental Results

The planner C1 that we consider is a simple forward-state backtracking planner that repeats this computation in every state visited, pruning the actions that do not head any consistent path (the inconsistent actions). Notice that $h_{max}(s)$ is not used as an estimator of the goal distance, but only to retrieve the minimal paths. We will see that this planner, while simple, is very effective, solving more problems than the basic architecture of FF captured by the EHC search, taking only 20% more time. From a pool of 546 problems, FF(EHC) solves 78% while C1 solves 80%, more than half of them backtrack-free. The results appear in the columns for FF(EHC) and C1 of Table 2.1.

We evaluate the planner C1 in relation to FF using only EHC, which is the incomplete planner that constitutes the basic architecture of FF and accounts for its speed. In FF, a complete but slower best-first search (BFS) mode is triggered when EHC fails. We do not compare with FF running in both modes, as one could also switch from C1 to such BFS when it fails after a few minutes or simply when it has to backtrack. Furthermore, a standard greedy best-first search (GBFS) guided by the landmark heuristic or by h_{FF}, either using only helpful actions pruning or not, performs worse than FF(EHC) and C1 in terms of coverage. Note that these GBFS correspond to each search queue used by LAMA, without interaction between them, and to the complete mode of FF (Section 1.3.4).

C1 is written in C++ and uses the parser from Metric-FF. The experiments below were conducted on a CPU with a clock speed of 2.33 GHz and 8 GB of RAM with cutoffs in time and memory of 2 hours and 2GB.

Table 2.1 shows the coverage of both planners on a collection of 546 instances from previous International Planning Competitions. Remarkably, only pruning actions that do not head minimal consistent causal chains are as important as the use of h_{FF} heuristic to distinguish good from bad helpful actions. If helpful actions are used without the heuristic, the performance of FF(EHC) is very poor. FF(EHC) solves 78% of the problems while C1 solves 80%, 47% backtrack-free without any heuristic estimator. In terms of overall time, FF(EHC) is 19% faster than C1. FF(EHC) does significantly better in Free-Cell, Rovers, Grid, and TPP,

		FF(EHC)		C1			
Domain	I	S	T	S	BF	NS	T
Blocks World	50	42	0.22	46	26	4M	1.63
Depots	22	19	44.08	18	11	4T	36.82
Driver	20	6	41.28	12	8	8T	21.65
Ferry	50	50	< 1 msec	50	6	–	0.03
Free Cell	20	14	39.88	2	2	18M	6.58
Grid	5	5	< 1 msec	3	–	1T,1M	186.26
Gripper	50	50	< 1 msec	50	–	–	0.16
Logistics	28	28	< 1msec	28	28	–	0.11
Miconic	50	50	< 1 msec	50	50	–	0.01
Mystery	30	15	323.08	20	8	1R,9T	4.83
Open Stacks	30	30	7.12	28	28	2T	381.04
Pipes World	50	4	18.01	10	4	9T,31M	150.32
Rovers	40	40	26.97	36	36	4T	448.96
Satellite	20	20	0.02	20	20	–	2.13
Storage	30	3	15.00	27	11	2T,1M	150.28
TPP	30	30	426.90	16	0	3T,11M	170.01
Zeno Travel	20	18	2.04	20	19	–	79.25
Total	546	425	78.72	436	257		96.47
Percentage	100%	78%		80%	47%		

Table 2.1: Coverage of FF-EHC and C1: S is the total number of solved instances, NS stands for the unsolved instances with nT, nM, and nR meaning the number of time outs, memory outs, and no solutions found after finishing the (incomplete) search. T is the average time in seconds and BF stands for the number of instances solved backtrack-free.

while C1 does best in Blocks, Driver, Mystery, Pipes World, and Storage.

In terms of plan quality, the plans found by C1 tend to be very long, which is not surprising, as C1 does not use any criterion for ordering the consistent actions. In the problems that it solves backtrack-free, C1 does better, where the lengths of the plans are slightly above the lengths of the plans found by FF.

2.6 Summary

We have approached the problem of inference in planning from a different perspective, building on the notion of *causal chains;* sequences of causal links. We have shown that the semantics of causal links along such chains can be used to detect that some of the chains are inconsistent and cannot be true in any plan, and furthermore, that actions that do not head any consistent causal chain leading to the goal can be pruned. We showed that while simple, this inference rule is quite powerful, as a plain backtracking forward-state search planner using a version of this rule, that considers only the *minimal paths,* solves as many benchmark problems as the effective Enforced Hill Climbing search of FF, many of them backtrack-free.

At the same time, this perspective opens new doors to the problem of inference in planning that can lead to improvements in current planning technology on the one hand, and to a better understanding of the types of planning problems that are simple, on the other. It appears, for example, that in simple problems, there are always minimal consistent paths that provide a route to the goal, while in puzzle-like problems, the minimal paths are often inconsistent. Interestingly, the EHC search in FF relies also on paths that are minimal, and hence, the range of problems that are solved by (minimal) consistent pruning and by FF's EHC appear to be closely related, even if in the former there is no explicit heuristic measure of progress. Most of the information that is captured by the computation of the consistent minimal paths is thrown away in each node, except for the first action or link. In the following chapter we show how to make further use of this information.

Chapter 3

Exploiting Causal Chains

> Man is so intelligent that he feels impelled to invent theories to account for what happens in the world. Unfortunately, he is not quite intelligent enough, in most cases, to find correct explanations. So that when he acts on his theories, he behaves very often like a lunatic.

Texts and Pretexts.
Aldous Huxley

This chapter presents different techniques to exploit further the information encoded by causal consistent chains, and extensions to make stronger inferences. We first introduce the planner C3 which competed in the International Planning Competition 2008 (IPC-6). The planner uses a stronger definition of consistency and a first attempt to exploit all the causal links of consistent chains. We then refine further the ideas of C3 and present an algorithm that uses *paths as decomposition backbones* and a *heuristic estimate* of the cost of achieving the goal *along such paths*, resulting in a planner that solves most of the benchmarks with no search at all, suggesting that planning with paths may be an interesting idea from both a cognitive and computational standpoint. Finally we explain how causal chains can be used to build a path dependent heuristic that while being more computationally intense, takes deletes into account, and expands an order of magnitude less nodes than a standard delete-based relaxation heuristic.

3.1 The Classical Planner C3 in IPC-6

The classical planner C3 competed in the sequential satisficing track of the international planning competition 2008 (IPC-6). This track covered classical STRIPS with non-negative action costs. The goal of the track was to find the lowest-cost plan in 30 minutes, although C3 returns only the first solution. The planner was a proof-of-concept to illustrate how causal chain inference can be integrated in a classical planner (Lipovetzky et al., 2008). Anytime behavior was out of our scope.

c3 is a complete classical planner supporting action costs, where the search consists of two stages:

- A hill-climbing search is conducted, pruning actions a applicable on the current state s that are not a prefix for a minimal consistent causal chain.

- If hill-climbing fails, it tries to solve the problem from the initial state using a complete heuristic search algorithm.

The first stage is similar to $C1$ but stops when the first backtrack occurs. In addition c3 uses a lazy scheme for computing the minimal consistent chains in every state, introducing an approach to exploit all the causal links of consistent chains rather than only the first one, and defining a stronger consistency criterion.

The complete heuristic search algorithm implemented is *Weighted A^**, with the evaluation function $f(n) = g(n) + (w * h(n))$, where w is set to 5. We commit to this particular weight since it is the same as that used by Metric-FF (Hoffmann, 2003), and we have observed Metric-FF's own WA^* implementation to behave quite well on existing IPC benchmarks. The heuristic function $h(n)$ is similar to h_{FF}, but the relaxed plan is extracted from the h_{add} best supporters, which tend to be more cost sensitive (Keyder and Geffner, 2008; Keyder, 2010).

3.1.1 Refining $C1$

c3 incomplete search is derived from doing three refinements and optimizations in the C1 basic scheme. We optimize consistent causal chains computation by finding these lazily in order to avoid the overhead of computing all of them. When a consistent causal chain is computed, the sub-goaling information inherent in it is explicitly used during the search. Finally, we strengthen the notion of causal consistency to account for negation, and *joint persistency* to strengthen the atoms Q that persist along a causal chain from a given state s. All three refinements are discussed next.

Lazy Computation of Consistency and Ordering

The algorithm for pruning inconsistent actions computes all the minimal consistent chains at once and discards applicable actions that do not head any such chain. Then it applies any of the consistent actions and starts the process again. The lazy computation aims to minimize the computational cost of this pruning technique since there is no need to compute all consistent chains aside from one in order to prove that an applicable action is consistent. Thus the label propagation scheme described in Algorithm 1 is replaced by a "lazy" scheme where for each action a_0 that starts one or more minimal paths, as soon as one path is found to be consistent, it stops the propagation for the paths starting in a_0. Since only one consistent action is needed in order to progress the search, c3 applies the action a_0 as soon as a consistent minimal path is found and does not compute the other possible consistent paths starting with other applicable actions a_0'.

In order to account for non-uniform cost problems, C3 sorts actions a applicable on a state s by computing the additive relaxed plan heuristic on state s', the state resulting from action a on s. Applicable actions a are sorted according to these estimated values, so that the first action proven to lead a consistent causal chain is also the best action according to the relaxed plan heuristic. This simple scheme has the effect of improving notably the quality of the plans obtained.

Causal Chain Subgoaling

Generally, if the planning problem is not trivial, many consistent causal chains can be found in every state and many actions can lead to the goal. The complexity of the search space decreases if one is able to decompose the problem into subproblems by finding intermediate subgoals. Some systems generate automatic abstractions for defining subproblems, mostly known as abstraction hierarchies (Knoblock, 1994) and other planners, like SHOP2, rely on being provided with these decompositions as part of the problem description (Nau, 2003). We approach planning decomposition by enforcing the semantics of consistent chains.

Consider the consistent chain $a_0, p_1, a_1, \ldots, p_n, a_n$. Once a_0 is applied, C3 commits to the complete chain by changing the goal of the problem. Search nodes n keep track of the index i of the next action in the causal chain, so that the goal, for the search subtree rooted at n becomes $Pre(a_i)$. For instance, once a_i is applicable in s, it is executed and the goal of the search for its successor is set to $Pre(a_{i+1})$. Once all the actions in the chain have been executed, the goal of the search is set to the precondition of the End dummy action, which corresponds with the original goal of the problem. When the goal is set to $Pre(End)$, C3 then computes a new consistent chain and commits to it, decomposing the problem again.

An applicable action a_0 is consistent in a given state s when it heads a minimal consistent causal chain up to a fluent $p \in Pre(a_i)$, where the preconditions of a_i are the current goals. Consistency is checked not only along the chain $a_o, p_1, a_2 \ldots, p_i, a_i$ but also along the remainder of the chain $a_i, p_{i+1}, \ldots, p_n, a_n$ where a_n is the End action.

Taking into account all the information of the causal chains through this subgoaling scheme, makes the search more focused, with as few oscillations as possible among different possible paths to the goal.

This hill-climbing scheme will fail when no applicable action is found to be the head for a consistent chain. In order to avoid switching to the slower best-first search stage, the causal chain driving the search is reset, when either of the two following conditions apply:

- If no action is consistent with the tail, C3 resets the tail and computes a new minimal path to the original goal.

- C3 resets the tail if the state s' resulting from action a in state s has $h(pre(a_t)|s') > h(pre(a_t)|s)$.

The first decision avoids quitting the search when the tail [1] cannot be made consistent and there are still other consistent paths to the original goal that can repopulate the tail. The second decision generally improves plan quality, avoiding plateaus induced by the tail.

Consistency: Negation and Joint Persistence

Two simple ways for strengthening the notion of path consistency while keeping it sound result from using *negative literals* in labels in addition to atoms, and a stronger function $Persist(p; s)$ to detect what set of literals q in s are required to persist if an atom p is to be preserved.

Negative literals can be introduced in the labels of chains $t = a_0, p_1, a_1, \ldots, p_n, a_n$ through a slight change in the Definition 2.6 of the *Label* function (the change in the *LBS* functions of Algorithm 1 is then direct).[2] First, negative literals $\neg L$ that are true in the seed state s are added to $Label_t^-(a_0)$. Second, the $Update(a; s)$ function is revised so that negative literals $\neg L$ in s are removed when a adds L, while negative literals $\neg L$ are added when a deletes L. Finally, $Persists(p; s)$ is revised as well, so that negative literals $\neg L$ in s are allowed to persist when all actions a that add L, either add or e-delete p. Once negation is added, two complementary literals must be taken as mutex too.

For a stronger definition of the function $Persists(p; s)$, c3 takes *the maximal subset $Q \subseteq s$* such that for every $q \in Q$, all the actions a that delete q, add or e-delete p, or have a *precondition that is mutex with an atom $q' \in Q$*. The only novelty from the previous definition is the last condition, which allows one to identify more atoms which persist as a consequence of maintaining p. It is straightforward to extend this stronger definition to both positive and negative literals. The set Q can then be computed iteratively, initializing Q to s, and removing from Q every atom q that violates the above condition until no more such atoms are left in Q. The computation of this stronger form of *joint persistence* is more costly but in many cases, pays off.

3.1.2 Experimental Results

Like C1, c3 is written in C++ and uses the parser from Metric-FF. The experiments below were conducted on a CPU with a clock speed of 2.33 GHz and 8 GB of RAM with cutoffs in time and memory of 2 hours and 2GB.

Table 3.1 shows the coverage of the c3 and FF over a collection of 545 instances over 17 benchmarks, many of them used in previous International Planning Competitions. All of the problems solved by hill-climbing in c3, indicate that these problems were solved backtrack-free, as hill-climbing aborts when no more actions are consistent. FF(EHC) solves 78% of the problems while c3(HC) solves 77%. Overall, with the complete best-first search, c3 outperforms FF solving 90% of the problems, 2% more than FF. This difference is due mainly to the

---

[1] The tail refers to the actions of the causal chain committed in the node that have not been applied yet.   [2] Alternatively, the same definition of labels can be used, but assuming that atoms $\bar{p}$ representing the negation of the atoms $p \in F$ in the problem have been added, as when negation is compiled away (Gazen and Knoblock, 1997). The result is equivalent.

			c3					
Domain	I	S	HC	BFS	TO	MO	Avg. Time	Q
Blocks World	50	50	46	4	–	–	2.38	216%
Depots	22	22	18	4	–	–	58.88	113%
Driver	20	17	6	11	3	–	103.52	107%
Ferry	50	50	50	0	–	–	0.02	114%
Free Cell	20	17	5	12	2	1	80.79	126%
Grid	5	5	5	0	–	–	10.97	112%
Gripper	50	50	50	0	–	–	0.06	132%
Logistics	28	28	28	0	–	–	0.04	136%
Miconic	50	50	50	0	–	–	< 1 msec	141%
Mystery	30	27	19	8	2	1	4.79	103%
Open Stacks	30	27	27	0	2	1	60.42	101%
Pipes World	50	18	6	12	32	–	104.66	96%
Rovers	40	40	40	0	–	–	25.37	110%
Satellite	20	20	20	0	–	–	0.46	101%
Storage	30	19	10	9	11	–	63.27	120%
TPP	30	30	30	0	–	–	47.10	119%
Zeno Travel	20	19	11	8	1	–	98.47	127%
Totals	545	489	421	68	53	3	38.89	
Percentage		90%	77%	12%	13%	4%		122%

			FF 2.3				
Domain	I	S	EHC	BFS	TO	MO	Avg. Time
Blocks World	50	42	42	0	–	8	0.22
Depots	22	22	19	3	–	–	44.08
Driver	20	16	6	10	3	–	41.28
Ferry	50	50	50	0	–	–	< 1 msec
Free Cell	20	20	14	6	–	–	39.91
Grid	5	5	5	0	–	–	0.30
Gripper	50	50	50	0	–	–	< 1 msec
Logistics	28	28	28	0	–	–	0.00
Miconic	50	50	50	0	–	–	< 1 msec
Mystery	30	19	15	4	10	1	323.078
Open Stacks	30	30	30	0	–	–	7.116
Pipes World	50	22	4	18	28	–	18.0125
Rovers	40	40	40	0	–	–	26.97
Satellite	20	20	20	0	–	–	0.10
Storage	30	18	3	15	–	12	15.00
TPP	30	30	30	0	–	–	426.90
Zeno Travel	20	20	18	2	–	–	2.15
Totals	545	482	424	58	41	21	55.60
Percentage		88%	78%	11%	10%	36%	

Table 3.1: Coverage of c3 and *FF* 2.3: S is the total number of solved instances, BF stands for the number of instances solved backtrack-free, HC stands for hill-climbing, EHC stands for enforced hill-climbing, BFS stands for best-first search, TO and MO stands for the number of time outs and memory outs found after finishing the (complete) search, and Q stands for c3 average plan quality with respect to FF, e.g., 200% stands for plans twice as long as those of FF.

heuristic used in C3(BFS). FF does better in Free-Cell, Zeno and Open Stacks while C3 does better in Blocks, Mystery, Pipes World, and Storage. In terms of overall time, C3 needs almost half the time FF needs to solve the same instances. FF is very slow in Mystery and TPP (323 s. and 426 s) compared to C3 (4 s. and 63 s.). C3 has 53 timeouts, 49 of them happen in the BFS mode. The number of memory outs is reduced compared to C1 due to the lazy computation of consistent chains. In terms of plan quality, C3 finds longer plans in every benchmark but in Pipes World, on average returning plans 22% longer than FF.

3.1.3 Conclusions

We have introduced a planner based on causal consistent chains pruning and subgoaling as a proof of concept for the international planning competition. The resulting planner is composed of a hill-climbing search that prunes inconsistent actions while decomposing the original problem. It uses a stronger consistency definition, improves the computational time of consistency and exploits further the information contained by consistent chains. If hill-climbing fails to find a solution, a complete search is triggered. In the next section we formalize further the use of consistent causal chains in order to decompose the problem and a heuristic to assess the cost of achieving the goal along such paths.

3.2 Paths as Decomposition Backbones

Based on the good performance of C3, in this section we develop three techniques for performing inference over causal chains from which a path-based planner is obtained. We first refine the conditions under which a path is consistent, provide a heuristic estimate of the cost of achieving the goal along a consistent path, and introduce a planning algorithm that uses paths as decomposition backbones. The resulting planner, called C3 (version 2), is not complete and does not perform as well as recent planners that carry extensive but extremely efficient searches such as LAMA, but is competitive with FF and in particular, with FF running in EHC mode which yields very focused but incomplete searches, and thus provides, a more apt comparison. Moreover, more domains are solved backtrack-free, with no search at all, suggesting that planning with paths may be a meaningful idea both cognitively and computationally.

3.2.1 Consistency: Forward and Backward

We assume that the reasons for performing an action take the form of a sequence of causal links, that we call *causal chains*. When these causal chains reach the goal, we call them paths. They are not plans but rather *plan skeletons*, where actions may have to be filled in for achieving *all* the preconditions of the actions in the path.

A path starting with an action a that is applicable in the state s is said to be applicable in s. Such a path can be taken to suggest that a may be relevant for achieving the goal in s (Nebel et al., 1997). However, as argued before, it can be shown that certain paths, understood as sequences of causal links, cannot occur in any plan. We have seen an example in Tower-n, where blocks $1, \ldots, n$ initially on the table are to be arranged so that i is on top of $i+1$ for $i = 1, \ldots, n-1$. For this problem, the paths

$$t : pick(k), hold(k), stack(k, k+1), on(k, k+1), End$$

for any $k \neq n-1$ can be shown not to be true in any plan.[1] Indeed, if there is any plan where the path holds, one can show that $ontable(k+1)$ will be true when End is executed, but this atom is mutex with the precondition $on(k+1, k+2)$ of End because $ontable(k+1)$ is initially true and remains true when $hold(k)$ is preserved (first causal link), and when $on(k, k+1)$ is preserved (second causal link). This sort of inference, that captures *side-effects* along causal chains was formalized in Section 2.3.

We characterize the sets of fluents that must be true *before* and *after* applying each action a_i in a causal chain t, for *any plan* complying with the chain, as in Definition 2.6 but with joint persistence (Section 3.1.1). Thus the sets $F_t^-(a_i)$ and $F_t^+(a_i)$ are defined as follows:

Definition 3.1. *The sets $F_t^-(a_i)$ and $F_t^+(a_i)$, for a causal chain $t : a_0, p_1, a_1, \ldots, p_n, a_n$ applicable in a state s, $0 \leq i \leq n$, are*

- $F_t^-(a_0) = s$

- $F_t^+(a_i) = Update(a_i; F_t^-(a_i))$

- $F_t^-(a_{i+1}) = Persist(p_{i+1}; F_t^+(a_i))$

where $Update(a; s)$ is the set of facts

$$(s \cup Pre(a) \cup Add(a)) \setminus Del(a)$$

and $Persist(p; s)$ is the maximal subset $Q \subseteq s$, *such that for every $q \in Q$, all the actions a that delete q, either add or e-delete p, or have a precondition that is mutex with a $q' \in Q$.*

This definition does not provide a complete characterization but can be computed efficiently in low polynomial time. The only subtlety is in the computation of $Persists(p; s)$ that must be done iteratively, in no more iterations than fluents in the problem, and usually much fewer.

The definition above captures side effects by reasoning forwards along a causal chain. It is also possible to infer necessary side effects by reasoning backwards. The definition of the backward labels $B_t^+(a_i)$ and $B_t^-(a_i)$ proceeds in an analogous way:

Definition 3.2. *The sets $B_t^-(a_i)$ and $B_t^+(a_i)$, for a causal chain $t : a_o, p_1, a_1, \ldots, p_n, a_n$ $0 \leq i < n$, are*

---

[1] A causal link a, p, b is true in a sequential plan when a precedes b in the plan, a adds p, p is a precondition of b, and no action between a and b either adds or deletes p. If there are many occurrences of a and b in the plan, then the CL is true in the plan when it is true for one pair of such occurrences. It is direct to extend this to sequences of causal links being true in a plan.

- $B_t^-(a_n) = Pre(a)$

- $B_t^+(a_i) = PersistB(p_{i+1}; B_t^-(a_i + 1))$

- $B_t^-(a_i) = UpdateB(a_i; B_t^+(a_i))$

where $UpdateB(a; s)$ is the set of facts

$$(s \cup Pre(a)) \setminus Add(a))$$

and $PersistB(p; s)$ is the maximal subset $Q \subseteq s$, such that for every $q \in Q$, all the actions a that add q, either add or e-delete p.

Indeed, in the same way that the atom $ontable(k + 1)$, for $k \neq n$, can be propagated forward along the path t into the set $F_t^-(End)$, the atom $on(k+1, k+2)$ can be propagated backwards from $Pre(End)$ into $B_t^-(pick(k))$. This is because the only action that adds $on(k + 1, k + 2)$, namely $stack(k + 1, k + 2)$, e-deletes $on(k, k + 1)$, as its precondition $clear(k+1)$ is mutex with this atom, while it also e-deletes $hold(k)$. The atom $on(k + 1, k + 2)$ in $B_t^-(pick(k))$ thus means that in any plan complying with the chain t, the atom $on(k + 1, k + 2)$ must be true just before the first action of the chain; an inference that can be understood as a form of goal ordering along a chain (Koehler and Hoffmann, 2000). We will indeed refer to the fluents p in a label $B_t^-(a_i)$, such that $p \notin Pre(a_i)$, as the *implicit preconditions* of the action a_i along the chain t. These conditions are needed at the time a is executed, not by a, but by the actions that follow a along the path.

Forward and backward inference along a chain can be combined to interact synergistically. For example, knowing that a certain fluent p must persist backwards along an interval, can help to establish that a certain other fluent q must persist forward along the same interval, if the actions that delete q, e-delete p. This combination of forward and backward inference yields fixed point labels that we will refer to as the final labels $L_t^-(a_i)$ and $L_t^+(a_i)$. The consistency of a path is defined as follows:

Definition 3.3. *A causal chain applicable in a state s is inconsistent in s if one of the final labels along the chain include a mutex pair. If the chain is not inconsistent, it is said to be consistent.*

Note that the previous definition of path consistency (Definition 2.7) checked explicitly if $pre(a_i)$ was mutex with $L_t^-(a_i)$ as the labels were only propagated forwards.

The notion of *implicit preconditions* along a path and the notion of *path consistency*, will be two of the building blocks of the planning algorithm below.

3.2.2 Minimality

The only paths considered are the minimal paths (Definition 2.3). This is what makes the planner incomplete, in the same way that the EHC search with only helpful actions is incomplete in FF. There is a difference though: while FF computes the helpful and hence minimal actions without restriction, we will see that c3 computes the minimal actions in the context of a set of commitments. As a consequence, the minimal actions are not necessarily the same actions that are minimal when no commitments are made. A simple example illustrates the difference.

A simple problem that requires non-minimal actions is what we call the 'suit-case' problem. A passenger is at location L_1 with a suitcase on the floor, and he must get to location L_{10} holding the suitcase. For getting from L_1 to L_{10} there are two paths: a direct one L_2, L_3, ..., L_{10} and a longer one. On the shorter path, however, there is a catch: the passenger cannot pass from L_4 to L_5 while hold-ing the suitcase. No such restriction exists on the longer path. The solution to the problem is to pick up the suitcase, and head to L_{10} through the longer path. The minimal and helpful actions in the initial state, however, are to pick up the suitcase and head for the shorter path. FF will thus solve the problem once the helpful action restriction is dropped. A different approach is taken in c3.

In the new c3 algorithm that we introduce next, we always stick to the min-imal actions but commit to paths, and therefore, to causal links. So all actions that constitute 'threats' to a causal link a, p, b that has been temporarily commit-ted to, i.e. that delete or e-delete p, are excluded until the action b is executed. By excluding some actions, paths that were not minimal in the original problem P, may become minimal in the modified problem. In the problem above, once the suitcase is picked up to support the precondition 'holding suitcase' of the action End, this causal link is maintained by dropping from the problem all the actions that 'threat' (delete or e-delete) the causal link. The action of moving from L_4 to L_5 is then excluded as it e-deletes 'holding suitcase'. Once the suitcase is picked up and this action is excluded, the longer path to L_{10} becomes the minimal path, leading to a plan without backtracks.

We will say that a path t is minimal in a state s in the context of a set of atoms p that must be preserved, if t is minimal in the modified problem where the actions that delete or e-delete p are excluded. Such paths are obtained from the minimal graph induced by the h_{max} heuristic with the exclusion of those actions, by tracing backward from the goal all their best supporters and the best supporters of their preconditions recursively.

3.2.3 Decomposition: The Planning Algorithm

The plan algorithm in c3 regards a consistent path $t : a_0, p_1, a_1, \ldots, p_n, a_n$ in a state s as a recipe for a *decomposition* where the actions a_0, a_1, etc. are executed in that order by solving a series of subproblems: after applying the action a_i, the preconditions of the next action a_{i+1} become the goal, and so on, until reach-ing the End action a_n. In this decomposition, the *implicit preconditions* of each action a_i in the path, derived backward from the goal, are included among the explicit preconditions $Pre(a)$. A planning problem is solved by finding first a con-sistent path to decompose the problem, and using the same method recursively to decompose the first subproblem until the path can be reduced.

We refer to the operation of applying the action a_i after its (explicit and implicit) preconditions have been achieved, as a *reduction* step. In the reduction of a path $a_i, p_{i+1}, a_{i+1}, \ldots, p_n, a_n$, the current state is progressed through the action a_i, and the algorithm is then called on the subproblem with path $a_{i+1}, \ldots, p_n, a_n$, where the atom p_i is *maintained* until the action a_{i+1} is executed.

A reduction is not possible when the preconditions of the first action do not hold in the current state s. If $t : a_i, p_{i+1}, a_{i+1}, \ldots, p_n, a_n$ is the path, then a new path t' is created by composing a minimal chain for an 'open' precondition of a_i (that is not true in s), and the 'tail' t. This operation is called an *extension*. For the construction of the minimal chain, the actions that delete or e-delete conditions that must be maintained until a_i is executed, are excluded.

The paths that are created by the *extensions* are always checked for consistency: inconsistent paths are skipped over while the implicit preconditions are computed for the paths found to be consistent.

The state of the planning algorithm or solver is a tuple comprising the current state s, the committed path t, the set K of pairs $\langle p, a \rangle$ so that p needs to be preserved until a is applied, and the plan prefix π. Initially, $s = s_0$, $t = \{End\}$, and $K = \pi = \{\}$.

The reduction and extension steps modify the state of the solver. The algorithm terminates when the tail $t = \{End\}$ is reduced. On the other hand, when the current path t cannot be reduced or extended with a consistent path, the commitments, i.e., t and K, are *reset*. The option here is to backtrack rather than to reset, yet this option produces weaker empirical results. The solver backtracks though when there is nothing to reset; namely, when the solver state is a reset state with $K = \{\}$ and $t = \{End\}$ in which the path cannot be reduced or extended consistently.

Pseudo-code for the planning algorithm is shown in Figure 3.1. The minimal chains in the extend operation are computed very much like relaxed plans, in two phases: in the forward phase, the heuristic $h_{max}(p)$ is computed for all fluents p from the current state s; in the second phase, all the best h_{max} supporters of the goals are marked, and the process is applied recursively to the preconditions of such actions, excluding the goals and preconditions that are true in s. In this process, actions a that e-delete an atom p that must be preserved at that stage, i.e. atoms p for a pair (p, b) in K, are excluded. The minimal chains compatible with the commitments in K that extend the current path t can then be obtained starting with the actions applicable in s that are marked. The CHOOSEMINPATH construct in the algorithm expresses a non-deterministic choice that is critical for the actual performance of the algorithm: the order in which consistent minimal paths are constructed and considered, given by the best supporter marks. We address this issue next.

There are two sources of incompleteness in the algorithm. First, the exclusion of paths that are not minimal in the extension operation, and second, the interpretation of paths as sequential decompositions. Neither choice, however, turns out to be as restrictive as it may appear. In the first case, because the minimal paths are computed given a set of commitments; in the second, because the implicit preconditions take into account not only the immediate goals, given by the preconditions of the first action in the path, but further goals down the path as well.

Input: An initial state $s = s_0$; initial path $t = \{End\}$; atoms to keep $K = \{\}$;
plan prefix $\pi = \{\}$
Output: A plan π

function $\mathtt{Solve}\,(s, t, K, \pi)$:
begin
    $G \leftarrow$ Prec of first action in t
    if G *true in s* **then**
        if $t = End$ **then**   (⋆ Plan found ⋆)
            return π
        else
            $\mathtt{Solve}\,(s', t', K', \pi + a)$ (⋆ Reduce ⋆)
                where $t = a, p, t'$
                  $s' = do(a, s)$
                  $K' = (K - \forall(q, a) \in K) + (p, b)$
                  s.t. b is the first action in t'
    else
        $\mathtt{ComputeMinGraph}$ excluding actions that e-delete q for $(q, b) \in K$
        $\mathtt{ChooseMinPath}$ a, p, t_1 for G in min graph that is consistent, computing
        implicit preconditions
        $\mathtt{Solve}\,(do(a, s), t_1 + t, K + (p, b), \pi + a)$ (⋆ Extend ⋆)
        if *no consistent path left* **then**
            if *if $t = \{End\}$ and $K = \{\}$* **then**
                return fail   (⋆ Backtrack ⋆)
        else
            $\mathtt{Solve}\,(s, \{END\}, K = \{\}, \pi)$ (⋆ Reset ⋆)

Figure 3.1: *C3* Decomposition Planning Algorithm

3.2.4 Preferences: Sorting Causal Chains

The order in which the consistent minimal paths are constructed after marking the best h_{max} supporters backwards from the goal, has a significant impact on the performance of the algorithm. This operation is needed when the current path t needs to be extended. Ideally, we would like to find quickly a minimal path $t' + t$ that is consistent and which yields a good decomposition towards the goal. The criterion that we use to achieve this is heuristic, and the strategy greedy.

The building block for ordering the paths in the extension step, is a new heuristic $h(t|s)$ built from a known base heuristic, that estimates the cost of achieving the goal *along the path* t. The interesting thing about this new heuristic is that it takes deletes into account, even if the base heuristic does not, and it penalizes paths t that provide bad decompositions. Moreover, $h(t|s) = 0$ if and only if the sequence of actions in t constitutes a plan from s, as the heuristic excludes the cost of the actions already committed (actions in t). The base heuristic is the additive heuristic, but other heuristics could be used as well.

Let t be the consistent path $a_1, p_2, \ldots, p_n, a_n$. This path does not have to be applicable in the state s, but as any path, it must reach the goal (i.e. $a_n = End$). For any such path, we provide first an (heuristic) estimation of the state s_{i+1} that results right after the action a_i in the path is applied. We use the expression $\pi(a_i; s_i)$ to denote a relaxed plan that achieves the (explicit and implicit) preconditions of action a_i in the state s_i along the path. This relaxed plan is obtained by collecting the best supporters according to the base heuristic, backwards from the goal (Keyder and Geffner, 2008).

If $\pi_i = \pi(a_i, s_i)$ is the relaxed plan for achieving the preconditions of a_i from s_i, then the state s_{i+1} *projected* after applying the action a_i is estimated as

$$s_{i+1} = (((s_i \setminus Del(\pi_i)) \cup Add(\pi_i)) \setminus eDel(a_i)) \cup Add(a_i) \qquad (3.1)$$

where $Add(\pi_i)$ is the set of fluents added by the actions in π_i, $eDel(a_i)$ is the set of fluents e-deleted by the action a_i and $Del(\pi_i)$ refers to a *subset* of the fluents deleted by actions in π_i. This subset is defined as the fluents that are deleted not just by one action in π_i, that is a best supporter of some fluent p in the the relaxed plan, but by *all* the best supporters of p, whether they made it in the relaxed plan or not. The reason is that the choice of best supporters in the relaxed plan is rather arbitrary, and deleting a fluent because an arbitrary best supporter deletes it turns out to be more critical than adding a fluent that an arbitrary supporter adds. So these deletions aim to be cautious.

A state sequence $s_1, \ldots, s_n$ is then generated for a consistent chain $t : a_1, p_2, \ldots, p_n, a_n$ in a state s, according to the formula above by setting s_1 to s, $\pi(a_i, s_i)$ to the relaxed plan for obtaining the preconditions of a_i from s_i, and s_{i+1} as in the formula above. This sequence is used to compute the heuristic $h(t|s)$, that estimates the cost of achieving the goal along the path t and can be expressed as

$$\sum_{i=1}^{n} h(Pre(a_i)|s_i)$$

where implicit preconditions in the path are treated as action preconditions. This estimate is just the sum of the estimated costs of solving each of the subproblems along the path, assuming that the states s_i along the path are those in the projected state sequence.

A problem with this estimate, however, is that due to the use of deletes, it is often infinite. This may reflect the fact that the projected state sequence is misleading, but more often, that the decomposition expressed by the path t is not perfect. For example, if precondition p of an action a_i cannot be established from the state s_i, yielding $h(a_i|s_i) = \infty$, it is possible that such a precondition can be established in the previous subproblem from the state s_{i-1} and maintained into the following subproblem if the action a_{i-1} does not e-delete it.

With this in mind, we define the estimated cost of achieving the goal through a consistent path $t : a_1, \ldots, p_n, a_n$ as

$$h(t|s) = \sum_{i=1}^{n} h_i(Pre(a_i)|s_i)$$

where h_1 is equal to the base heuristic h, and h_{i+1} is

$$h_{i+1}(p|s_{i+1}) - \min\left[\, h(p|s_{i+1}),\ h_i(p|s_i) + \Delta_i(p)\,\right]$$

where $\Delta_i(p)$ is a penalty term for bringing p from the subproblem i along the path t to subproblem $i+1$. We have set $\Delta_i(p)$ to a large constant, independent of i and p (10 in our experiments), except when the action a_i e-deletes p where $\Delta_i(p)$ is set to ∞. In the computation of the base heuristic $h(p|s_i)$ for all fluents p in the subproblem that corresponds to $s = s_i$, all the actions that e-delete a fluent in the label $L_t^-(a_i)$ are excluded, as those are the fluents that must hold prior to a_i in any plan that complains with the path t.

Provided with this heuristic function, the extensions $t' = b_1, q_1, b_2, \ldots, q_m, b_m$ of a path t in a state s in the planning algorithm, are constructed incrementally, starting with the actions that are applicable in s that have been marked as best supporters in the extension step in the algorithm. The action b_1 is chosen as the action that minimizes $h(t|s_1)$ where s_1 is the state that results from applying b_1 in s, and given the action b_i and the state s_i projected along the t' path, the action b_{i+1} is chosen as the one that minimizes $h(t|s_{i+1})$, among the actions in the min graph with a precondition q_i that is added by b_i.

In these extensions, we prune the chains that contain actions b_i that either appear already in one of the relaxed plans $\pi(b_k, s_k)$, for some $k < i$, or that support an atom q_i in the path that some action in those relaxed plans add. This is because when the planner commits to a path like $b_1, q_1, b_2, q_2, \ldots$ where b_i is a best supporter for q_i, it is reasonable to assume that in the plans that comply with this path, b_i and q_i do not occur prior to their occurrence in the path. In other words, the assumption of best supporters in the path, is also an assumption of first supporters in the plans complying with the path.

3.2.5 Examples

The c3 planner is supposed to be a transparent planner where the choice for the actions selected can be explained in terms of reasons given by paths. Thus, before reporting the tables that are standard in the experimental evaluation of planners, we analyze the behavior of c3 over two examples.

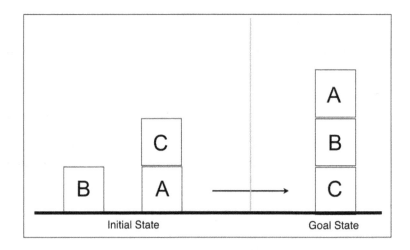

Figure 3.2: A blocks-world instance requiring goal interleaving

Blocks World

The so-called Sussman Anomaly is a small instance of the Blocks-World domain known because it requires some form of goal interleaving. The instance is shown in Figure 3.2: the problem has two goals, b on c, and a on b, but no goal can be tackled first while leaving the other goal aside; the subgoals of the two problems need to be interleaved, something that appears to defy the decomposition in the c3 planner.

The first consistent path that extends the initial path given by the End action, in the initial state, is

$$t_1 : unstack(c, a), clear(a), pick(a), hold(a),$$
$$stack(a, b), on(a, b), End$$

with the goal $on(b, c)$, which is the other precondition of End, inferred to be an implicit precondition of $pick(a)$, as the actions that add $on(b, c)$ e-deletes both $hold(a)$ and $on(a, b)$. This is the second path considered in the extension step, because the first path

$$t_2 : pick(b), hold(b), stack(b, c), on(b, c), End$$

is found to be inconsistent: the precondition $on(a, b)$ is mutex with the atom $ontable(a)$ that is propagated along the path from the initial state to the End action.

Once the path t_1 is returned, it is then reduced by applying its first action $unstack(c, a)$ in the initial state $s = s_0$. This reduction implies a commitment to the fluent $clear(a)$ until $pick(a)$ is executed, and a new path t_1' given by the tail of t_1 starting with $pick(a)$. This new path cannot be reduced because $pick(a)$ has explicit and implicit preconditions that do not hold in the resulting state s_1 where

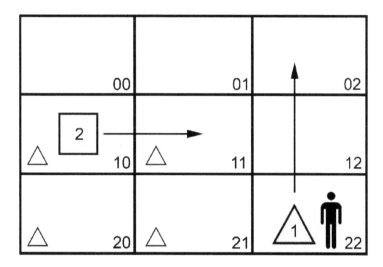

Figure 3.3: A Grid instance: key 1 needed to unlock positions 11 and 10 to reach key 2. Key 2 must be placed at 11 and key 1 at 02.

block c is being held. The planner then extends t'_1 with the chain

$$t_3 : putdown(c), handfree, pick(b), hold(b),$$
$$stack(b, c), on(b, c)$$

that supports one of open (implicit) preconditions of $pick(a)$ and yields the consistent path $t_3 + t'_1$. It turns out that the actions in this path form a plan from the state s_1, and thus, the problem is solved after 6 successive reductions. Since no more extensions are needed, the problem is solved backtrack-free in two extensions: the first that generated the path t_1 that extended the initial path $t = \{End\}$; the second, that generated the path $t_3 + t'_1$ that extended the tail t'_1 of t_1.

Grid Problem

The Grid domain consists of an agent, that can carry a key, moving around in a grid. Some of the cells in the grid are locked and can be opened by keys of a certain shape. Before moving into a locked place, however, the agent has to unlock it from an adjacent position. The lower-right numbers are the cell indexes in the grid, and the lower-left shapes indicate whether or not the positions are locked and the shape needed to unlock them. The square at position 10 is the shape of key 2 ($k2$) and the triangle is the shape of key 1 ($k1$) at position 22. The arrows indicate where the keys have to be moved (Figure 3.3).

Before finding the first consistent path from the initial state s_0 in the instance shown, the following paths are generated

$$t_1 : pick(22, k1), hold(k1), put(02, k1), k1@02, End.$$
$$t_2 : pick(22, k1), hold(k1), put(11, k1), k1@11,$$
$$pick\&lose(11, k1, k2), k2@11, End.$$

and pruned, although this time not because they are inconsistent but because both have heuristic values $h(t_i|s_0) = \infty$. In the first case, because of the last sub-problem, where the precondition $k2@11$ must be achieved from a projected state where $k2$ is at the (still) locked position 10, while the atom $k1@02$ is preserved. In the second, because of the subproblem where the precondition $hold(k2)$ of $pick\&lose(11, k1, k2)$ must be achieved from a projected state where $k2$ is at the locked position 10 while maintaining the atom $k1@11$. Actually, the generation of the path t_2 is pruned at that point and never reaches the End action.

The third path generated turns out to be consistent and is

$$t_3 : pick(22, k1), hold(k1), unlock(12, 11, k1),$$
$$open(11), move(12, 11), atrobot(11),$$
$$unlock(11, 10, k1), open(10), move(11, 10),$$
$$atrobot(10), pick\&lose(10, k2, k1), hold(k2),$$
$$put(11, k2), k2@11, End,$$

that describes a *plan skeleton* where after picking up $k1$, the robot unlocks 11 from 12, moves then to 11, unlocks 10, moves then to 10, exchanges $k1$ with $k2$, and places $k2$ at its target cell. This is a plan skeleton as some actions need to be filled in by suitable extensions. Indeed, this path can be reduced up to End after two successive and successful extensions calls, involving the action $move(22, 12)$ before $unlock(12, 11, k1)$, and the action $move(10, 11)$ before $put(11, k2)$.

After this reduction, the tail contains the End action only, that cannot be reduced since its other precondition $k1@02$ does not hold, and then an extension call that keeps the atom $k2@11$, results in the following consistent path:

$$t_4 : move(11, 10), atrobot(10), pick(10, k1),$$
$$hold(k1), put(02, k1), k1@02, End$$

whose first two actions can be reduced right away, and where the 'open' precondition $atrobot(02)$ of the third action, $put(02, k1)$, results in an extension call that fills in the moves needed to apply this action and get to the goal. The plan is thus obtained after 3 main extensions, the first one extends the initial path that just contains the End action and results in the path t_2, the second that extends the initial path but in a different state and with the commitment to keep $k2@11$, and the third that extends the tail $put(02, k1), k1@02, End$ of t_4 with the move actions to get to $atrobot(02)$.

Domain	I	FF			c3				LAMA		
		S	EHC	T	S	BF	T	Q	S	T	Q
Blocks World	50	42	42	0.22	50	50	8.79	114%	50	0.87	187%
Depots	22	22	19	44.08	22	22	107.82	90%	20	46.58	102%
Driver	20	16	6	41.28	20	17	41.02	118%	20	4.67	104%
Ferry	50	50	50	< 1msec	50	50	0.07	117%	50	0.18	104%
Free Cell	20	20	14	38.80	6	3	26.21	139%	20	34.30	115%
Grid	5	5	5	< 1msec	5	3	107.72	98%	5	5.58	95%
Gripper	50	50	50	< 1msec	50	50	0.98	132%	50	0.00	100%
Logistics	28	28	28	< 1msec	28	28	0.76	135%	28	0.25	101%
Miconic	50	50	50	< 1msec	50	50	0.02	154%	50	0.15	100%
Mystery	30	19	15	323.08	23	14	2.44	103%	22	15.31	93%
Open Stacks	30	30	30	7.12	29	29	557.51	99%	30	12.80	102%
Pipes World	50	22	4	18.01	28	22	957.33	152%	28	112.25	118%
Rovers	40	40	40	26.97	39	39	548.88	102%	40	13.44	103%
Satellite	20	20	20	0.02	20	20	3.24	101%	20	0.90	107%
Storage	30	18	3	15.00	29	10	446.06	100%	18	1.62	121%
TPP	30	30	30	426.90	27	25	586.84	122%	30	13.11	87%
Zeno Travel	20	20	18	2.14	20	20	53.15	129%	20	3.55	117%
Total	545	482	424	78.63	496	452	202.87		501	15.62	
Percentage		88%	78%		91%	83%		118%	92%		109%

Table 3.2: c3 vs. FF and LAMA on instances of previous IPCs: *S* is the number of solved instances, *EHC* is the number of problems solved by EHC, *BF* is the number of instances solved *Backtrack-free*, *T* is the average time in seconds, and *Q* is the plan quality ratio; e.g. 200% means plans twice as long as those reported by FF on average

3.2.6 Experimental Results

We compare c3 with FF and LAMA over a broad range of planning benchmarks.[1] c3 is written in C++ and uses Metric-FF as an *ADL* to *Propositional* STRIPS compiler (Hoffmann, 2003). LAMA is executed without the plan improvement option, reporting the first plan that is found. All experiments were conducted on a dual-processor Xeon Woodcrest running at 2.33 GHz and 8 GB of RAM. Processes time out or memory out after 2 hours or 2 GB. All action costs are assumed to be 1 so that plan cost is plan length.

Table 3.2 compares c3 with *FF* and *LAMA* over 545 instances from previous IPCs. In terms of coverage, c3 solves 5 fewer problems than LAMA but 14 more than FF, and more remarkably, it solves 452 problems (30 fewer than FF and 28 more than FF in EHC) *backtrack-free*, that is, heading directly to the goal, without ever having to revise a plan prefix. There are several domains where c3 solves more problems than both FF and LAMA, the largest difference being in Storage, where c3 solves 29 problems, and FF and LAMA 18. On the other extreme, FF and LAMA solve all the 20 Free Cell instances, while c3 solves only 6.

The average quality of the plans found by c3 is 18% worse than those found by FF, and 9% worse than those found by *LAMA*, with the largest differences in *Miconic* and *Pipesworld*. In some cases, however, it delivers shorter plans, like in

---

[1] FF is FF2.3, while LAMA is the version used in the 2008 IPC.

Domain	I	FF			c3				LAMA		
		S	EHC	T	S	BF	T	Q	S	T	Q
Cybersecure	30	4	4	0.74	20	20	170.71	100%	25	402.26	100%
Elevator	30	30	30	1.34	30	29	226.25	125%	30	3.28	103%
Openstacks	30	30	30	0.59	30	30	180.84	100%	24	0.48	105%
ParcPrinter	30	30	21	0.05	30	30	6.03	102%	30	3.53	104%
Pegsol	30	30	0	9.87	21	4	70.67	104%	28	25.84	100%
Scanalyzer	30	30	22	55.57	25	25	173.31	94%	30	41.02	97%
Transport	30	30	30	355.50	24	14	806.67	125%	30	9.83	85%
Wood	30	17	12	5.08	8	8	34.70	98%	30	3.68	104%
Total	240	201	149	53.59	188	160	208.65		227	61.24	
Percentage	100%	84%	62%		78%	67%		106%	95%		100%

Table 3.3: c3 vs. FF and LAMA on instances from the 2008 IPC

Depots, where it delivers plans that are 10% shorter.

Table 3.3 compares c3 with *FF* and *LAMA* over 240 instances of the IPC-6 held in 2008. In this set of benchmarks, c3 does relatively worse, with LAMA solving 227 of the problems, FF solving 201, and c3 solving 188; 85% backtrack-free.

Domains like *M-Prime*, *Pathways*, *Pipes-NT*, and *Psr-Small*, are not included in the tables because one or more of the planners had problems parsing the instances. On the other hand, in *Sokoban*, c3 could not solve *any instance*, very similar to FF in EHC mode. In both, the problem arises from the focus on the paths that are minimal. The version of c3 used in IPC-6 solves these instances by triggering a best-first search when the basic algorithm fails, very similar to FF. For clarity, however, we have excluded this option here.

A measure of the number of choices made in FF and LAMA is given by the number of nodes expanded. In c3, this measure is given by the number of extension operations. As we have seen, the number of extension operations can be smaller than the number of actions in the plan, as often many of the actions in a path can be reduced one after the other. While in many cases, FF and LAMA expand thousands of nodes as shown in Table 3.4, c3 appear to solve a similar number of problems by performing a much reduced number of extensions in all domains but Pegsol, where c3 falls in many deadends. This, however, does not mean that c3 is faster; actually, it is not, due to the overhead in the ordering, filtering, and selection of paths.

Overall, these results are surprisingly good, as c3 did not aim to compete with state-of-the-art planners, but with algorithms such as FF's EHC that provide very focused but incomplete searches, and that work very well in problems that are not particularly hard. In this sense, c3 does extremely well, solving more problems backtrack-free than those solved by FF in EHC mode. Moreover, overall c3 solves more instances than FF, 684 vs. 683, although LAMA does better than both, solving 728 instances in total.

Domain	I	FF Expands	c3 Extends	LAMA Expands
Blocks World	50	9,193	23	1,496
Cybersecure	30	228	15	151
Depots	22	57,777	23	42,609
Driver	20	7,062	21	7,892
Elevator	30	1,254	61	666
Ferry	50	50	17	108
Free Cell	20	5,573	28	3,091
Grid	5	301	12	174
Gripper	50	102	51	80
Logistics	28	94	29	97
Miconic	50	52	26	37
Mystery	30	75,031	4	63,597
Openstacks	30	993	87	162
OpenstacksIPC6	30	866	78	397
Parc Printer	30	252	18	13,980
Pegsol	30	32	4,021	873
Pipes World	50	36,572	37	36,140
Rovers	40	10,341	42	1,750
Satellite	20	389	21	412
Scanalyzer	30	2,166	14	4,882
Storage	30	142,526	45	3,348
Transport	30	105,754	77	6,828
TPP	30	116,904	63	1,805
Wood	30	1,027	21	146
Zeno Travel	20	135	21	482
Total	785	22,987	194	7,648

Table 3.4: c3, FF and LAMA on instances of previous IPCs: *Expands* is the average number of expanded nodes and *Extends* is the average number of path extensions.

3.2.7 Conclusion

We have focused on the study of paths for planning and developed three techniques for performing inference over them. We refined the conditions under which a path is consistent, provided an heuristic estimate of the cost of achieving the goal along a consistent path, and introduced a planning algorithm that uses paths recursively as decomposition backbones. The resulting planner is not complete and does not perform as well as recent planners, but surprisingly, does not lag far behind. Moreover, of the collection of 728 problems, 78% of them are solved backtrack-free.

The use of causal links is a feature of POCL planners (McAllester and Rosenblitt, 1991), and some recent POCL planners perform various forms of inference over them (Nguyen and Kambhampati, 2001; Younes and Simmons, 2003; Vidal and Geffner, 2006). The proposed planner, however, is not a POCL planner but a path-based planner, as it explores, evaluates, and commits to complete paths rather than to individual causal links. As hinted above, some of the inference

over these paths are structural rather than heuristic. Other forms of structural
inference in modern planners are the notion of helpful actions in FF, and the
use of landmarks in LAMA (introduced in Hoffmann et al. (2004)). Many of these
notions have been incorporated in various planners as they are compatible with
the use of heuristic estimators and different search strategies. The same is true
for the forms of inference over paths that we consider, some of which can find
uses in other contexts.

3.3   Path-Based Heuristic

The version of c3 just introduced, computes paths $a_0, p_1, a_1, \ldots, p_n, a_n$ with $a_n = End$ from the current state, and uses them to decompose the problem into subproblems: achieving first the preconditions of a_0, then from the resulting state
the preconditions of a_1 while preserving p_1, etc. Moreover, this decomposition is
recursive, and thus if the preconditions of the first action in the path are true,
the action is applied and otherwise, the problem of achieving them is handled in
the same manner by finding a path to an open precondition of the first action,
and so on.

A key aspect of the algorithm is the way paths t are ranked and constructed
in a given state s. This is done by means of a new heuristic $h(t|s)$, built from
a known base heuristic, that *estimates the cost of achieving the goal along the
path t*. Since the path t is built incrementally, in order to define this heuristic on
paths, we let t range not only on full paths that reach the goal through the End
action, but also over partial paths or chains that do not. The new state heuristic
that we want to define and evaluate here can be roughly stated as $h_{path}(s)$:

$$h_{\text{path}}(s) = \min_t h(t|s) \tag{3.2}$$

where t ranges among the paths applicable in s; namely, the causal chains that
connect s with the goal. This is the general idea, although later we will restrict the
space of paths to be considered. We take the basic building blocks from previous
sections.

3.3.1   Ranking Chains and Projected States

Let t be a causal chain $a_1, p_2, \ldots, p_n, a_n$. For generality, we do not assume that the
first action is applicable in s nor that the last action is the End action. We want
the heuristic $h(t|s)$ to estimate the cost of achieving the goal along this chain. For
defining this heuristic, we estimate the sequence of states $s_1, \ldots, s_n$ induced by
the chain so that s_i is the state that is estimated to be true right after the action
a_i in the chain that is applied.

The sequence of states induced by a chain is defined in Equation 3.1 from
Section 3.2.4. The heuristic $h(t|s)$ for the chain $t : a_1, p_2, \ldots, p_n, a_n$ in a state s is
defined in terms of a base heuristic h, and a sequence $s_1, \ldots, s_n$ of states induced
by t

$$h(t|s) = \sum_{i=1}^{n} [\, cost(a_i) + h(Pre(a_i)|s_i)\,] \tag{3.3}$$

where in the computation of the heuristic $h(Pre(a_i)|s_i)$ for $1 < i \leq n$, all the actions that interfere with the causal link a_{i-1}, p_i, a_i in t are excluded (actions that e-delete p_i). This estimate is thus the sum of the estimated costs of solving each of the subproblems along the path, assuming that the states s_i along the path are those projected and that causal links are respected.

As stated in Section 3.2.4, a problem with this estimate, however, is that due to the use of deletes in the projection and the preservation of causal links, it is often infinite. For example, if a precondition p of an action a_i cannot be established from the state s_i, yielding $h(a_i|s_i) = \infty$, it is possible that such a precondition can be established in the previous subproblem from the state s_{i-1} and maintained into the following subproblem if the action a_{i-1} does not e-delete it. With this in mind, the estimated cost of achieving the goal through the chain $t : a_1, \ldots, p_n, a_n$ is defined as

$$h(t|s) = \sum_{i=1}^{n} [cost(a_i) + h_i(Pre(a_i)|s_i)] \tag{3.4}$$

where h_1 is equal to the base heuristic h, and h_{i+1} is

$$h_{i+1}(p|s_{i+1}) = \min [h(p|s_{i+1}), h_i(p|s_i) + \Delta_i(p)] \tag{3.5}$$

where $\Delta_i(p)$ is a penalty term for bringing p from the subproblem i along the path t to subproblem $i + 1$. We have set $\Delta_i(p)$ to a a constant, independent of i and p, except when the action a_i e-deletes p where $\Delta_i(p)$ is set to ∞. This is the same heuristic used by C3 for sorting causal chains but takes into account action costs.

3.3.2 Computing $h_{path}(s)$

Given the heuristic $h(t|s)$ for causal chains t, the path-based heuristic $h_{path}(s)$ over states is defined as $\min_t h(t|s)$, where t ranges over a suitable class of paths applicable in s.

In C3, the path t is constructed by computing the measure $\min_t h(t|s)$ greedily. Here, we instead use the A* algorithm over a graph where *nodes* are causal chains whose first action applies in the state s, and *goal nodes* represent (full) paths. For uniformity, we take the *source nodes* in this search to be the chains a_0, p_1, a_1 where a_0 is the dummy *Start* action, a_1 is an action applicable in s, and p_1 is a dummy atom not deleted by any action in the problem. Last, the children of a node $t = a_0, p_1, \ldots, p_n, a_n$ such that $a_n \neq End$, are the nodes $t' = a_0, p_1, \ldots, p_n, a_n, p_{n+1}, a_{n+1}$ where p_{n+1} is a precondition of action a_{n+1} added by action a_n.

For the A* search, in this graph of causal chains, the evaluation function $f(n) = g(n) + h(n)$ is defined so that for n representing the path $t = a_0, p_1, \ldots, p_n, a_n$, $g(n) = h(t|s)$ and $h(n) = h(End|s_n)$, where $h(t|s)$ is defined as in Equation 3.4 and $h(End|s_n)$ is the base heuristic with s_n being the last state projected along the chain t.

This search is not guaranteed to yield the exact minimum $\min_t h(t|s)$ over all the paths t because the heuristic $h(n) = h(End|s_n)$ is not always a lower bound,

Domain	I	h_{add}			h_{path}			Quality
		S	D	T	S	D	T	
Blocks World	50	50	0	13.89	48	45	126.18	65%
Depots	22	11	3	184.69	9	3	79.20	87%
Driver	20	16	0	28.70	14	6	20.36	90%
Ferry	50	50	6	0.06	50	43	0.57	95%
Grid	5	2	0	3.12	2	1	72.81	100%
Gripper	50	50	50	0.39	50	2	33.85	100%
Logistics	28	28	1	0.45	28	11	53.15	87%
Miconic	50	50	20	0.02	50	50	0.50	77%
Mystery	30	26	9	13.47	22	12	38.94	94%
Open Stacks	30	20	0	184.55	10	0	201.43	100%
Rovers	40	17	1	125.05	13	4	102.78	98%
Satellite	20	20	14	9.42	12	7	268.79	101%
Storage	30	17	3	59.24	14	5	72.12	97%
TPP	30	15	5	110.30	10	5	168.31	89%
Zeno Travel	20	19	2	185.12	13	6	33.28	95%
Totals	475	391	114	61.23	345	200	84.82	
Percentage		82%	24%		73%	42%		92%

Table 3.5: Additive heuristic vs. Path-based heuristic in a standard greedy best-first search on instances from previous IPCs: I is the number of instances, S is the number of solved instances, D is the number of instances where search goes straight to the goal, T is the average time in seconds, and *Quality* is the plan quality ratio; e.g. 200% means that it plans twice as long as those reported by h_a on average

even if $h(n) = 0$ when n represents a path. Moreover, we consider two pruning techniques for speeding up the search that affect the optimality of the resulting measure as well.

First, in order to restrict the size of the search graph, we prune the nodes n representing a path $t = a_0, p_1, \ldots, p_i, a_i$ if there is another node n' representing a path that ends in the same pair p_i, a_i such that $f(n') < f(n)$. Second, we prune from the search all causal links a_i, p_{i+1}, a_{i+1} that do not lie along a *minimal path* from s. Recall that a minimal path $a_0, p_1, a_1, \ldots, p_i, a_i$ is one where the actions a_i are best (h_{max}) supporters of the fluent p_{i+1}.

The value of the heuristic $h_{path}(s)$ is then set to the value $f(n) = g(n)$ of the first goal node n found in the A* search. This value stands for the heuristic value $h(t|s)$ associated to some minimal path t from s, and is only an approximation of the optimal value $\min_t h(t|s)$ when t ranges over all paths.

3.3.3 Experimental Results

In order to test the quality and cost-effectiveness of the new heuristic h_{path}[1], we compared it with the additive heuristic h_{add} in the context of a greedy best-first state search. The planners were evaluated with a timeout of 1800 seconds and a

---

[1] We use as the base heuristic for $h(t|s)$ the same heuristic that we compare with, the additive heuristic.

Domain	I	h_{add}		h_{path}	
		Ex	Ev	Ex	Ev
Blocks World	50	1,912	14,834	41	402
Depots	22	13,369	165,834	45	667
Driver	20	548	17,679	78	995
Ferry	50	65	462	29	186
Grid	5	72	389	22	124
Gripper	50	98	2,726	121	1,692
Logistics	28	75	1,256	55	1,031
Miconic	50	81	725	30	289
Mystery	30	60	2,141	5	84
Open Stacks	30	3,916	126,393	75	606
Rovers	40	4,791	159,923	123	3,106
Satellite	20	36	5,066	25	1,775
Storage	30	2,065	31,449	67	739
TPP	30	8,982	111,056	1,910	21,236
Zeno Travel	20	58	3,601	17	415
Totals	475	2,409	42,902	176	2,223

Table 3.6: Additive heuristic vs. Path-based heuristic search effort in a standard greedy best-first search on instances from previous IPCs: I is the number of instances, S is the number of solved instances, Ex and Ev stand for the average number of nodes expanded and evaluated

memory limit of 2GB. The experiments were run on Xeon Woodcrest computers with clock speeds of 2.33 GHz.

The results are shown in Table 3.5. In terms of coverage, h_{path} solves 9% fewer problems than h_{add}, but at the same time, the solutions that it obtains are 8% shorter on average (35% shorter in Blocks). In terms of time, the search with h_{path} is slower than with h_a because of the higher overhead, yet this is compensated by the additional information gained, that translates in a highly reduced number of expanded nodes (Table 3.6). Indeed, in 42% of the problems, the heuristic h_{path} takes the plan straight to the goal without expanding any node off the solution. This is shown in the D column. The corresponding number for the h_{add} heuristic is 24%.

Table 3.7 shows an experiment aimed at making the search more focused by considering only the actions applicable in states that are minimal. These are the actions that head the applicable minimal paths. Compared to Table 3.5, the coverage is improved, h_{path} solving 50% of the problems straight to the goal. The minimality requirement increases the number of expanded nodes by h_{path} in Driver and Storage while it decreases in TPP, suggesting how suitable a focused search is for certain domains (Table 3.8). On the other hand, h_{add} expands just half of the nodes compared to Table 3.6.

| Domain | I | h_{add} | | | h_{path} | | | Quality |
		S	D	T	S	D	T	
Blocks World	50	49	0	15.22	43	30	35.18	65%
Depots	22	12	2	50.11	16	4	50.51	88%
Driver	20	18	1	152.34	14	6	157.50	93%
Ferry	50	50	4	0.04	50	49	0.08	97%
Grid	5	2	0	1.65	4	1	276.54	117%
Gripper	50	50	50	0.22	50	50	1.75	76%
Logistics	28	28	2	0.22	28	1	25.08	86%
Miconic	50	50	12	0.01	50	48	0.05	100%
Mystery	30	25	12	1.87	21	11	65.42	96%
Open Stacks	30	20	0	99.60	17	0	233.29	100%
Rovers	40	34	4	102.63	26	5	85.38	97%
Satellite	20	20	9	1.07	19	17	11.36	100%
Storage	30	16	4	3.47	8	4	228.91	111%
TPP	30	16	5	68.00	12	4	27.36	84%
Zeno Travel	20	20	5	81.30	18	9	171.36	94%
Totals	475	410	110	38.29	376	239	91.32	Average
Percentage		86%	23%		79%	50%		94%

Table 3.7: Additive heuristic vs. Path-based heuristic in a standard greedy best-first search considering only *minimal actions* applicable in a state: I is the number of instances, S is the number of solved instances, D is the number of instances where search goes straight to the goal, T is the average time in seconds, and *Quality* is the plan quality ratio; e.g. 200% means plans twice as long as those reported by h_a on average

3.3.4 Discussion

We have presented a new heuristic for a forward state-based planner and empirical results. The heuristic is defined on top of a delete-relaxation heuristic and yet takes deletes into account by means of the notion of paths. The other heuristics that take deletes into account are (1.) the admissible h^m heuristics (Haslum and Geffner, 2000), used mainly in the context of optimal planning, (2.) the semi-relaxed plan heuristic that introduces special fluents that explicitly represent conjunctions of fluents in the original planning task (Emil Keyder and Haslum, 2012), and (3.) the causal graph heuristic (Helmert, 2004), that is closely related to the additive heuristic, but is defined over multivalued variables and keeps track of side effects pertaining to each variable's parents (Helmert and Geffner, 2008). The path heuristic h_{path}, keeps track of side effects through the states that are projected along paths. From this perspective, it is fruitful to look at the enforced hill-climbing (EHC) search procedure in FF, not as a search procedure, but as a lookahead device for producing a more informed heuristic value for the seed state. This lookahead is common in chess playing programs where the backed-up value is assumed to be more reliable that the root value. From this point of view, while the EHC lookahead considers paths in the (local) state space until a state with a better value is found, the lookahead in the path-based heuristic considers paths in an abstraction, where all but one of the preconditions and positive effects are thrown away, but which are evaluated with all the informa-

Domain	I	h_{add}		h_{path}	
		Ex	Ev	Ex	Ev
Blocks World	50	2,145	13,931	87	889
Depots	22	5,670	45,741	43	535
Driver	20	3,693	30,405	3,080	23,318
Ferry	50	68	284	29	100
Grid	5	39	142	79	347
Gripper	50	101	1,426	77	807
Logistics	28	70	557	219	3,318
Miconic	50	46	221	35	199
Mystery	30	7	49	8	58
Open Stacks	30	1,195	28,894	289	1,259
Rovers	40	185	3,664	64	955
Satellite	20	38	617	36	697
Storage	30	821	3,996	2,346	12,875
TPP	30	4,137	28,489	564	3,483
Zeno Travel	20	59	1,211	34	656
Totals	475	1,203	10,539	466	3,300

Table 3.8: Additive heuristic vs. Path-based heuristic search effort in a standard greedy best first search considering only *minimal actions* applicable in a state. *I* is the number of instances, *S* is the number of solved instances, *Ex* and *Ev* stand for the average number of nodes expanded and evaluated

tion available in the original problem. The paths in the state-space considered in EHC have the benefit that the local states are true, reachable states. On the other hand, projected states along the abstract paths considered in this section, may represent Âťunreal' states that cannot be reached. However, while EHC looks over real states in the local neighborhood, the abstract paths are forced to reach the goal, and thus, can probe much more deeply.

Chapter 4

Searching for Plans with Probes

Tiger got to hunt, bird got to fly; Man got to sit and wonder, 'Why, why, why?' Tiger got to sleep, bird got to land; Man got to tell himself he understand.

Cat's Cradle.
Kurt Vonnegut

In this chapter, we explore further the synergy between different type of inferences, by formulating and testing a new dual search architecture for planning that is based on the idea of *probes*: single action sequences computed without search from a given state that can quickly go deep into the state space, terminating either in the goal or in failure. We show experimentally that by designing these probes carefully using a number of existing and new polynomial inference techniques, most of the benchmarks can be solved with a single probe from the initial state, with no search. Moreover, by using one probe as a lookahead mechanism from each expanded state in a standard greedy best first search, the number of problems solved increases and compares well to state-of-the-art planners like FF and LAMA. The success of probes suggests that many domains can be solved easily once a suitable serialization of the landmarks is found, a finding that may open new connections between recent work in planning and more classical work concerning goal serialization and problem decomposition in planning and search.

4.1 Introduction

Heuristic search has been the mainstream approach in planning for more than a decade, with planners such as FF, FD, and LAMA being able to solve problems with hundreds of actions and variables in a few seconds (Hoffmann and Nebel, 2001; Helmert, 2006; Richter and Westphal, 2010). The basic idea behind these planners is to search for plans using a search algorithm guided by heuristic estimators derived automatically from the problem (McDermott, 1996; Bonet and Geffner, 2001). State-of-the-art planners, however, go well beyond this idea, adding a number of techniques that are specific to planning. These techniques, such as helpful actions and landmarks (Hoffmann and Nebel, 2001; Hoffmann et al., 2004; Richter et al., 2008), are designed to exploit the *propositional structure* of planning problems; a structure that is absent in traditional heuristic search where states and heuristic evaluations are used as *black boxes*. Moreover, new search algorithms have been devised to make use of these techniques. FF, for example, triggers a best-first search when an incomplete but effective greedy search that uses helpful actions only, fails to find a solution. In FD and LAMA, the use of helpful or preferred operators is not restricted to the first phase of the search, but to one of the open lists maintained in a multi-queue search algorithm. In both cases, dual search architectures that rely on either two successive searches or to a single search with multiple open lists, are aimed at quickly solving large problems that are simple, without giving up completeness on problems that are not.

In this chapter, we formulate and test a new dual search architecture for planning that is based on the idea of *probes*: single action sequences computed without search from a given state that can quickly go deep into the state space, terminating either in the goal or in failure. We show that by designing these probes carefully using a number of existing and new polynomial inference techniques, 683 out of 980 benchmarks (70%) can be solved with a single probe from the initial state. Moreover, by using one probe as a lookahead mechanism from each expanded state in a standard greedy best-first search informed by the additive heuristic, the number of problems solved jumps to 900 (92%), a number that compares well to state-of-the-art planners like FF and LAMA that solve 827 (84%) and 879 (89%) problems respectively.

The main contribution is the design of these effective probes. A probe is an action sequence computed greedily from a seed state for achieving a *serialization of the problem subgoals* that is computed dynamically along with the probe. The next subgoal to achieve in a probe is chosen among the first unachieved landmarks that are *consistent*. Roughly, a subgoal that must remain true until another subgoal is achieved, is consistent, if once it is made true, it does not have to be undone in order to make the second subgoal achievable. The action sequence to achieve the next subgoal uses standard heuristics and helpful actions, while maintaining and enforcing the reasons for which the previous actions have been selected in the form of *commitments* akin to causal links. The computational value of the subgoal serialization, the consistency checks, and the use of commitments, is evaluated empirically as well.

The success of probes, like the improvements of FF and LAMA over HSP before, suggest that effective heuristic search planning is more than heuristic search with automatically derived estimators. Structural inference techniques in the form of helpful actions or landmarks, play an important role as well. The probes are designed to take advantage of these and other inference techniques. Critical for the effectiveness of the probes is the use of *causal commitments* of the form $\langle a, p, B \rangle$ to express that a fluent p was made true by action a in order to achieve one of the fluents in B.[1] Nodes generated during the probes do not only maintain the state of the fluents but also the reasons for which these fluents were made true. Then in a node where the causal commitment $\langle a, p, B \rangle$ is true, actions that delete p without adding one of the fluents in B are pruned. The result is that probes are more goal-directed than arbitrary sequences of helpful actions in FF that tend to exhibit more 'oscillations' on the way to the goal when multiple goals are in 'conflict' (Section 4.2). Moreover, probes are not used to improve the heuristic value of the seed state, but to reach the goal, and thus can go arbitrarily deep. They terminate like the EHC search, however, when the goal is reached (success), or when the helpful actions yield no new states, or the heuristic becomes infinite. An important difference, however, is that the heuristic used in the probes takes the causal commitments into account, and hence, reports infinite values much more often.

In the remainder of this chapter, we first illustrate the limitations of heuristic search planners using a simple example. We then introduce the new planner PROBE, present the experimental results, illustrate the behavior of PROBE over two specific problems, and finish with a brief summary.

4.2 Effects of Multiple Conflicting Goals

The heuristics used in state-of-the-art (satisficing) planners are a decade old and are based on the delete-relaxation.[2] Several heuristics that take deletes into account have been formulated but they have not been shown to be cost-effective (Haslum and Geffner, 2000; Emil Keyder and Haslum, 2012). One problem that surfaces with delete-relaxation based heuristics, that approximate the optimal delete free heuristic h^+, appears in instances with multiple 'conflicting' goals. In these very common cases, progress towards one goal means diverting from other goals. Such instances produce large plateaus where the heuristic is almost useless. Indeed, in some cases, state-of-the-art heuristics are no better than *heuristics that ignore the problem structure completely* and just count, for example, the *number of unachieved goals*.

As an illustration, consider the Visit-All domain from the 2011 International Planning Competition (IPC7) where an agent in the middle of a square grid $n \times n$ must visit all of the cells in the grid. This is an extremely simple problem to solve non-optimally, and a version of this problem is related to one of the domains used in the Conformant track of the 2008 IPC (Bryce and Buffet, 2008).[3]

Table 4.1 shows the results for several planners over this domain. Although being intractable, solving optimally the delete relaxation, h^+ gives the exact goal distance as long as there exists a hamiltonian path visiting every cell[4]. Interestingly, the planner that does best in this domain is based on a greedy best-first

---

[1] The causal commitments are similar to causal links in partial order planning (Tate, 1977; McAllester and Rosenblitt, 1991), but are used in a forward state search in a different way. [2] The exception is the landmark heuristic in LAMA, discussed below. [3] We are referring to the Dispose domain where an agent has to pick up objects in a grid without knowing their locations, and thus has to attempt a pick up action in each cell. In this domain, a conformant planner guided by the 'number of unachieved goals' heuristic did much better than the classical FF planner over a suitable translation. Table 4.1 explains how this can happen. [4] In the simplest version of Visit-All, a $1 \times n$ grid, no hamiltonian path exists.

I	LAMA		LAMA-ff		LAMA-lm		FF	
	time	cost	time	cost	time	cost	time	cost
5	0.15	26	0.22	36	0.17	26	0.05	38
10	0.43	128	0.55	352	0.40	111	0.16	177
15	1.39	270	118.60	1,258	1.00	271	15.38	428
20	3.42	493	M	M	2.92	453	M	M
25	10.32	757	M	M	5.98	732	M	M
30	26.38	1,149	M	M	14.10	1,082	M	M
35	R	R	R	R	R	R	M	M
40	R	R	R	R	R	R	M	M
45	R	R	R	R	R	R	M	M
50	R	R	R	R	R	R	M	R

I	GBFS-hadd		GBFS-hgoals		PROBE	
	time	cost	time	cost	time	cost
5	0.02	98	0.01	30	0.02	24
10	7.15	883	0.04	104	0.21	99
15	M	M	0.32	276	1.4	224
20	T	T	1.14	417	8.52	399
25	T	T	3.58	660	20.32	624
30	T	T	9.07	956	76.58	899
35	T	T	20.65	1330	146	1220
40	T	T	47.43	1920	320.28	1600
45	T	T	74.04	2140	557.44	2020
50	M	M	122.19	2550	805.47	2500

Table 4.1: Planners performance over the Visit-all domain. The planners are *LAMA* and versions of it using only the FF and Landmark heuristic respectively, *FF*, two greedy best-first search planners using the additive and number of unachieved goal heuristics respectively, and the new planner PROBE. The size of the grids are $n \times n$, with the number n reported in each row. For the non-solved problems, M, T, and R stand for memory-out (2GB), time-out (30min.), and grounding error respectively.

search using *the number of unachieved goals heuristic (hgoals)*, that manages to solve the larger 50×50 instance in 122 seconds. The greedy best search using the *additive heuristic* does much worse, and cannot even solve the 15×15 instance. FF, like LAMA[1] when run with the FF heuristic only, does not perform much better and does not solve the 20×20 instance. On the other hand, LAMA and the version of LAMA that uses the *landmark heuristic* only, do quite well and break over the 35×35 instance due to 'grounding errors'. The performance of LAMA, however, is not surprising as the landmark heuristic in this case is quite close to the 'number of unachieved goals' heuristic. Finally, the planner PROBE to be explained below, which also uses landmarks, does well too, scaling up well and producing plans of slightly better quality. A key aspect in PROBE is the selection of the action for extending the current probe in a state s. One could select, for example, the action a that minimizes the distance to the joint goal G from the resulting state s_a as captured by the heuristic $h(s_a, G)$. The problem, as argued above, is that planning heuristics used in this form are non-informative in situations such as this one, where the goals are in conflict, and approaching one goal means to divert from other goals. Thus, rather than selecting the action that minimizes the distance to the joint goal $h(s_a, G)$, PROBE selects the action that minimizes the distance to the nearest 'first' unachieved landmark L; i.e., $\arg\min_a \min_L h(s_a, L)$. This is an important idea that is present in LAMA and does not follow directly from the use of the delete-relaxation or the landmark heuristic.

We emphasize that domains like Visit-All show that some of the problems that are difficult for 'pure' heuristic search planners are not hard at all, they are just the result of multiple easy but conflicting goals that can often be achieved trivially, once they are serialized. The use of delete-relaxation heuristics to appraise the cost of achieving all goals together runs into a situation resembling Buridan's ass: where a hungry and thirsty donkey, placed between a bundle of hay and a pail of water, dies of hunger and thirst for not finding a reason to choose one over the other. The action selection criterion based on the distance to the nearest landmark achieves some form of serialization. Yet, as it is known, not every serialization works, and thus additional criteria are needed to rule out some of the nearest landmarks as possible subgoals.

4.3 PROBE: **Dual Search Architecture**

Heuristic search planners that plug a delete-relaxation heuristic into a well known search algorithm are useful, as they can be easily understood. As we have shown in Section 4.2, one problem that they face, however, is that the search plateaus. This situation arises when goals are in 'conflict', and approaching one goal means to move away from the others. Since the formulation of *more effective estimators* has not been simple after more than a decade, the solution to this problem has given rise to other types of inferences and techniques. These techniques are absent in the first generation of planners such as UNPOP and HSP, but are present in FF, FD, and LAMA. These planners are less monolithic, and their details are

---

[1] LAMA is the version used in IPC6.

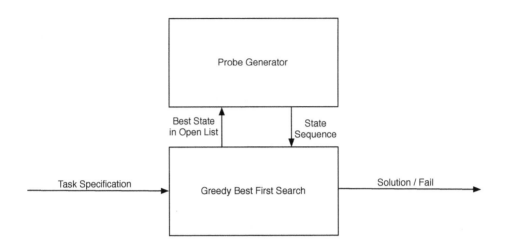

Figure 4.1: PROBE's base dual architecture

often more difficult to follow, but it is precisely those 'details' that make the difference. The planner PROBE is no exception to this trend towards 'finer-grained planning', and incorporates a number of design decisions that we explain below.

PROBE is a complete, standard greedy best-first (GBFS) STRIPS planner using the standard additive heuristic, with just *one difference*: when a state is selected for expansion, it first launches a *probe* from the state to the goal. If the probe reaches the goal, the problem is solved and the solution is returned. Otherwise, the states expanded by the probe are added to the open list, and control returns to the GBFS loop (Figure 4.1). *The crucial and only novel part in the planning algorithm is the definition and computation of the probes.*

We assume a STRIPS problem whose top goals G are the preconditions of a dummy End action that adds a dummy goal G_d. As in POCL planning, this is needed due to the use of causal commitments that are similar to causal links (Tate, 1977; McAllester and Rosenblitt, 1991).

4.3.1 Probe Construction

A *probe* is an action sequence $a_0, a_1, \ldots, a_k$ that generates a sequence $n_0, n_1, \ldots, n_{k+1}$ of nodes, each of which is a pair $n_i = \langle s_i, C_i \rangle$ made up of the problem state s_i and a set of *causal commitments* C_i. The initial node of a probe is $n_0 = \langle s, \emptyset \rangle$ where s is the state from which the probe is triggered, and $\emptyset$ is the empty set of commitments. The *action selection* criterion decides the action a_i to choose in node $n_i = \langle s_i, C_i \rangle$ greedily without search. This action generates the new node to $n_{i+1} = \langle s_{i+1}, C_{i+1} \rangle$, where s_{i+1} is the result of progressing the state s_i through a_i, and C_{i+1} is C_i updated with the causal commitments *consumed* by a_i removed, and the causal commitments *produced* by a_i added.

The actions in a probe are selected in order to achieve *subgoals* chosen from *the landmarks that are yet to be achieved.* A number of techniques are used to make the greedy selection of the *next subgoal* to achieve and *the actions for achieving it* effective. A probe that reaches the goal is the composition of the action sequences selected to achieve the next subgoal, the one following it, and so on, until all landmarks including the dummy goal G_d are achieved. Probes are not complete; yet they are supposed to capture the plans that characterize 'simple domains' even if a formal characterization of such domains is still missing.

The subgoal to pursue next is selected in a node n in two cases: when n is the first node of the probe, or when the subgoal g associated with its parent node n' in the probe is achieved in n. Otherwise, n *inherits the subgoal from its parent node*. The action a selected in a node n is then the action that appears to be 'best' for the subgoal g associated with n. If a does not achieve g, then g stays active for the next node, where the action to include in the probe is selected in the same way.

The formal definition of the subgoal and action selection criteria below uses notions that will be made fully precise later on, like the *heuristic* $h(G|s,C)$ that takes both the state s and the *commitments* C into account, the precomputed *partial ordering among landmarks*, and the conditions under which a subgoal is deemed as *consistent* from a given node.

4.3.2 Subgoal and Action Selection

The criterion for selecting the subgoal g in node $n = \langle s, C \rangle$ is the following. First, the set S of *first unachieved landmarks* that are *consistent* in $n = \langle s, C \rangle$ is computed. Then, the landmark $p \in S$ that is *nearest* according to the heuristic $h(p|s,C)$ is selected as the subgoal for n.

The selection of the action a in n is in turn the following. First, the set of actions a that are deemed *helpful* in $n = \langle s, C \rangle$ for either the subgoal or commitments associated with n are computed, and those that lead to a node $n' = \langle s', C' \rangle$ for which either $h(G|s', C')$ is infinity or s' has been already generated are pruned.[1] Then, among the remaining actions, if any, the action that minimizes the heuristic $h(g|s', C')$ is selected.[2] In the case of a tie, two other criteria are used lexicographically: first 'min $\sum_L h(L|s', C')$', where L ranges over the first unachieved landmarks, then 'min $h(G_d|s', C')$', where G_d is the dummy goal. Thus, the action selection mechanism tries to achieve a subgoal while preferring those actions that minimize the distance to next subgoal candidates.

In the next few sections, we specify fully the notions assumed in these definitions.

4.3.3 Enhanced Helpful Actions

Only the actions deemed to be helpful are considered along the states of a probe. Such actions are those used in the solution to the relaxed problem found by the

---

[1] Notice that we are forcing probes to explore new states only. This is a heuristic decision that does not compromise the completeness of the best-first search algorithm that uses probes. [2] Except for a few details, this criterion is similar to the one used by LAMA for preferring actions in the landmark heuristic queue; namely, that "if no acceptable landmark can be achieved within one step, the preferred operators are those which occur in a relaxed plan to the nearest simple acceptable landmark" (Richter and Westphal, 2010).

heuristic $h(s, C)$ that are applicable in the state s. The relaxed solution π^+ is extracted backwards from the goals G recursively adding to π^+ each action a that adds a goal $g \in G$ with the lowest $h(pre(a)|s, C)$ value, i.e. the best supporter a for each goal g, and by adding the best supporters of preconditions $p \in pre(a)$ of actions a in the relaxed solution $a \in \pi^+$; until all preconditions and goals p are either supported by one action $a \in \pi^+$ or belong to the state $p \in s$. When more than one action can be the best supporter for an atom p, that is, more than one action a adding p has the same $h(pre(a)|s, C)$ value, ties are broken randomly. Thus, the set of helpful actions considered in each state s is not uniquely defined when more than one action can be the best supporter according a heuristic h.

In order to overcome the stochastic nature of the set of helpful actions H, we define a sequence of enhanced helpful actions that systematically collect all possible helpful actions in the following way:

Definition 4.1 (Enhanced Helpful Actions). *The enhanced helpful actions $EH_0, \ldots,$ EH_n over $\Pi = \langle F, I, O, G \rangle$ induced by heuristic h in state s consists of a sequence of helpful actions $H(s, \Pi_i)$ over problems $\Pi_i = \langle F, I, O_i, G \rangle$ where:*

1. $EH_0(s) = H(s, \Pi)$

2. $EH_{i+1}(s) = H(s, \Pi_{i+1})$, *with* $O_{i+1} = O \setminus \{a \mid a \in \cup_{k=0,\ldots,i} EH_k(s)\}$

3. $EH_n(s) = \emptyset$, *no relaxed solution exists for Π_n, such that $h(G|s, C) = \infty$*

The first set EH_0 is the set of helpful actions from the original problem. Each EH_i is extracted from the relaxed plan induced by heuristic h in problem Π_i, where actions considered to be helpful previously are excluded, until no relaxed solution is possible and the heuristic $h(G|s, C) = \infty$.

Thus, probes incrementally go beyond helpful actions. While constructing a probe, if a node $n = \langle s, C \rangle$ is reached such that all helpful actions EH_0 are pruned, a second attempt to extend the current probe is made before giving up. PROBE recomputes the relaxed plan from n with those actions excluded, resulting in a new set of helpful actions EH_1 if the heuristic does not become infinite. The new set of helpful actions EH_1 is pruned again as above, and the process is iterated, until a non-pruned helpful action $a \in EH_i$ is obtained at s, or the heuristic becomes infinite. In the latter case, the probe *terminates* with *failure*. If before failing, it reaches a goal state, it terminates *successfully* with the problem solved.

4.3.4   Causal Commitments

A node $n = \langle s, C \rangle$ along a probe is a pair consisting of state s and causal commitments C, similar to the notion of a causal link (Tate, 1977; McAllester and Rosenblitt, 1991). While causal link $\langle a, p, c \rangle$ encodes that an action a adds a fluent p required by some action c, causal commitments do not commit to a single action c but to a disjunctive set of fluents added by some action that requires p:

Definition 4.2 (Causal Commitment). *Given a planning problem $\Pi = \langle F, I, O, G \rangle$, a causal commitment is a triple $C = \langle a, p, B \rangle$ where $a \in O$ is an action, $p \in add(a)$ is a fluent added by a, and $B \subseteq F$ is a set of fluents.*

The intuition is that fluent p was added by a in order to achieve (at least) *one* of the fluents in B, and hence that p should remain true until an action adds some fluent in B, *consuming* the causal commitment. Consequently, in a node $n = \langle s, C \rangle$ with a commitment $\langle a, p, B \rangle$ in C, any action a applicable in s that deletes p but does not add any fluent in B, is taken to *threat* the commitments in C, and is pruned from the set of applicable actions.

Definition 4.3 (Causal Commitment Threat). *Given a node* $n = \langle s, C \rangle$, *an action a applicable in s is a threat to a causal commitment* $\langle a_i, p_i, B_i \rangle \in C$, *if a deletes p_i and does not add any fluent* $q \in B_i$.

There are two differences with a causal link threat: only applicable actions can threat a causal commitment, and actions that add a fluent p but do not add any fluent in B are not considered as a threat for $C = \langle a, p, B \rangle$.

We now show how a causal commitment is consumed and generated by an action a in node $n = \langle s, C \rangle$.

Definition 4.4 (Consume(a,n)). *An action a consumes a commitment* $\langle a_i, p_i, B_i \rangle$ *in* $n = \langle s, C \rangle$ *if a adds a fluent in B_i (whether or not a deletes p_i).*

Definition 4.5 (generate(a,n)). *An action a generates the commitments* $\langle a, p, B \rangle$ *in* $n = \langle s, C \rangle$, *if p is a fluent added by a, and B is the set of fluents added by actions in the relaxed plan π^+ in n that have p as a precondition.*

An action a selected in a node $n = \langle s, C \rangle$ generates the new node $n' = \langle s', C' \rangle$ where s' is the result of progressing s through a, and C' is the result of removing the commitments consumed by a in n, and adding the commitments generated by a in n, that is, $s' = (s \cup add(a) \setminus del(a))$ and $C' = (C \setminus consume(a, n)) \cup generate(a, n)$.

The *relaxed plan* associated with a node $n = \langle s, C \rangle$ and a goal G is obtained by collecting backwards from G, the best supporters a_p for each p in G, and recursively the best supporters for their preconditions that are not true in s (Keyder and Geffner, 2008). The best supporter for an atom p is an action a that adds p and has minimum $h(a|s, C)$ value. The *helpful actions* for a subgoal g in a node $n = \langle s, C \rangle$ are defined then as in FF, as the actions a with heuristic $h(a|s, C) = 0$ that add a precondition or goal in the relaxed plan. For convenience, however, this relaxed plan is not defined as the relaxed plan for g in n, but as the relaxed plan for the joint goal formed by g and *the (disjunctive) targets* B_i in the commitments $\langle a_i, p_i, B_i \rangle$ in C. This reflects the notion that such targets also represent subgoals associated with the node $n = \langle s, C \rangle$, even if unlike g, they do not have to be achieved necessarily.[1]

In order to take advantage of the information contained in the causal commitments, we introduce a heuristic $h(G|s, C)$ that estimates the cost to a set G of fluents from a node $n = \langle s, C \rangle$. This heuristic takes the set of causal commitments C into account and is defined like the standard additive heuristic (h_{add}):

$$h(G|s, C) = \sum_{p \in G} h(p|s, C) \tag{4.1}$$

---

[1] Indeed, a probe may reach the goal with a non-empty set of commitments.

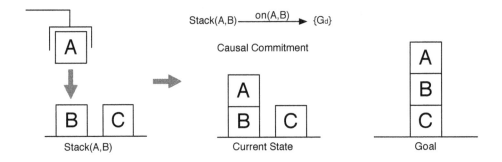

Figure 4.2: Blocks world example where the goal is reachable but $h(G|s, C) = \infty$. The figure in the middle shows the state s with commitment C that results from action $stack(A, B)$.

where

$$h(p|s, C) = \begin{cases} 0 & \text{if } p \in s \\ \min_{a \in O(p)} [cost(a) + h(a|s, C)] & \text{otherwise} \end{cases} \qquad (4.2)$$

and

$$h(a|s, C) = \delta(a, s, C) + h(Pre(a)|s, C) \qquad (4.3)$$

where $O(p)$ range over the actions adding p and $Pre(a)$ are the preconditions of action a.

Compared to h_{add}, the only novelty in this definition is the offset term $\delta(a, s, C)$ that penalizes actions a that *threat* causal commitments $\langle a_i, p_i, B_i \rangle$ in C. The offset for such actions is the cost of achieving one of the fluents in B_i, as the action a cannot be executed until those commitments are consumed. More precisely:

$$\delta(a, s, C) = \begin{cases} 0 & \text{if } a \text{ threat no commitment in } C \\ \max_i \min_{q \in B_i} h(q|s, C) & \text{otherwise,} \end{cases} \qquad (4.4)$$

where B_i are the sets of fluents in the commitments $\langle a_i, p_i, B_i \rangle$ in C threatened by a. Intuitively, the offset $\delta(a, s, C)$ delays the application of action a at least until the first action that consumes the threatened commitment can be applied ($\min_{q \in B_i}$ term). Moreover, if a threatens more than one commitment it has to be delayed until the last commitment can be consumed ($\max_i$ term). The result of the offsets arising from the commitments C is that actions a *applicable* in s may get heuristic value $h(a|s, C)$ greater than zero when they threaten a commitment in C.

The offset δ causes $h(G|s, C)$ to be unsafe, that is, a goal G reachable from s may get an infinite heuristic value $h(G|s, C)$. This situation arises when G

requires an action a with an infinite offset $\delta(a, s, C)^1$. For example, consider the blocks world instance shown in Figure 4.2. Goal G stands for the atoms $on(A, B)$ and $on(B, C)$, and G_d is the dummy goal added by action END with precondition G. The heuristic $h(G_d|s, C)$ associated with the node $n = \langle s, C \rangle$ shown in the figure that results from stacking A on B when B is not on C, has infinite value. The reason is that the offset $\delta(a, s, C)$ for action $a = unstack(A, B)$ is infinite and no solution exists if a is not applicable. More precisely, a threatens the commitment $\langle stack(A, B), on(A, B), \{G_d\} \rangle$, and the offset $\delta(a, s, C)$ implied by Equation 4.4 is at least $h(G_d|s, C)$. As every sequence of actions that achieves G_d contains action a^2, and a cannot come before G_d is added, G_d is unreachable and $h(G_d|s, C) = \infty$.

4.3.5 Disjunctive Commitments

For the purpose of the presentation, we have made a simplification that we now correct. From the description above, it is clear that an action a can introduce commitments $\langle a, p_i, B_i \rangle$ for more than one effect p_i of a. This will be the case when the preconditions of the actions in the relaxed plan involve more than one effect of a. The heuristic $h(G|s, C)$ and the notions above are all correct provided that this situation does not arise. On the other hand, when it does, the above definitions interpret multiple commitments $\langle a, p_i, B_i \rangle$ in C for a common action a *conjunctively*, as if each such commitment must be respected. This, however, is too restrictive. If a adds two relevant effects p_1 and p_2, this rules out the possibility that a is the causal support of p_1 in the plan but not of p_2.

For example, consider the instance shown in Figure 4.3 where a block A must be placed on top of block C, given that A is on B, and B on C. In such a case, the action $a = unstack(A, B)$ is done in order to get the precondition $clear(B)$ of $unstack(B, C)$, but not for getting the precondition $hold(A)$ of $stack(A, C)$. Thus, in PROBE, multiple commitments $\langle a, p_i, B_i \rangle$ for the same action a in C are treated not *conjunctively*, but *disjunctively*. Based on the relaxed plan in the figure, action a adds the disjunctive commitment $\langle a, clear(B), \{clear(C)\} \rangle \vee \langle a, hold(A), \{on(A, C)\} \rangle$. It is assumed that every action in a probe is made with *some* purpose encoded by a commitment, but not with all purposes that are possible.

We adapt previous definitions in order to account for disjunctive commitments. First, an action threatens a disjunctive commitment if it violates every commitment of the same disjunction.

Definition 4.6 (Disjunctive Causal Commitment Threat). *Given a node* $n = \langle s, C \rangle$, *an action* a *applicable in* s *is a* threat *to a disjunctive commitment* $\langle b, p_i, B_i \rangle$, $i = 1, \ldots, n_b$, *where these are all the commitments involving the action* b *in* C, *when* a *threatens each one of them; i.e. it deletes each* p_i *without adding any fluent in* B_i, *for* $i = 1, \ldots, n_b$.

---

1 $\delta(a, s, C) = \infty$ if in order to consume any of the commitments $\langle a_i, p_i, B_i \rangle$ in C threatened by a, it is necessary to violate one of such commitments   2 The dummy goal G_d is added only by action END with preconditions $on(A, B)$ and $on(B, C)$, thus given Equations 4.1 and 4.3 $h(G_d|s, C) = h(END|s, C) = h(on(A, B)|s, C) + h(on(B, C)|s, C)$. The fluent $on(B, C)$ is reachable only if we allow sequences that contain $unstack(A, B)$.

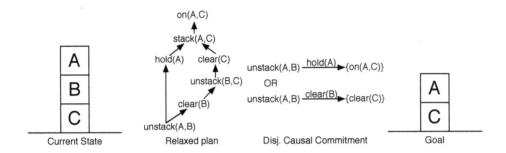

Figure 4.3:   Blocks world example of a disjunctive causal commitment.   The relaxed plan is induced by $h(G|s, C)$.

The offsets $\delta(a, s, C)$ for the heuristic $h(G|s, C)$ must be defined as:

$$\delta(a, s, C) \overset{\text{def}}{=} \begin{cases} 0 & \text{if } a \text{ violates no } \textit{disjunctive} \text{ commitment in } C \\ \max_b \max_{i=1,n_b} \min_{q \in B_i} h(q|s, C) & \text{otherwise} \end{cases} \quad (4.5)$$

where $\langle b, p_i, B_i \rangle$, $i = 1, \ldots, n_b$, $n_b \geq 1$, constitute the disjunctive commitments threatened by action a. The new term $\max_{i=1,n_b}$ states that the delay of a disjunctive commitment is the maximum among the elements of the disjunction. Finally, a commitment is consumed or generated as follows:

Definition 4.7 (Consume(a,n)). *An action a consumes a disjunctive commitment $\langle b, p_i, B_i \rangle$ with a common action b in $n = \langle s, C \rangle$ if a adds a fluent in some B_i (whether or not a deletes p_i). If a is not a threat to any disjunctive commitment $\langle b, p_i, B_i \rangle$ in C, $i = 1, \ldots, n_b$, these are updated by removing from C the individual commitments $\langle b, p_i, B_i \rangle$ violated by a.*

Note that after an action a updates individual threatened commitments $\langle b, p_i, B_i \rangle$, at least one such commitment must remain in the disjunction involving action b, otherwise according to Definition 4.6 a will be considered to violate the disjunctive commitment. Moreover, a cannot be a helpful action in this case, as the heuristic will be $h(G|s, C) \neq 0$ due to the delay imposed by $\delta(a, s, C)$. Thus, disjunctive commitments may eventually evolve into single commitment as actions discard incompatible possible commitments from previous actions.

Definition 4.8 (generate(a,n)). *An action a generates a disjunctive commitment $\langle a, p_i, B_i \rangle$ in $n = \langle s, C \rangle$, if p_i is a fluent added by a, and B_i is the set of fluents added by actions in the relaxed plan π^+ in n that have p_i as a precondition.*

The size of the disjunction generated by an action a is at least 1 and at most the number of fluents p_i added by a that appear in the relax plan π^+. If no fluent p_i appears in π^+, a is not helpful and it is not considered as a possible successor of a probe.

The commitments C' in the node $n' = \langle s', C' \rangle$ that follows the action a in node $n = \langle s, C \rangle$ are formed from C by removing the disjunctive commitments consumed by a (the set of commitments $\langle b, p_i, B_i \rangle$ with a common action b such that a adds a fluent in some B_i), by updating the rest of the disjunctive commitments in C, and last, by adding the disjunctive commitments made by a (as already defined).

4.3.6 Subgoal Candidates

The subgoal candidates are the fluent landmarks of the problem. The overall picture for landmarks and their ordering is not too different from LAMA except that we do not deal with disjunctive landmarks, nor with a landmark-based heuristic. A minor difference is that we define and compute landmarks using a formulation that is a slight variation of the set-additive heuristic (Keyder and Geffner, 2008; Keyder et al., 2010).

The landmarks are computed as a preprocessing step using the equations below, where $L(p)$ and $L(a)$ stand for the landmarks of fluent p and action a from the given initial state s, and $O(p)$ stands for the actions that add p:

$$L(p) = \begin{cases} \{p\} & \text{if } p \in s \\ \cap_{a \in O(p)} L(a) & \text{otherwise} \end{cases} \tag{4.6}$$

where

$$L(a) = \cup_{q \in Pre(a)} L(q)$$

Provided that all labels $L(p)$, except for $p \in s$, are initialized to $L(p) = \perp$ ('undefined'), and that no 'undefined' label is propagated, the computation converges to labels $L(p)$ that are sound and complete relative to the delete-relaxation. The landmarks of the problem are then those in $L(G_d)$, where G_d is the dummy goal.

Furthermore, landmarks can have precedence relations. Orderings over landmarks are statements about the order in which they must be made true. In the following definition, we use the notation $s[o_1, \ldots, o_n]$ to denote the state that results from applying the sequence of actions $\langle o_1, \ldots, o_n \rangle$. While many ordering criteria have been proposed by Hoffmann et al. (2004), we take into account only sound orderings that are valid in every possible plan:

Definition 4.9 (Orderings between landmarks). *Given a planning problem $\Pi = \langle F, I, O, G \rangle$ and two landmarks L_1 and L_2.*

- *There is a natural ordering $L_1 \to L_2$ if for any plan $\pi = o_1, \ldots, o_n$, $I[o_1, \ldots, o_j] \models L_2$ implies it exists $i < j$ such that $I[o_1, \ldots, o_i] \models L_1$.*

- *There is a necessary ordering $L_1 \to_n L_2$ if $L_1 \to L_2$ and for any plan $\pi = o_1, \ldots, o_n$, $I[o_1, \ldots, o_j] \models L_2$ implies $I[o_1, \ldots, o_{j-1}] \models L_1$.*

- *There is a greedy necessary ordering $L_1 \to_{gn} L_2$ if $L_1 \to_n L_2$ and for any plan $\pi = o_1, \ldots, o_n$, $I[o_1, \ldots, o_j] \models L_2$, $I[o_1, \ldots, o_i] \not\models L_2$ for all $i < j$ implies $I[o_1, \ldots, o_{j-1}] \models L_1$.*

- *There is a goal ordering $L_1 \to_g L_2$ if all actions adding L_1 e-delete L_2 and $L_1, L_2 \in G$.*

Intuitively, $L_1 \to L_2$ states that L_1 must be true before L_2 is made true, $L_1 \to_n L_2$ states that L_1 is true immediately before L_2, and $L_1 \to_{gn} L_2$ states that L_1 must be made true immediately before L_2, but only the first time L_2 becomes true. Every necessary ordering is greedy necessary but not vice versa, and every necessary or greedy necessary ordering is natural but not vice versa (Hoffmann et al., 2004).

Taking advantage of the notion that top goals must all be true at the same time, *goal orderings* are computed for all pairs $p, q \in G$ based on the notion of e-deletes[1]. This is due to the fact that if all actions adding p e-delete q, one can show then that the *last action* in a plan that achieves p and q jointly, must be the action that adds q.

Natural orderings are inferred from labels $L(p)$ such that $p \to q$ if $p \in L(q)$. *Necessary* and *greedy necessary orderings* can also be inferred from these labels: $p \to_n q$ if $p \in L(q)$, and all achievers of q have p in their preconditions; and $p \to_{gn} q$ if $p \in L(q)$, and all the first achievers of q have p in their preconditions. The first achievers of q are those actions a for which $q \in add(a)$ and $q \notin L(a)$, i.e, q must not be achieved before a adds q.

Other commonly used precedences between landmarks are the reasonable and obedient reasonable orderings. We omit them from this work for two reasons: these orderings are heuristic, they do not hold in every plan, and more importantly, we subsume them through a more powerful heuristic method called consistency that we introduce in the next section.

The landmarks in $L(G_d)$ are ordered by means of a directed acyclic graph with landmark orderings as arcs. In order to avoid redundant edges, natural orderings $p \to q$ are added to the graph only if $p \in L(q)$, and p is not a landmark for another $r, r \in L(q)$. Namely, we can infer these orderings from the transitive closure of the graph.

The set of achieved landmarks $Achieved(L(G_d))$ contains initially the landmarks that are true in the initial state. A landmark L is added to the set when an action adds it, and when all landmarks preceding L in the graph are in the set. A landmark L is deleted from the set when an action deletes it, and L is a top goal or L is a greedy necessary landmark $L \to_{gn} L'$ for an unachieved landmark $L' \notin Achieved(L(G_d))$. Analogously, The set $Unachieved(L(G_d)) = L(G_d) \backslash Achieved(L(G_d))$ of unachieved landmarks in a state s are the landmarks in $L(G_d)$ that are not in the set of achieved landmarks.

Then, the subgoal candidates considered in nodes along the probe are extracted from the set of *first unachieved* landmarks $FirstUnachieved(L(G_d))$. These are the unachieved landmarks that are not strictly preceded by any other unachieved landmark, that is, $FirstUnachieved(L(G_d)) = \{ L \mid L \in Unachieved(L(G_d)) \land \forall L' \to_x L : L' \in Achieved(L(G_d)) \}$. If every achieved landmark is deleted from the landmark graph, the first unachieved landmarks would correspond to the roots of the graph.

---

[1] An action e-deletes a fluent when the fluent must be false after the action, or more precisely, when the action either deletes the fluent, has a precondition that is mutex, or adds a mutex.

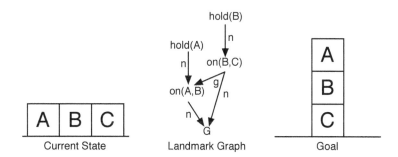

Figure 4.4: Blocks world example of a Landmark Graph. The labels on edges stand for the ordering type: n for necessary, g for goal. Landmarks in the current state are omitted.

4.3.7 Consistent Subgoal Candidates

When a subgoal must be selected in a node n, it is chosen as the nearest first unachieved landmark that is *consistent* relative to n. The notion of consistency, adapted from Chapter 2, was previously used to prune applicable actions in arbitrary states. Here we explore instead the conditions under which a subgoal candidate can be pruned. We start with the notion of *landmark chain* induced by the ordering relations in the landmark graph of the problem.

Definition 4.10 (Greedy Necessary Chain). *A Greedy necessary landmark chain is a sequence $p_1, p_2, ..., p_k$, $k \geq 1$ of landmarks $p_i \in Unachieved(L(G_d))$, where $p_1 \in FirstUnachieved(L(G_d))$, $p_i \rightarrow_{gn} p_{i+1}$, and $p_k \rightarrow_x r, r \in L(G_d)$ such that $x \neq gn$ or $p_k = G_d$.*

In other words, a greedy necessary chain is a sequence of unachieved landmarks $p_1, p_2, ..., p_k$, $k \geq 1$, where p_1 is a first unachieved landmark, p_i is greedy necessary for p_{i+1}, and p_k precedes a landmark but is not greedy necessary for it or p_k is the dummy goal G_d.[1]

A first unachieved landmark g is *consistent* in $n = \langle s, C \rangle$ if it heads a *consistent greedy necessary chain of unachieved landmarks*. Intuitively, exploiting the semantics of greedy necessary orderings, a greedy chain $p_1, ..., p_k$ is *consistent* when it does not need to be broken; i.e, when the landmark p_{i+1} can be achieved from the state s_i that results from achieving the precedent landmark p_i, *while keeping p_i true until p_{i+1} is true* for $i = 1, ..., k-1$. Recall that all landmarks in the chain are greedy necessary and have to be true until the next one is made true. Indeed, it does not make sense to choose p_1 as the next subgoal, in order to achieve then $p_2, ..., p_k$, if this chain of causal commitments cannot be sustained.

For example, given the landmark graph of Blocks World problem shown in Figure 4.4, where $on(A, B)$ and $on(B, C)$ must be achieved starting with both blocks on the table; it does not make sense to adopt the 'first unachieved landmark' $hold(A)$ that heads the greedy chain $hold(A), on(A, B), G_d$ as a subgoal. Indeed,

---

[1] A greedy chain can contain a single atom p_1 if p_1 complies with the conditions on p_k. Recall also that all necessary orderings are greedy necessary.

after achieving $hold(A)$, either $hold(A)$ or $on(A, B)$ will have to be *undone* in order to achieve G_d. Thus, while a greedy chain headed by a landmark p_1 provides a potential reason for selecting p_1 as the next subgoal, the notion of consistency is aimed at detecting that some of these reasons are spurious.

The definition of the conditions under which a greedy chain is consistent borrows a number of ideas from Section 3.2, in particular, the notion of *projected states* that provide a fast approximation of the state that results from the achievement of a given goal.

The criterion for checking if p_{i+1} can be achieved while preserving p_i, is based on projecting the node $\langle s_{i+1}, C_{i+1} \rangle$. It approximates the fluents that will be true when p_{i+1} is achieved from s_i, without violating the commitments in C_i, and the set of commitments that no action can consume.

Input: A planning problem $\Pi = \langle F, I, O, G \rangle$
Input: A relaxed plan extractor function $\texttt{RelPlan} : \mathcal{P}(F) \mapsto \mathcal{P}(O)$
Input: A mutual exclusivity function $\texttt{Mutex} : \mathcal{P}(F) \mapsto \mathcal{P}(F)$
Output: A relaxed plan π

$\pi \leftarrow \emptyset$
to-support $\leftarrow G$
while *to-support* $\neq \emptyset$ **do**
$\qquad \pi \leftarrow \pi \cup \{\texttt{RelPlan}\,(\textit{to-support})\}$
$\qquad$ *to-support* $\leftarrow \emptyset$
$\qquad$ **foreach** $p \in add(a)$ such that $a \in \pi$ **do**
$\qquad\qquad$ **if** $p \in \texttt{Mutex}(G)$ *and* $\not\exists b \in \pi$ such that $p \in del(b)$ **then**
$\qquad\qquad\qquad$ *to-support* $\leftarrow$ *to-support* $\cup \neg p$
return π

Figure 4.5: The mutually exclusive extended relaxed plan extraction algorithm.

Given a greedy necessary landmark chain $p_1, \ldots, p_k$, $k \geq 1$ relative to a node $n = \langle s, C \rangle$, the projected nodes $n_i = \langle s_i, C_i \rangle$, are obtained differently for $i = 1$ and $i > 1$. The projected node $n_1 = \langle s_1, C_1 \rangle$ is obtained from the relaxed plan π for the goal $G_1 = \{p_1\}$ from n. The state s_1 is defined as s extended with the atoms p *added* by the actions in π. Since some of these atoms are mutex with p_1 they are not added to s_1 and, the process is iterated, as shown in Figure 4.5, by extending the goal G_1 and the relaxed plan π, until π includes actions that delete the atoms in s_1 that are mutex with p_1; a process that can potentially add new atoms into s_1. Likewise, the set of commitments C_1 true in the projected node n_1 are those in C, but with the commitments consumed by actions in π removed, and the commitment $\langle \emptyset, p_1, \{p_2\} \rangle$ added if p_1 is not the last landmark in the chain.

The projected node $n_{i+1} = \langle s_{i+1}, C_{i+1} \rangle$ for the greedy chain $p_i, \ldots, p_k$ is defined in a slightly different way for $i > 1$, as while the choice of the chain makes p_1 the first unachieved subgoal, it does *not* necessarily make p_2 the second. Instead, after achieving p_1, the probe may select other landmarks to achieve and only then come back to p_2. For this reason, s_{i+1} is defined as the set of atoms reachable

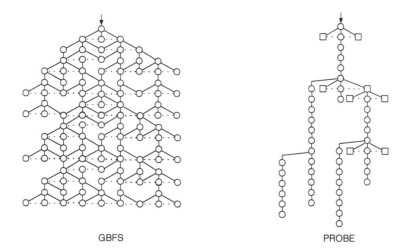

GBFS   PROBE

Figure 4.6: Sketch of GBFS' and PROBE's state space expansion. In PROBE, Squares are nodes generated by greedy best-first procedure, and circles by probes.

from s_i that are not mutex with p_{i+1}. Three type of actions a must be excluded in this reachability analysis: those with infinite offsets $\delta(a, s_i, C_i)$, those that make p_i false without making p_{i+1} true, and those with p_{i+1} in the precondition. Similarly, C_{i+1} is obtained from C_i by removing the commitments consumed by the remaining reachable actions, and adding the commitment $\langle \emptyset, p_{i+1}, \{p_{i+2}\}\rangle$.

A greedy chain is defined to be consistent in node $n = \langle s, C\rangle$ as follows:

Definition 4.11 (Consistent Greedy Chain). *Given the projected nodes $n_i = \langle s_i, C_i\rangle$ for $i = 1, \ldots, k$ along a greedy chain $p_1, \ldots, p_k$, with $n_0 = \langle s, C\rangle$, the chain is consistent if $h(G_d|s_k, C_k) \neq \infty$ and $h(p_i|s_{i-1}, C_{i-1}) \neq \infty$, for $i = 1, \ldots, k$.*

Note that if the last landmark p_k of a chain $p_1, \ldots, p_k$ is the dummy goal G_d, then $h(G_d|s_k, C_k)$ for that chain is either infinite, if it is inconsistent, or zero if it is consistent.

Then, PROBE selects a subgoal g in $n = \langle s, C\rangle$ among the nearest first unachieved landmarks according to $h(g|s, C)$ that head a consistent greedy chain.

4.3.8 Summary

PROBE is a greedy best-first planner that, throws a probe from the node $n = \langle s, C_0\rangle$ where C_0 is the empty set of commitments each time that a state s is expanded. In order to understand the intuition on how PROBE explores the state space, Figure 4.3.8 gives a visual sketch of the state space generated by a standard greedy best-first search and PROBE. The best-first search makes the planning algorithm complete, while the probes are designed to reach the goal greedily and fast. A probe is a sequence of actions that is computed without search by selecting at each node $n = \langle s, C\rangle$ the action that is helpful to the subgoal g associated with n or

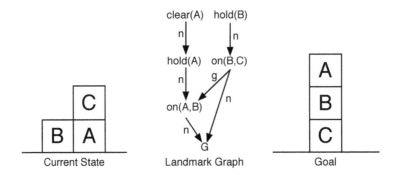

Figure 4.7: The landmark graph for Sussman's anomaly. The labels on edges stand for the ordering type: n for necessary, g for goal. Landmarks in current state are omitted.

the commitments C in n. A node $n = \langle s, C \rangle$ inherits the subgoal g from its parent node in the probe, except when s achieves g or n is the first node of the probe. In these two cases, the subgoal g is selected as the nearest first unachieved landmark that heads a consistent greedy chain. Probes terminate in the goal or in failure, and they are not allowed to visit states in memory (open or closed). All the states expanded by failed probes are added nonetheless to the open list of the best-first search algorithm. As we will see in the next section through some examples, a single probe can solve problems with multiple conflicting goals without search, choosing always the correct subgoals and action sequences to achieve them.

4.3.9 Examples

PROBE is a 'fine-grained' planner that can solve many problems without search, and thus it is illustrative to see its behavior over concrete instances. We discuss 3 different instances solved by a single probe from the initial state and 1 instance solved by two probes.

Blocks World

The Sussman Anomaly is a Block World problem that starts with blocks b and a on the table, and c on top of a, and requires some form of goal interleaving for achieving the goals b on c and a on b. Indeed no goal can be tackled first while leaving the other goal aside; progress towards the two subgoals needs to be interleaved, which can defeat naive serialization schemes.

The landmark graph generated for this problem is shown in Figure 4.7. The goal *on(b,c)* must be achieved before *on(a,b)*, as the actions that add the first goal e-delete the second. The landmarks of *on(a,b)* are $hold(a)$, which is necessary for *on(a,b)*, and $clear(a)$ which is necessary for $hold(a)$. The goal *on(b,c)* is preceded only by the necessary landmark $hold(b)$. The two goals are in turn necessary for the dummy end goal G_d.

As described above, the first probe is launched from the initial state. First, it must select a subgoal. The selection process computes the set of consistent first unachieved landmarks and chooses the one with the lowest heuristic value. In this case, the only consistent landmark is $clear(a)$. The other first unachieved landmark $hold(b)$ is not consistent, as the heuristic $h(G_d|s_2, C_2)$ over the pair $\langle s_2, C_2 \rangle$ that results from the projection when $on(b, c)$ is achieved in the greedy chain $hold(b), on(b, c), G_d$, is infinite, meaning that from that state $on(a, b)$ cannot be achieved by maintaining $on(b, c)$.

Once the subgoal $clear(a)$ is selected, the action selection process is triggered. There is one helpful action with respect to $hold(a)$, $unstack(c, a)$, which leaves the subgoal at distance 0. The action $a_0 = unstack(c, a)$ adds the commitment

$$\langle a_0, clear(a), \{hold(a)\}\rangle$$

that can only be consumed by the action $pickup(a)$ given that a is on the table. Notice that committing to maintain $clear(a)$ until $hold(a)$ is achieved results in all possible $stack(X, a)$ actions being penalized with an offset by the heuristic.

In the resulting node, goal selection is triggered because the previous subgoal has been made true in the parent node. Among the two first unachieved landmarks $hold(a)$ and $hold(b)$, only the latter is consistent. $hold(a)$ is not consistent as $h(G_d|s_3, C_3) = \infty$, where the pair $\langle s_3, C_3 \rangle$ represents the state and set of commitments resulting from the projection along the chain $p_1, p_2, p_3 = hold(a), on(a, b), G_d$[1]. Once $hold(b)$ is selected as the new subgoal, the helpful actions with respect to $hold(b)$ and $hold(a)$ are computed. Notice that though $hold(a)$ is not the current subgoal, helpful actions are computed for it as well, as it is a goal of one of the active commitments. The only action that respects the current commitments is then $a_1 = putdown(c)$, adding the commitment

$$\langle a_1, freearm, \{hold(a), hold(b)\}\rangle \ .$$

As the current subgoal is not yet achieved in the resulting node, goal selection is skipped and the action selection procedure computes the helpful actions with respect to $hold(b)$ and $hold(a)$. There are two actions: $pickup(b)$ which leaves the subgoal at distance 0, and $pickup(a)$ that leaves the subgoal at distance 2. Therefore, $a_2 = pickup(b)$ is selected, consuming the last commitment and adding instead the commitment

$$\langle a_2, hold(b), \{on(b, c)\}\rangle \ .$$

In the resulting node, goal selection is triggered again, selecting the top goal $on(b, c)$ and discarding $hold(a)$, because it still does not begin a consistent greedy chain. The only helpful action for $on(b, c)$ and $hold(a)$ is $a_3 = stack(b, c)$, which consumes the last commitment, and adds the disjunctive commitment

$$\langle a_3, on(b, c), \{g\}\rangle \vee \langle a_3, freearm, \{hold(a)\}\rangle \ .$$

The probe continues, selecting the only possible new subgoal $hold(a)$, which is consistent because $on(b, c)$ is already true in the current state. It then selects the

---

[1] It is not possible to reach G_d because the precondition $on(b, c)$ of the only action that adds G_d is unreachable

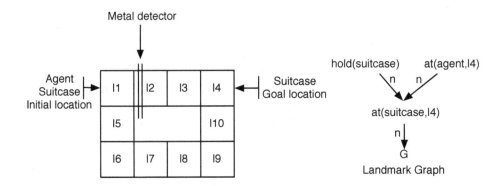

Figure 4.8: The landmark graph for the Suitcase problem. The label n on edges stand for necessary ordering. Landmarks in current state are omitted.

helpful action $a_4 = pickup(a)$ that consumes the two existing commitments $(a_0,$ $a_3)$, and adds

$$\langle a_4, hold(a), \{on(a,b)\}\rangle \ \ .$$

Finally the subgoal $on(a,b)$ is selected, and the helpful action $a_5 = stack(a,b)$ is applied, consuming the last commitment and adding $\langle a_5, on(a,b), \{G_d\}\rangle$. The probe ends successfully with the selection of the *End* action that adds that last landmark, that stands for the dummy goal G_d.

Suitcase

The Suitcase benchmark consists of an agent whose goal is to move a metallic suitcase. The agent can move through all connected cells except for those with a metal detector if he is carrying the suitcase, and he can pickup the suitcase only if he is at the same location. The actions available for the agent are *Move* from one cell to another connected cell, *pick* up suitcase and *put* down suitcase. Movement to cells with metal detectors has the precondition *not holding* in the *Move* actions. For example in the instance shown in Figure 4.8, the action $move(l1, l2)$ has the preconditions $at(robot, l1)$ and $(notholding \ suitcase)$. Delete relaxation based heuristics will guide the search towards the shortest path connecting the suitcase to its goal location without taking into account whether or not the path has a metal detector. Thus, if the solution implies taking the longest path, it will be typically the last one to be explored.

The landmark graph generated for the problem shown in Figure 4.8 consists of the landmarks $holding(suitcase)$ and $at(agent, l4)$, which are necessary for the goal landmark $at(suitcase, l4)$.

The first probe is launched from the initial state where the agent and the suitcase are at location $l1$. It first selects the subgoal $holding(suitcase)$, since the other first unachieved landmark $at(agent, l4)$ is inconsistent. The only chain $at(agent, l4)$, $at(suitcase, l4)$, G_d headed by $at(agent, l4)$ is inconsistent since the heuristic $h(G_d|, s_1, C_1)$ over the pair $\langle s_1, C_1 \rangle$ that results from the projection when the first landmark is achieved, is infinite, meaning that once $at(agent, l4)$ is achieved and maintained until $at(suitcase, l4)$, there is no way to achieve $holding(suitcase)$. The projected pair $\langle s_1, C_1 \rangle$ is constructed from the initial state s_0 plus the atoms added in the relaxed plan $\pi^+ = \{move(l1, l2), move(l2, l3), move(l3, l4)\}$ for $at(agent, l4)$ extended with actions that delete the mutex atoms of $at(agent, l4)$: $at(agent, x)$ for $x = l1, l2, l3$. In this case no new actions are added into the relaxed plan, as all the mutex atoms are already deleted by some action. The resulting projected state is $s_1 = \{at(suitcase, l1), at(agent, l4)\}$ with commitment $C_1 = \langle \emptyset, at(agent, l4), \{at(suitcase, l4)\} \rangle$ from which $h(at(suitcase, l4)|s_1, C_1) = \infty$.

Once the subgoal $holding(suitcase)$ is selected, the only helpful action is $a_0 = pickup(l1)$, which achieves the subgoal and adds the commitment

$$\langle a_0, holding(suitcase), \{at(suitcase, l4)\} \rangle$$

that can only be consumed by the action $putdown(l4)$. The only atom appearing in the set B of the commitment $\langle a, p, B \rangle$ is $at(suitcase, l4)$ because the only action in the relaxed plan for the dummy goal G_d that requires $holding(suitcase)$ is $drop(suitcase, l4)$. Notice that this commitment results in all $drop(suitcase, x)$ for any x different from $l4$ being penalized with an offset by the heuristic.

In the next node, goal selection is triggered as the previous subgoal is true in n_1. The first unachieved landmark $at(agent, l4)$ is now consistent, and it is selected as the next subgoal. The action selection mechanism is triggered again and the only helpful action is $a_1 = move(l1, l5)$, adding the commitment

$$\langle a_1, at(agent, l5), \{at(agent, l6)\} \rangle$$

Note that the action $move(l1, l2)$ is not applicable as it is penalized for e-deleting $holding\ (suitcase)$ and not adding $at(suitcase, l4)$. The action selection is triggered again six times until the subgoal $at(agent, l4)$ is achieved, resulting in the action sequence $a_2 = move(l5, l6)$, $a_3 = move(l6, l7)$, $a_4 = move(l7, l8)$, $a_5 = move(l8, l9)$, $a_6 = move(l9, l10)$ and $a_7 = move(l10, l4)$ consuming the last commitment and adding

$$\langle a_7, at(agent, l4), \{at(suitcase, l4)\} \rangle$$

Finally the subgoal $at(suitcase, l4)$ is selected and the action $a_8 = drop(suitcase, l4)$ is suggested by the action selection process as the only helpful action for the active subgoal. Action a_8 consumes the two active commitments and adds $\langle a_8, at(suitcase, l4), \{G_d\} \rangle$. The probe ends successfully with the selection of the End action that adds that last landmark, standing for the dummy goal G_d.

Gripper Unit and Gripper Infinite

Gripper Unit and Gripper Infinite are variations of the Gripper classical benchmark. It consists of a gripper with a single hand that can move to adjacent cells, grab balls and deposit them in other locations. The difference between Gripper Unit and Infinite, is the number of balls that a gripper can hold; in the former a single ball while in the later an unlimited number of balls. Both examples have the same single line grid initially with one ball in every cell and the gripper standing in the middle of the line. The goal of both problems is to drop all of the

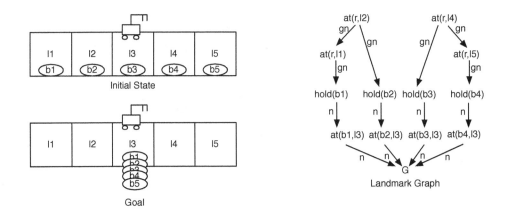

Figure 4.9: Landmark graph for Gripper Unit and Infinite. The labels on the edges stand for the ordering type: *n* for necessary, *gn* for greedy necessary. Landmarks in the current state are omitted.

balls into the middle cell, where the gripper is initially located. Both problems pose a challenge similar to the one posed by the Visit-All domain from Section 4.2, where heuristics based on the delete relaxation find themselves constantly in search plateaus. Instead of illustrating the solution of a single probe over Visit-All, we prefer to show the solutions for these two variations, as solutions to Visit-All are achieved backtrack free only due to the nature of selecting the closest subgoal and the action to achieve it, where commitments and the heuristic do not play an important role.

The landmark graph shown in Figure 4.9 for the problem over a line of five cells $l_1, \ldots, l_5$, with the gripper located at l_3 and balls located at every l_i for $i = 1, \ldots, 5$, is the same for both gripper unit and infinite, where the goal is to place every object in cell l_3, which is the cell in the middle of the line. The objects are denoted by b, r and l standing for ball, robot and location respectively. The goals $at(b_x, l_3)$ are necessary landmarks for G_d[1], and $hold(b_x)$ are necessary landmarks for their respective $at(b_x, l_3)$ for $x = 1, \ldots, 5$. The landmark $at(r, l1)$ is greedy necessary for $hold(b_1)$, and $at(r, l2)$ is greedy necessary for both $at(r, l1)$ and $hold(b_2)$. Similarly, $at(r, l5)$ is greedy necessary for $hold(b_5)$, and $at(r, l4)$ is greedy necessary for both $at(r, l5)$ and $hold(b_4)$. Note that the last ordering relations are greedy necessary because they hold only the first time that the landmark is achieved. For example, the first time $hold(b1)$ is achieved, the robot has to be at l_1, which is the initial location of b_1, but once b_1 is held and moved to another location, this relation does not stand anymore since $at(r, l_1)$ will not be true necessarily right before holding the ball again.

Gripper Unit. First, we start explaining the behavior of a probe in the gripper unit variation. The probe is launched from the initial state while selecting the first

---

[1] Goal $at(b3, l3)$ is omitted from the landmark graph because it is already true in the initial state and does not affect the behavior of the probe in this example.

subgoal. Both first unachieved landmarks $at(r, l2)$ and $at(r, l_4)$ are consistent, and at distance 1 according to the heuristic, thus one of them is selected randomly, for example $at(r, l_4)$. Once the subgoal is selected, the action selection procedure is triggered, applying the only helpful action $a_1 = move(l_3, l_4)$, which adds the commitment

$$\langle a_0, at(r, l_4), \{hold(b_4), at(r, l_5)\}\rangle$$

that can only be consumed by $pick(b_4)$ or $move(l_4, l_5)$.

As the subgoal is already true in the resulting node, the subgoal selection computes the consistent first unachieved landmarks. Again landmarks $at(r, l_5)$ and $hold(b_4)$ are consistent and at the same distance 1, so $at(r, l_5)$ is chosen randomly. The action $a_1 = move(l_4, l_5)$ is selected, consuming the previous commitment and adding

$$\langle a_1, at(r, l_5), \{hold(b_5)\}\rangle$$

that can be consumed by $pick(b_5)$. Note that all *move* actions from l_5 will be penalized by this commitment while $hold(b_5)$ is not true.

The subgoal selection then sets $hold(b_5)$ as the next subgoal for being the closest consistent first unachieved landmark at distance 1. The other two consistent first unachieved landmarks $at(r, l_4)$ and $at(r, l_2)$ are at distance 2 and 4 respectively. Note that while $at(r, l_4)$ is really at distance 1, (i.e., only action $move(l_5, l_4)$ needs to be applied) a penalty of 1 is added by the heuristic because this action threatens the active commitment. [1] Once $hold(b_5)$ is selected, the only helpful action $a_2 = pick(b_5)$ is applied, consuming the active commitment and adding

$$\langle a_2, hold(b_5), \{at(b_5, l_3)\}\rangle$$

The next consistent subgoal is $at(b_5, l_3)$ and the action selection applies the sequence $a_3 = move(l_5, l_4)$, $a_4 = move(l_4, l_3)$ and $a_5 = drop(b_5)$ consuming all active commitments and adding

$$\langle a_5, at(b_5, l_3), \{G_d\}\rangle$$

The next subgoal is selected among $at(r, l2)$ and $at(r, l_4)$ again as both are consistent and at distance 1, choosing $at(r, l_4)$ randomly. The action $a_6 = move(l_3, l_4)$ is applied, adding the commitment

$$\langle a_6, at(r, l_4), \{hold(b_4)\}\rangle$$

This commitment is similar to the first commitment added in the probe, but without $at(r, l_5) \in B$ because the atom not longer appears in the relax plan. The closest consistent subgoal is $hold(b_4)$ and the action $a_7 = pick(b_4)$ is applied consuming the last commitment and adding

$$\langle a_7, hold(b_4), \{at(b_4, l_3)\}\rangle$$

The next subgoal selected is then $at(b_4, l_3)$, and the actions $a_8 = move(l_4, l_3)$ and $a_9 = drop(b_4)$ are applied, consuming the last commitment and adding

$$\langle a_9, at(b_4, l_3), \{G_d\}\rangle$$

---

[1] The penalty is given by the cheapest $h(p|s, C)$ among $p \in B$ over the commitments threatened in C. The only atom in B is $p = hold(b_5)$ with $h(p|s, C) = 1$, thus the penalty is 1.

The other two balls b_2, b_1 located at l_2, l_1 respectively are achieved by following a similar chain of decisions. Briefly, the subgoal $at(r, l_2)$ is selected and the action $a_{10} = move(l_3, l_2)$ is applied, adding $\langle a_{10}, at(r, l_2), \{hold(b_2), at(r, l_1)\}\rangle$. The subgoal $hold(b_2)$ then, is selected randomly among $hold(b_2)$ and $at(r, l_1)$ for being both consistent and at distance 1. Then, the action $a_{11} = pick(b_2)$ is applied, consuming last commitment and adding $\langle a_{11}, hold(b_2), \{at(b_2, l_3)\}\rangle$, and the subgoal $at(b_2, l_3)$ is selected and achieved by actions $a_{12} = move(l_2, l_3)$ and $a_{13} = drop(b_2)$, consuming last commitment, and adding $\langle a_{13}, at(b_2, l_3), \{G_d\}\rangle$. The last subgoals $at(r, l_1)$, $hold(b_1)$, and $at(b_1, l_3)$ are selected sequentially and achieved by the sequence of actions $a_{14} = move(l_3, l_2)$, $a_{14} = move(l_2, l_1)$, $a_{15} = pick(b_1)$, $a_{16} = move(l_1, l_2)$, $a_{17} = move(l_2, l_3)$, and $a_{18} = drop(b_1)$.

Gripper Infinite. We now explain the differences involved in solving the gripper infinite variant. The first subgoals, commitments and actions are the same up until the node resulting from the sequence $a_0 = move(l_3, l_4)$, $a_1 = move(l_4, l_5)$, $a_2 = pick(b_5)$, with the active commitment $\langle a_2, hold(b_5), \{at(b_5, l_3)\}\rangle$.

The next subgoal is $at(r, l_4)$, as it is the closest consistent first unachieved landmark. Recall that previously this landmark was not consistent, and the closest one was instead $at(b_5, l_3)$. The landmark $at(r, l_4)$ leads the chain $at(r, l_4)$, $hold(b_4)$, $at(b_4, l_3)$ that is consistent now because the gripper can hold more than one ball without threatening the active commitment. The action $a_3 = move(l_5, l_4)$ is applied and adds the commitment

$$\langle a_4, at(r, l_4), \{hold(b_4), at(r, l_3)\}\rangle$$

The closest consistent landmark then is $hold(b_4)$ at distance 1 while $at(b_5, l3)$ lays at distance 2. The first landmark is selected and achieved through action $a_5 = pick(b_4)$, which adds the commitment

$$\langle a_5, hold(b_4), \{at(b_4, l_3)\}\rangle$$

Then all first unachieved landmarks are consistent and at distance 2: $at(b5, l_3)$, $at(b4, l_3)$ and $at(r, l_2)$. If the last landmark is selected, the probe will proceed by grabbing the other two balls located at l_1 and l_2. If either $at(b_5, l_3)$ or $at(b_4, l_3)$ is selected, the probe will drop the ball at l_3 and it will be one step closer and continue grabbing the other balls.

Bribery

The Bribery domain consists of an agent that has to get from one location to another and may have to bribe police officers in some known locations. In order to bribe a police officer, there may be some goods that the agent can grab. Consider an instance where two paths $x_1, \ldots, x_{10}$ and $y_1, \ldots, y_{10}$ connect an initial location a with a final location b. Starting from a the agent can go either to x_1 or y_1 and from x_{10} or y_{10} to b, but at the beginning and end of both paths there is an officer to bribe. The agent starts at location a holding res_1 and there is another resource res_2 laying on the ground of location a. The agent can grab an infinite number of resources, and indeed, it needs at least two resources to cross from a to b.

Heuristics based on the delete relaxation do not realize the need to grab both resources, and moreover, grabbing the second resource is not even considered to be a helpful action while the agent holds the other. As probes rely on helpful actions, they fail too. Aside from the helpful actions failing to suggest grabbing the other resource, two other reasons make the probe fail: once it makes the wrong choice of moving without grabbing the second resource, the probe is not allowed to go back and amend the mistake in the same probe, as it is only allowed to visit new states; and, there is no landmark other than the goal $at(agent, b)$, because there are two paths that the agent can take. This shows that the more landmarks the problem has, the merrier, (i.e., as more subgoals are available, the inference done by PROBE can be stronger). Indeed more subgoals such as disjunctive landmarks of the form $x_i \vee y_i$ for $i = 1, \ldots, 10$ can be inferred (Porteous and Cresswell, 2002), and later we will discuss in Section 4.5 a simple way to compile them into the problem in order to keep probe's inference techniques unchanged. Nevertheless, we now show how PROBE solves the problem with 2 probes.

The first probe is triggered from the initial state. We skip the goal selection mechanism since the only available goal $at(agent, b)$ is selected. The action selection suggests the helpful action $move(a, x_1)$. Action $move(a, y_1)$ is not helpful because the relaxed plan breaks ties randomly and chooses the path $x_1, \ldots, x_{10}$. Neither is action $pick(res2)$ helpful, as the relaxed plan does not realize that $res1$ is deleted. The action $a_0 = move(a, x_1)$ is applied and adds the commitment

$$\langle a_0, x_1\{x_2\}\rangle$$

Yet the subgoal is still active and the sequence of actions $move(x_i, x_{i+1})$ for $i = 1, \ldots, 8$ is applied, resulting in the robot at location x_9 and commitment $\langle a_8, x_9\{x_{10}\}\rangle$, from which the only helpful action $a_9 = move(x_9, x_{10})$ results in a state with an infinite heuristic. The reason for the heuristic to be infinite is due to the commitment $\langle a_9, x_{10}\{b\}\rangle$ added by the last action, which implies that x_{10} can be consumed only by the action $move(x_{10}, b)$. As crossing to b requires a resource that is not available without moving from x_{10}, the goal $at(agent, b)$ is unreachable and the probe fails. At this point, every state along the probe is added to the open list of the greedy best first search without recomputing their heuristic value. We could indeed recompute the heuristic $h(G_d|s, C)$ with $C = \emptyset$ before adding those states, but it has almost no impact on the overall performance. All states other than the initial one have the same heuristic value of 13. For example, at every state where the agent is at x_i for $i = 1, \ldots, 10$ without an available resource, the distance from x_i to the goal $at(agent, b)$ as well as holding the resource located at a, is always 12 plus a penalty of 1 for the action used to go back and violate the commitment $\langle a_{i-1}, x_i, \{x_{i+1}\}\rangle$. The distance from the initial state where the agent is at a holding one resource is 11: the distance from a to b.

Once all states are in the open list, the greedy best-first search picks the initial state as the most promising one. It then expands all its possible successors resulting from actions $pick(res2)$ and $move(a, y1)$, (the two actions not considered in the expansion done by the probe) and adds the expanded node into the closed list. The node resulting from the first action is at distance 11, and the second is at distance 12 given by $h(G_d|s, C)$ with $C = \emptyset$. Both nodes are inserted in the open

Domain	I	FF			LAMA		PROBE			
		S	EHC	EX	S	EX	S	1P	EX	#P
Blocks World	50	42	42	9,193	**50**	1,077	**50**	50	40	1.0
Cyber	30	4	4	228	**25**	73	24	13	30	111.5
Depots	22	**22**	19	71,649	20	44,738	**22**	14	108	11.8
Driver	20	16	6	11,476	**20**	2,445	**20**	15	54	2.1
Elevator	30	30	30	1,429	30	666	30	25	114	1.2
Ferry	50	50	50	50	50	108	50	50	29	1.0
Freecell	20	**20**	14	1,506	**20**	2,071	18	7	261	35.1
Grid	5	5	5	301	5	174	5	5	59	1.0
Gripper	50	50	50	102	50	**79**	50	50	101	1.0
Logistics	28	28	28	94	28	97	28	28	55	1.0
Miconic	50	50	50	52	50	**37**	50	50	45	1.0
Mprime	35	**34**	34	23	4	12	**34**	33	7	1.0
Mystery	30	18	15	258	22	238	**25**	23	8	1.1
Openstacks	30	30	30	504	30	124	30	30	121	1.0
Openstacks-IPC6	30	30	30	968	30	146	30	30	139	1.0
Parc-Printer	30	**30**	21	173	24	409	27	21	49	9.7
Pegsol	30	**30**	0	15,287	**30**	5,174	29	1	1,681	864.7
Pipesworld-No-Tan	50	35	17	3,540	44	1,363	**45**	19	65	6.4
Pipesworld-Tan	50	22	4	46,189	39	40,015	**41**	16	1,055	108.7
PSR-Small	50	41	0	39,533	**50**	276	**50**	0	70	30.8
Rovers	40	40	40	10,341	40	1,750	40	38	114	1.1
Satellite	20	20	20	389	20	412	20	20	41	1.0
Scanalyzer	30	**30**	22	1,905	28	257	28	26	39	2.8
Sokoban	30	**27**	0	19,355	26	16,066	14	0	12,027	11,120.6
Storage	30	18	3	261,299	18	3,645	**21**	15	15	2.5
TPP	30	28	28	28,388	**30**	1,340	**30**	30	119	1.0
Transport	30	29	29	45,593	**30**	4,964	**30**	24	157	1.2
Trucks	30	11	6	135,863	**16**	**169**	9	0	2,762	2,818.4
Woodworking	30	17	12	1,329	**30**	7,040	**30**	30	31	1.0
Zeno Travel	20	20	18	148	20	482	20	20	50	1.0
Total	980	827	627	23,572	879	4,515	900	683	648	
Percentage		84%	64%		89%		92%	70%		

Table 4.2: PROBE vs. FF and LAMA on instances of previous IPCs: *I* is the number of instances, *S* is the number of solved instances, *EHC* is number instances solved by EHC, *EX* is the average number of expanded nodes, *1P* is the number of instances solved with *one* probe, *#P* is the average number of probes triggered. *EX* is reported for problems solved by all three planners.

list and the second probe is triggered from the most promising one.

The node with the lowest value is the one resulting from action $pick(res2)$ applied in the initial state. Thus, the second probe is launched from the state where the agent is at a holding both resources. The second probe selects the only available goal $at(agent, b)$ and finds the sequence that successfully achieves it: $move(a, x_1)$ followed by $move(x_i, x_{i+1})$ for $i = 1, \ldots, 9$ and $move(x_{10}, b)$. Note that none of those nodes have been expanded in the first probe, as these states contain the atom $hold(res2)$.

As we will see in the next section, most IPC domains are solved with a single probe, and only two domains require thousands of expansions and probes.

Domain	I	FF			LAMA			PROBE		
		Q		T	Q		T	Q		T
Blocks World	50	**39**	(9)	0.22	86	(1)	0.69	40	(2)	**0.21**
Cyber	30	30	(0)	**0.74**	30	(0)	48.48	30	(0)	1.46
Depots	22	47	(0)	38.28	52	(1)	46.58	**42**	(6)	**3.01**
Driver	20	**34**	(2)	11.73	37	(4)	1.32	50	(1)	**0.99**
Elevator	30	86	(4)	**1.34**	88	(0)	3.28	110	(0)	30.81
Ferry	50	**28**	(0)	**0.01**	29	(0)	0.18	29	(1)	0.02
Freecell	20	**55**	(7)	**2.81**	64	(0)	19.78	67	(1)	45.45
Grid	5	61	(1)	**0.30**	**56**	(1)	6.43	59	(1)	7.74
Gripper	50	**76**	(0)	**0.01**	**76**	(0)	0.26	101	(0)	0.06
Logistics	28	**41**	(1)	**0.01**	42	(0)	0.25	55	(0)	0.13
Miconic	50	**30**	(0)	**0.01**	**30**	(0)	0.15	45	(0)	0.02
Mprime	35	**6**	(1)	**0.03**	**6**	(0)	3.72	7	(0)	2.62
Mystery	30	7	(0)	**0.08**	**6**	(4)	2.36	8	(0)	1.21
Openstacks	30	**136**	(0)	**0.46**	145	(0)	3.03	139	(0)	20.22
Openstacks-IPC6	30	**156**	(0)	**0.59**	159	(0)	3.68	158	(0)	54.76
Parc-Printer	30	32	(0)	**0.03**	34	(0)	0.41	**31**	(0)	0.26
Pegsol	30	**34**	(0)	1.35	35	(0)	**1.34**	**34**	(0)	2.10
Pipesworld-No-Tan	50	**28**	(5)	0.45	37	(1)	1.04	33	(5)	**0.35**
Pipesworld-Tan	50	**30**	(8)	62.23	31	(2)	**32.41**	55	(5)	59.14
PSR-Small	50	**17**	(1)	60.96	**17**	(0)	0.89	20	(0)	**0.07**
Rovers	40	**100**	(4)	26.97	106	(1)	**13.44**	113	(0)	28.16
Satellite	20	**38**	(0)	**0.10**	39	(0)	0.90	41	(0)	0.86
Scanalyzer	30	24	(1)	1.89	24	(2)	8.52	24	(4)	6.15
Sokoban	30	141	(2)	**0.82**	**138**	(4)	3.52	160	(0)	96.71
Storage	30	16	(0)	49.90	20	(0)	1.62	**15**	(6)	**0.08**
TPP	30	122	(0)	42.41	**104**	(8)	**6.91**	119	(0)	20.88
Transport	30	28	(1)	133.52	27	(0)	**41.23**	**26**	(4)	42.27
Trucks	30	**23**	(0)	5.66	24	(0)	**0.61**	26	(0)	20.55
Woodworking	30	117	(1)	**0.26**	**100**	(15)	5.84	154	(0)	5.45
Zeno Travel	20	**31**	(13)	**0.13**	36	(1)	3.55	50	(0)	6.21
Total	980	54		14.77	56		8.75	61		15.26

Table 4.3: PROBE vs. FF and LAMA on instances of previous IPCs: *I* is the number of instances, *T* is average time in seconds and *Q* is the average plan length. *T* and *Q* are reported for problems solved by all three planners. In parenthesis is the number of problems where each planner produces solutions that are at least 10% better than the other two planners

4.4 Experimental Results

We compare PROBE with FF and LAMA over a broad range of IPC domains. [1] PROBE is written in C++ and uses Metric-FF as an *ADL* to *Propositional* STRIPS compiler (Hoffmann, 2003). LAMA is executed without the plan improvement option, reporting the first plan that it finds. All experiments were conducted on a dual-processor Xeon Woodcrest running at 2.33 GHz and 8 GB of RAM. Processes time or memory out after 30 minutes or 2 GB. All action costs are assumed to be 1 so that the plan cost is equal to the plan length.

Table 4.2 compares PROBE with FF and LAMA over 980 instances from previous IPCs. In terms of coverage, PROBE solves 21 more problems than LAMA and 73 more than FF. More remarkably, 70% of problems are solved with just *one probe* (56 problems more than FF in EHC). Enhanced helpful actions provide more actions than just those that are helpful to a single probe before giving up and returning to GBFS. If enhanced helpful actions were not used, a single probe

---

[1] FF is FF2.3, while LAMA is the version used in the 2008 IPC.

Feature Off	S	1P	Q	T
None	92%	70%	67.0	34.8
Probes	75%	–	71.0	99.6
Consistency	91%	40%	91.4	56.9
Subgoaling	86%	44%	80.7	55.2
Commitments	90%	63%	85.0	39.0

Table 4.4: Ablation Study. The columns indicate the feature of PROBE that has been turned off, the % of problems solved (S) and solved by a single probe (1P), and the average plan length (Q) and time (T) in seconds. The averages are computed over all problems solved by PROBE.

would solve 40 fewer problems, but just 10 fewer in the general dual search architecture. There are several domains where PROBE solves more problems than LAMA or FF, the largest difference being in *Mprime* due to LAMA's parsing problems.[1] On the other hand, the largest gain of LAMA and FF over PROBE is in Sokoban, where LAMA and FF solve 12 and 13 more instances respectively.

Column #P shows the average number of probes required in each domain, which corresponds to the number of nodes expanded in the greedy best-first search (not the number of total expanded nodes that are shown). Interestingly, this number is one in most domains, and large in three domains only; Sokoban, Trucks, and Pegsol, where probes do not pay off.

A measure of the search effort is given by the number of nodes that each planner expands over the instances solved by all three planners. LAMA expands around 7 times more nodes than PROBE, and FF expands 36 times more. In some domains this difference is even larger. In Depots, for example, LAMA (FF) solves fewer instances than PROBE, but it expands 414 (663) times more nodes. This, however, does not mean that PROBE is faster. One reason is the use of deferred evaluation by LAMA, which leads to faster node expansions and fewer heuristic evaluations. Another reason is the overhead in PROBE. Interestingly, FF is the fastest in 18 out of the 30 domains, while LAMA and PROBE are each fastest in 6. The average plan length of the instances solved by the three planners is 61 for PROBE, 56 for LAMA and 54 for FF. PROBE performs the worst in *Sokoban* and *Gripper*, while best in *Depots* and *Blocks* (Table 4.3).

We have also evaluated the impact of the different design decisions made in PROBE. The results are summarized in Table 4.4, where the columns show the percentage of problems solved, the percentage of problems solved with a single probe, the average plan length and time that results from dropping some feature from PROBE; namely: the *probes* themselves, the subgoal *consistent tests*, the *subgoaling mechanism* itself, and the *commitments*.[2] In this table, the averages are computed over the problems solved by PROBE with all of these features, and thus they differ from the averages in the previous table computed over the prob-

---

[1] Changing the domain definition of Mprime, allows LAMA to solve 35 instances. Pipesworld domains were solved with LAMA 2010, as some bugs were fixed in order to parse them.   [2] The removal of the subgoaling mechanism means that the heuristic minimization used to select the next action, is not done for the selected subgoal, but over all the possible first subgoals.

lems solved by the three planners. As can be seen from the table, dropping the probes from PROBE, (i.e., making it a standard greedy BFS planner) reduces the coverage from 92% to 75%, while the times increase by a factor of 3. The removal of consistent tests and the removal of the whole subgoaling mechanism, in turn, do not affect coverage as much, but reduce the percentage of problems solved with a single probe from 67% to 40% and 44%, while increasing times and lengths by roughly 50% and 25% respectively. Likewise, if only commitments are dropped, the loss is mainly on the average length of plans which jumps up 26%.

From these figures, a number of conclusions can be drawn. First, the use of probes helps significantly along all relevant dimensions. Second, *subgoaling helps as well but only when used in combination with the consistency tests* (degradation from turning off consistency is similar to degradation from turning off whole subgoaling mechanisms). Third, commitments help, but mainly to improve the quality of the resulting plans; something that is achieved by keeping track of the reasons for the introduction of the actions in the plan.

4.5 Limitations and Extensions

In this section we discuss some of the limitations and improvements that we left out of PROBE to keep the design of probes as simple as possible. Generally, such improvements had a small impact on overall performance even if they tackle interesting limitations.

Probes map the original problem into a series of subproblems by inferring the next subgoal to achieve from the set of landmarks. Serializations are built heuristically by changing the original goal of the problem with a series of single landmark fluents. The experiments shown above suggest that most of the planning benchmarks accept such serializations, as most of the domains can be solved by single probes. When a probe fails it may be due to the non-decomposable structure of the goal in a domain, or if decomposable, it may be that finding a decomposition that renders the subproblems easy, involves more than the use of landmarks. Tower of Hanoi is an example of the first situation where once a subgoal is achieved, it has to be undone in order to achieve the remaining ones. Sokoban is an example of the last situation, where even if serializations are easy to find, the subproblems still contain many dead-ends and search plateaus. Generally, when more landmarks are available, the subproblems are more simple to solve. Determining whether or not a fluent is a Landmark is PSPACE-complete (Hoffmann et al., 2004), but if the problem does not contain deletes, determining whether or not a fluent is a landmark is in P (Hoffmann et al., 2004). The method we use for discovering single fluent landmarks finds the complete set relative to the delete relaxation of the original problem, although small variations of the same problem may render no fluent landmarks at all. For example, consider the gripper domain, where a gripper has to move a number of balls from one room to another. If the gripper has a single hand, every fluent such as $hold(hand1, ball)$ is a landmark, but if instead the gripper has two hands or more than one gripper exists, there is not a single fluent landmark but a disjunctive landmark such as $hold(hand_1, ball) \lor hold(hand_2, ball)$.

Disjunctive fluent landmarks capture a wider range of subgoals, and although being less committed than a single fluent subgoal, they may be useful for getting better serializations. We do not include them in probes for simplicity. Thus, instead of explicitly representing the knowledge of disjunctive landmarks, we use an extension of the original problem that encodes the disjunction of atoms with single fluents, (i.e., implicitly encoding disjunctive landmarks in the problem). State-of-the-art planners ground the actions of a PDDL problem before attempting to solve it, (i.e., they transform predicates, objects, and constants into a propositional representation). Predicates may have arguments as parameters specifying the set of objects that make the grounded fluents, (e.g., a predicate $pred(arg_1, arg_2)$ where arg_1 and arg_2 refer to different sets of objects, is grounded into propositional fluents taking the cross product of both sets). In order to introduce fluents that represent the disjunction of the objects' set (i.e., disjunction of grounded fluents), we add to each set the symbol $*$. We call such predicates the *star-predicates*. To enforce semantically that $*$ stands for *any object* of a set, every action that adds a grounded fluent that contains an object in the set, also adds the fluent with the symbol $*$. For example, in the Gripper domain, every time the action $pickup(arm_i, ball_i)$ adds the predicate $hold(arm_i, ball_i)$, it also adds the predicates $hold(*, ball_i)$, $hold(arm_i, *)$ and $hold(*, *)$. The number of fluents of the problem grows linearly. Note that we do not add such predicates in action preconditions and deletes, so they do not add extra complexity to the problem and they are just surrogates of the first time a disjunctive fluent is achieved. Not every possible disjunction is captured, rather those that come from the same predicate are, (i.e., we cannot capture disjunctions such as $pred_1(args) \vee pred_2(args)$). When the set of single fluent landmarks is computed over the transformed relaxed problem, *star-predicates* can appear as single fluent landmarks as well. Just a single change is needed in order to account for such predicates in the inferences done by the probes. When a star-predicate is selected as a subgoal and is achieved, the commitment added to the probe should refer to the real predicate represented by the star-predicate. As no action deletes any star-predicate, the commitment will not be threatened by any action if we state that the star-predicate should be true until some other predicate is made true. The impact of such disjunctions pay-off experimentally in specific instances, but overall the impact is not substantial, improving only slightly the overall plan quality.

Further heuristic orderings such as reasonable and obedient-reasonable orderings can be added to the landmark graph, but the results were not consistent. In some domains they render better overall performance, in some worse.

Probes use a small variation of the additive heuristic, were a penalty is added to actions that threaten active commitments. The definition of the penalty fits perfectly with other known heuristics such as h_{max} or h_{FF}, but none dominate h_{add} in our experiments. When a probe fails, the nodes are inserted into the open list of the greedy best-first search (GBFS) without recomputing their heuristic values. When a node is expanded by GBFS it computes the heuristic with an empty set of commitments. It is arguable that the heuristic value of such nodes are different from the heuristic value of the nodes in the open list that come from probes, where the set of commitments indeed is not empty. Thus, it may seem to be appropriate to recompute the heuristic value of the nodes that come from probes before inserting them into the open list of the GBFS. But, as heuristics are approximations of the distance from a given state to the goal, we treat the values obtained along the probe as a similar approximation of the same value, and indeed, in some instances, the penalties help to differentiate nodes that may be treated as equally distant if they were expanded by GBFS. More importantly, it is known that heuristic functions are computationally expensive, thus the outcome of recomputing heuristic values does not pay off in our scheme. A more in-depth analysis of the different strategies to incorporate nodes from the probes into another search algorithm is out of scope of this work.

The commitments taken into account by the heuristic $h(G|s, C)$ render the goal unreachable from many states, even if they are not real dead ends. If a state s is infinite given the set of commitments C but not if those commitments are omitted, the right interpretation is that state s is a dead-end given that each action a_i in the commitments $\langle a_i, p_i, B_i \rangle$ is the *last supporter* of the atom p for achieving an atom q in B. For example, consider a Blocks World instance where a set of blocks $x_1, \ldots, x_n$ are in the table and the goal is to build a tower with the block x_n on the table and each x_i on top of x_{i+1} for $i = 1, \ldots, n-1$. If the actions $pick(x_1)$ and $stack(x_1, x_2)$ are applied in the initial state, and the commitment $\langle stack(x_1, x_2), on(x_1, x_2), \{G_d\} \rangle$ is added, the resulting state is a dead-end given the semantics introduced above. The commitment states that the action $stack(x_1, x_2)$ is the last supporter of fluent $on(x_1, x_2)$ in order to achieve the dummy goal. Indeed, if at this point $on(x_1, x_2)$ is added for the last time, there is no possible way to achieve the other goal $on(x_2, x_3)$, as it would require undoing $on(x_1, x_2)$, violating the semantic implied by the commitment.

4.6 Conclusion

We have formulated and tested a new dual search architecture for planning based on the notion of probes: single action sequences constructed greedily but care-fully, that can quickly get deep into the state space, terminating in the goal or in failure. The probes are used as part of a greedy best-first search algorithm that throws a single probe from every state that is expanded. We have shown that most IPC domains are solved with a single probe, while in a few difficult do-mains such as Sokoban and Trucks, probes do not help and introduce overhead. Overall, the performance of the planner is comparable with state-of-the-art plan-ners such as FF and LAMA, while its coverage over the 980 planning instances considered is slightly better (92% for PROBE vs. 84% and 89% for FF and LAMA respectively).

The design of probes uses and extends a number of techniques developed in modern planners that go well beyond the use of heuristic functions to guide the search. They include helpful actions, landmarks, causal commitments, subgoals, and consistency tests, all of which help in the greedy selection of the subgoal to achieve next, and the actions needed to reach it.

From the success of probes and their computation, in which problems are mapped into a *series of subgoals* that are heuristically computed along with the probes, two conclusions can be drawn. The first is that most of the classical benchmarks admit good serializations of the landmarks under which the solution of the problems becomes simple. The second is that while not every serialization is good, the mechanisms in PROBE and in particular the consistency tests, appear to find good ones. These observations raise two questions. The first is which methods are good for finding good serializations when they exist? PROBE implements one such method but it is not necessarily the best such method, and moreover, probes are greedy and incomplete. In Chapter 8 we develop an alternative method for finding such serializations. The second question is which methods are good for finding and exploiting serializations in problems that have good but no perfect decompositions? The 8-puzzle is an example of this situation: one can place the tile 1 in position 1, the tile 2 in position 2, but then one needs to undo this last subgoal, in order to have tiles 2 and 3 at their target positions.

The ideas of goal serialization and problem decomposition have received a lot of attention in search and in the early days of planning (Korf, 1987), and it may be worth revisiting those ideas equipped with the techniques that have been developed more recently in planning research. The challenge is explicitly to recognize and exploit the structure of problems that are nearly-decomposable, even if they are not perfectly decomposable. Indeed, planning used to be defined originally as being mainly concerned with those problems (Newell and Simon, 1963). While the notion has practically disappeared from the modern language of planning, it is still very much there: classical planners do best on those problems[1], simply because the heuristics used, like delete-relaxation heuristics, assume that problems are in fact decomposable. Nonetheless, there is the possibility that modern planners could do better still on nearly-decomposable problems, if they would more explicitly address and exploit the good but not perfect serializations that such problems hide.

---

[1] Planners can solve other problems too, but expanding much larger number of nodes, and not scaling up as well.

Chapter 5

The Classical Planner PROBE in IPC-7

> 'Beware of the man who works hard to learn something, learns it, and finds himself no wiser than before,' Bokonon tells us. 'He is full of murderous resentment of people who are ignorant without having come by their ignorance the hard way.'
>
> *Cat's Cradle.*
> Kurt Vonnegut

In this chapter we explain the changes introduced to PROBE for the sequential satisficing track of the international planning competition IPC-7. The 14 domains with 20 instances each, including costs and planners, had 6 GB of available memory for reporting the best solution they found in 30 minutes.

5.1 Practical Improvements

The Sequential Satisficing track covers classical STRIPS planning (non-durative actions) with actions having associated non-negative costs (not necessarily uniform). The goal of the track is to solve and find low-cost plans, where the cost is defined as the sum of the costs of each plan's actions.

The evaluation criteria emphasizes good plan quality and puts less emphasis on solving time. If two plans are found within the time and memory limits, then a plan with better quality, as defined by the objective function, will have a better score. The objective function is the ratio between the best known solution divided by the solution of the planner $\frac{Q*}{Q}$ for every solved instance.

In order to improve the performance of PROBE for the planning competition we explain how probes are used in the dual search architecture, how costs are taken into account and how once the first solution is found, the planner continues the search in order to find better solutions.

5.1.1 GBFS + probes

In most classical benchmarks a single probe suffices to find a solution, suggesting that most problems admit good serializations of landmarks. In problems with no perfect serializations, such as Sokoban or 8-puzzle, many probes are needed to find a solution and rather than boosting the GBFS loop, they slow down the search algorithm. As puzzle-like problems tend to be solved by extensive search, it is better to decrease the number of launched probes and let the GBFS control the search. To behave properly in both kind of problems, we launch a probe every R expanded nodes by the GBFS. When the search begins, R is initialized to 1. R is increased according to the 'usefulnessÂt' of a probe when it fails. A simple approximation is to increase R by 1 when the tail state of the failed probe has an heuristic estimation greater than the seed state. Intuitively, we decrease the rate of probes launched in GBFS search, when a probe does not find the solution and it does not decrease the distance to the goal.

5.1.2 Anytime search

In order to convert PROBE into an anytime planner, once it finds the first solution, it iteratively triggers a Weighted A* with decreasing weights to get better plan qualities. Each WA* is bounded by the best solution founded so far. WA* uses $|\pi(h_{add})|$ heuristic, the size of the relaxed plan extracted by the cost sensitive additive heuristic (Keyder, 2010).

5.1.3 Costs

In planning with costs, rather than optimizing plan length the planner needs to optimize plan cost. In this planner, costs are treated in two different ways. First, costs are ignored in the GBFS+probes phase in order to get a first quick solution. Avoiding the extra complexity added by taking into account costs, increases coverage. The drawback is that the first solution quality may be worse. Thus, in the bounded WA* phase, costs are taken into account through the cost sensitive heuristic $|\pi(h_{add})|$. We found that some problems could be solved by the cost sensitive WA* only when they were bounded by the first solution that did not take costs into account. The second phase improves the solution quality of the first phase by taking costs into account.

An important issue appears with the presence of zero cost actions that can lead to heuristic plateaus, in which the application of such operators do not decrease the cost to the goal. In order to overcome those situations, we add a base cost of 0.01 to all zero cost actions (Keyder, 2010).

5.2 IPC-7 performance

PROBE is written in C++ and uses Metric-FF as an *ADL* to *Propositional* STRIPS compiler (Hoffmann, 2003). Results are taken from the 7th International Plan-

planner	pegsol	scan.	parc.	openst.	nomys.	tidybot	wood.	sokoban	trans.	visitall	elevators	parking	barman	floortile	total
lama-2011	20.00	18.12	19.30	18.58	9.92	14.71	14.64	17.22	15.74	16.51	10.28	18.11	17.70	5.49	216.33
fdss-1	18.49	18.52	18.68	16.86	11.26	16.09	19.99	17.05	12.22	3.97	12.52	14.79	16.34	5.30	202.08
fdss-2	14.44	17.86	18.31	16.94	11.21	16.08	19.82	16.67	9.37	2.12	14.50	15.28	16.81	6.60	196.00
fd-autotune-1	19.23	16.67	19.40	16.28	9.50	13.25	14.71	18.57	8.99	1.71	11.04	10.93	19.37	5.46	185.09
roamer	17.74	17.59	6.22	17.80	9.67	13.99	12.51	15.35	16.72	8.62	13.61	14.08	15.18	2.38	181.47
fd-autotune-2	19.95	15.95	13.57	19.09	18.36	15.89	10.24	15.93	8.79	4.14	16.17	7.19	4.01	8.87	178.15
forkuniform	19.90	14.88	19.28	16.22	10.45	12.44	14.49	17.35	6.61	5.19	18.01	14.59	4.47	4.02	177.91
probe	18.44	16.34	12.11	12.41	5.90	16.32	17.10	13.14	10.03	18.05	8.24	7.63	18.60	2.83	177.14
arvand	20.00	18.53	19.42	15.38	18.97	16.56	17.05	2.00	12.25	7.38	11.22	3.31	0.00	3.00	165.07
lama-2008	19.54	17.15	0.88	18.05	11.44	13.17	9.97	14.62	16.44	17.59	4.94	13.86	3.60	2.07	163.33
lamar	19.36	16.71	2.55	17.96	11.46	16.67	13.63	12.99	9.17	9.17	7.34	14.76	5.08	2.36	159.20
randward	19.58	15.68	1.00	18.93	8.55	15.57	13.83	14.01	4.46	10.92	4.29	10.55	2.06	2.00	141.43
brt	12.68	17.77	5.17	3.75	5.75	14.91	1.64	7.66	9.65	2.13	13.84	4.42	13.83	2.82	116.01
cbp2	16.64	2.29	5.00	13.29	4.00	13.78	1.63	11.39	12.16	10.82	7.34	0.00	0.00	0.00	98.34
daeyahsp	4.00	14.23	15.70	0.00	9.67	0.00	6.32	0.00	15.48	19.71	0.00	0.00	5.72	4.39	95.23
yahsp2	9.46	8.08	17.70	0.00	6.70	0.00	9.65	0.00	10.92	18.09	0.00	5.24	5.85	3.29	94.97
yahsp2-mt	7.43	7.63	10.95	0.00	9.61	0.00	12.41	0.00	11.39	18.18	0.00	1.73	7.55	4.08	90.95
cbp	16.58	2.29	5.00	11.30	4.00	13.83	0.49	10.55	5.73	10.82	4.86	0.00	0.00	0.00	85.43
lprpgp	12.43	10.63	6.86	7.21	7.26	0.00	0.00	8.51	0.00	2.82	4.56	3.89	1.81	1.09	67.07
madagascar-p	12.98	11.30	18.31	0.00	13.93	6.60	0.71	1.50	0.60	0.00	0.00	0.00	0.00	0.00	65.93
popf2	6.39	13.65	13.58	0.00	8.22	0.00	2.51	4.92	0.00	2.82	4.73	2.40	0.00	0.67	59.88
madagascar	11.83	7.11	18.88	0.00	12.98	0.73	0.45	0.00	0.00	0.00	0.00	0.00	0.00	0.00	51.98
cpt4	1.00	3.00	14.00	0.00	15.00	0.00	14.85	0.00	0.00	0.00	0.00	0.00	0.00	0.00	47.85
satplanlm-c	6.00	5.92	15.04	0.00	3.00	0.00	0.00	0.00	0.00	0.00	0.00	0.00	0.00	0.00	29.96
sharaabi	11.88	0.00	5.26	2.81	0.00	0.00	0.00	0.00	0.00	0.00	0.56	0.00	0.00	0.00	20.52
acoplan	17.92	0.00	0.00	0.00	0.00	0.00	0.00	0.00	0.00	0.00	1.41	0.00	0.00	0.00	19.33
acoplan2	17.75	0.00	0.00	0.00	0.00	0.00	0.00	0.00	0.00	1.34	0.00	0.00	0.00	0.00	19.09
total	391.63	307.90	302.18	242.85	236.79	230.58	228.65	219.43	196.71	193.49	168.04	162.78	157.98	66.73	

Table 5.1: Best quality ratio scores IPC-7

ning Competition official data. [1] Table 5.1 shows the performance of each participating planner using the objective function $\frac{Q^*}{Q}$ that takes into account only the quality of the best solutions found. Each column stands for a different domain and the last column shows the total score for each planner. The maximum score that a planner can get if it finds the best solutions for every instance of a domain is 20.00, as 20 instances are available for each domain. Thus the overall possible maximum score is 280.00. PROBE outperformed LAMA-2008 but did not perform as well as the last version of LAMA-2011, and in fact, 6 other planners also outperformed it. The best 10 planners were all implemented on top of the FD framework except for PROBE. As we will show in the next tables, PROBE performed poorly due mainly to the fact that the anytime algorithm responsible of improving the first solution was much slower than planners implemented on FD, where almost all of them adopted a similar anytime algorithm.

Table 5.2 shows the same quality ratio, but instead takes into account only the first solution reported by each planner. PROBE was the second best performer, outperformed only by LAMA-2011. The only difference from the previous table is that the anytime behavior is not taken into account. Thus, if only the greedy best first search with probes alone is compared to the first solutions found by other planners, the score is much higher, suggesting that indeed the anytime algorithm of PROBE did not compete well with the implementation of FD based planners.

Table 5.3 shows the ratio between the fastest solution and the solution given by each planner. PROBE is the second best performer with nearly the same score as LAMA-2011, suggesting that the computationally intense inferences employed during the construction of probes, pay off compared to planners that perform a more exhaustive search.

Finally, Table 5.4 shows the coverage of each planner, where again PROBE is the second best performer, solving 233 out of 280 instances.

---
[1] source: http://www.plg.inf.uc3m.es/ipc2011-deterministic/Results

planner	pegsol	scan.	parc.	openst.	nomys.	tidybot	wood.	sokoban	trans.	visitall	elevators	parking	barman	floortile	total
lama-2011	15.77	13.08	17.03	15.44	17.04	17.17	12.07	16.92	15.60	8.65	17.52	15.32	17.94	4.83	204.37
probe	16.35	11.66	8.73	18.48	14.21	9.25	16.82	13.56	13.77	4.35	13.21	17.71	19.40	4.02	181.54
fdss-2	15.32	10.95	15.24	18.40	16.68	13.21	13.40	8.57	17.57	9.26	15.75	2.20	14.22	6.55	177.33
fd-autotune-1	14.04	11.19	16.86	15.30	17.49	13.77	10.99	8.89	15.78	7.18	13.80	0.86	16.87	6.03	169.03
roamer	15.53	11.38	3.87	12.56	14.75	14.54	12.38	16.95	14.73	8.55	15.32	8.75	15.36	1.98	166.66
fdss-1	13.10	9.93	14.64	13.19	17.06	12.84	12.82	9.00	13.11	8.70	15.17	2.25	14.68	4.23	160.72
forkuniform	10.25	12.81	13.92	16.26	16.99	14.05	11.46	6.34	16.98	8.41	15.55	2.96	3.89	4.24	154.11
lama-2008	14.08	13.53	0.47	8.73	13.99	15.28	10.86	17.79	4.57	10.15	15.07	17.67	3.65	2.20	148.02
fd-autotune-2	10.74	12.86	10.48	9.26	14.32	16.71	13.13	6.51	15.32	16.59	6.83	1.98	4.33	8.78	147.84
lamar	13.86	12.73	1.78	13.38	12.63	15.24	14.46	9.87	8.81	10.17	18.03	9.00	5.02	1.91	146.88
randward	12.69	14.65	0.64	13.60	16.03	14.57	13.92	4.18	5.27	6.76	15.03	13.13	2.02	1.59	134.09
arvand	16.08	14.74	13.40	12.37	1.77	11.56	14.64	10.15	12.51	16.02	2.70	5.53	0.00	2.04	133.53
brt	14.04	8.49	3.38	1.50	6.61	2.83	15.10	11.30	16.38	4.15	6.25	3.65	15.67	3.07	112.42
yahsp2-mt	8.92	12.10	8.77	12.21	0.00	0.00	0.00	14.14	0.00	7.89	2.31	18.73	8.75	6.23	100.04
yahsp2	10.15	6.02	14.56	9.35	0.00	0.00	0.00	14.20	0.00	5.33	6.14	17.28	5.57	4.40	92.98
cbp2	1.63	9.24	3.80	1.69	10.39	12.59	12.71	12.38	9.21	3.62	0.00	9.47	0.00	0.00	86.74
daeyahsp	9.49	10.53	12.15	4.51	0.00	0.00	0.00	12.38	0.00	7.55	0.00	14.45	5.88	5.07	81.99
cbp	1.63	8.68	3.80	0.46	9.93	12.18	12.67	9.36	6.02	3.62	0.00	9.47	0.00	0.00	77.82
lprpgp	10.23	8.37	5.79	0.00	8.32	10.65	0.00	0.00	11.07	4.82	5.77	1.67	1.55	1.12	69.37
madagascar-p	12.04	9.82	17.37	1.00	1.64	0.00	6.99	0.94	0.00	12.15	0.00	0.00	0.00	0.00	61.95
popf2	11.22	3.60	10.32	2.12	4.63	0.00	0.00	0.00	5.64	5.76	3.01	1.67	0.00	0.67	48.62
madagascar	6.85	6.72	17.44	1.00	0.00	0.00	0.71	0.00	0.00	12.86	0.00	0.00	0.00	0.00	45.59
cpt4	2.03	0.00	11.17	15.48	0.00	0.00	0.00	0.00	0.00	13.81	0.00	0.00	0.00	0.00	42.49
satplanlm-c	4.26	2.26	11.98	0.00	0.00	0.00	0.00	0.00	0.00	3.00	0.00	0.00	0.00	0.00	21.50
sharaabi	0.00	6.75	4.22	0.00	0.00	3.64	0.00	0.00	0.43	0.00	0.00	0.00	0.00	0.00	15.04
acoplan2	0.00	8.95	0.00	0.00	0.00	0.00	0.00	0.00	0.00	0.00	0.48	0.00	0.00	0.00	9.44
acoplan	0.00	8.74	0.00	0.00	0.00	0.00	0.00	0.00	0.00	0.00	0.48	0.00	0.00	0.00	9.22
total	260.27	259.79	241.81	216.28	213.01	211.55	205.15	203.42	202.76	199.34	187.46	174.72	154.81	68.96	

Table 5.2: Quality of first solution ratio scores IPC-7

planner	pegsol	scan.	parc.	openst.	nomys.	tidybot	wood.	sokoban	trans.	visitall	elevators	parking	barman	floortile	total
lama-2011	11.33	19.77	10.42	16.86	6.41	17.15	11.98	10.35	10.99	7.34	7.79	8.72	13.99	2.17	155.27
probe	10.35	12.65	15.00	15.29	2.45	11.55	5.71	11.76	14.22	17.25	8.11	8.66	18.59	3.15	154.74
fdss-2	16.74	17.98	11.16	13.71	7.74	14.12	7.83	13.31	10.35	8.66	4.58	1.75	5.99	3.35	137.26
fd-autotune-1	8.77	18.60	10.81	14.33	6.23	15.45	12.18	10.63	8.98	6.71	4.80	0.60	8.77	2.74	129.59
roamer	10.00	2.98	9.42	11.23	8.31	11.63	11.08	9.69	11.08	8.08	7.36	7.31	10.69	0.94	118.81
lamar	10.91	1.34	10.57	15.53	10.31	6.45	10.96	8.87	16.10	8.76	4.87	6.15	3.96	0.91	115.68
forkuniform	11.42	9.93	6.53	16.92	6.75	11.49	10.20	12.41	10.13	7.86	4.36	1.84	1.73	2.08	113.67
fd-autotune-2	11.85	10.93	5.51	8.42	11.84	12.08	10.11	8.80	4.04	8.02	3.60	1.32	1.61	5.71	103.84
randward	14.13	0.47	8.08	15.12	6.45	3.72	9.13	11.15	13.10	8.87	2.60	7.89	1.00	0.68	102.40
yahsp2-mt	14.53	11.47	14.61	10.74	7.03	0.00	0.00	0.00	2.40	0.00	13.96	17.43	4.31	5.58	100.04
lama-2008	12.24	0.62	9.56	7.31	10.13	2.98	9.77	9.22	10.35	6.82	7.88	10.05	3.19	1.63	101.76
fdss-1	7.47	12.75	7.82	7.29	6.24	8.32	8.00	9.81	8.81	6.89	4.19	1.66	8.72	1.66	99.63
yahsp2	13.21	19.68	15.34	7.73	4.46	0.00	0.00	0.00	3.92	0.00	17.39	13.33	2.02	2.40	99.48
madagascar-p	19.17	20.00	14.90	1.00	14.27	0.00	0.00	1.43	0.00	6.38	0.76	0.00	0.00	0.00	77.91
arvand	12.63	5.80	8.11	7.40	9.23	8.07	7.23	0.78	1.65	8.04	4.44	3.27	0.00	0.80	77.46
brt	8.75	3.22	8.22	1.40	2.72	12.72	1.84	2.41	4.13	10.07	6.46	2.80	8.03	1.63	74.38
lprpgp	11.69	6.54	15.08	0.00	4.35	9.92	13.91	3.95	4.06	0.00	0.00	2.00	0.59	0.58	72.68
cbp2	8.70	2.70	1.39	1.63	2.66	5.99	12.37	6.22	0.00	7.40	5.90	4.97	0.00	0.00	59.92
cbp	8.15	2.74	1.48	0.60	3.10	4.62	13.01	5.60	0.00	7.34	5.24	4.97	0.00	0.00	56.84
madagascar	7.04	20.00	6.85	1.00	13.10	0.00	0.00	0.00	0.00	0.53	0.00	0.00	0.00	0.00	48.52
daeyahsp	6.49	9.68	4.90	2.66	4.73	0.00	0.00	0.00	0.00	0.00	5.37	5.65	2.12	2.17	43.76
popf2	6.29	9.93	9.49	2.20	3.65	4.02	0.00	2.00	2.15	0.00	0.00	1.87	0.00	0.35	41.93
cpt4	0.31	9.26	0.97	12.51	9.36	0.00	0.00	0.00	0.00	0.00	0.00	0.00	0.00	0.00	32.41
satplanlm-c	1.67	9.66	3.12	0.00	2.13	0.00	0.00	0.00	0.00	0.00	0.00	0.00	0.00	0.00	16.58
sharaabi	6.22	4.44	0.00	0.00	0.00	0.27	2.98	0.00	0.00	0.00	0.00	0.00	0.00	0.00	13.91
acoplan	8.57	0.00	0.00	0.00	0.00	0.00	0.00	0.00	0.00	0.00	0.00	0.48	0.00	0.00	9.05
acoplan2	7.64	0.00	0.00	0.00	0.00	0.00	0.00	0.00	0.00	0.00	0.00	0.48	0.00	0.00	8.12
total	266.29	243.11	209.34	190.88	163.67	160.54	157.30	138.39	136.45	135.00	119.67	113.21	95.30	38.53	

Table 5.3: First solution time ratio scores IPC-7

planner	pegsol	scan.	parc.	openst.	nomys.	tidybot	wood.	sokoban	trans.	visitall	elevators	parking	barman	floortile	total
lama-2011	20.00	20.00	20.00	20.00	20.00	19.00	20.00	16.00	10.00	20.00	20.00	19.00	20.00	6.00	250.00
probe	20.00	20.00	14.00	20.00	14.00	20.00	20.00	18.00	6.00	20.00	10.00	17.00	20.00	6.00	200.00
fdss-2	20.00	20.00	20.00	20.00	19.00	15.00	20.00	18.00	12.00	6.00	20.00	19.00	17.00	7.00	233.00
fdss-1	20.00	20.00	20.00	20.00	19.00	15.00	20.00	17.00	12.00	6.00	20.00	19.00	18.00	6.00	232.00
fd-autotune-1	20.00	20.00	20.00	20.00	20.00	11.00	20.00	15.00	10.00	2.00	19.00	19.00	20.00	7.00	223.00
roamer	18.00	20.00	7.00	20.00	20.00	19.00	17.00	16.00	10.00	10.00	19.00	16.00	18.00	3.00	213.00
forkuniform	20.00	18.00	20.00	20.00	18.00	10.00	20.00	15.00	11.00	7.00	19.00	18.00	5.00	6.00	207.00
lamar	20.00	20.00	3.00	20.00	20.00	14.00	13.00	19.00	12.00	11.00	20.00	14.00	0.00	3.00	195.00
fd-autotune-2	20.00	17.00	14.00	14.00	20.00	10.00	17.00	17.00	19.00	5.00	9.00	16.00	6.00	9.00	193.00
arvand	20.00	20.00	20.00	20.00	20.00	15.00	20.00	17.00	19.00	10.00	4.00	2.00	0.00	3.00	190.00
lama-2008	20.00	20.00	1.00	14.00	20.00	19.00	6.00	14.00	12.00	20.00	20.00	15.00	4.00	3.00	188.00
randward	20.00	18.00	1.00	20.00	20.00	8.00	9.00	18.00	9.00	20.00	20.00	16.00	3.00	2.00	184.00
brt	13.00	20.00	6.00	2.00	4.00	17.00	20.00	19.00	6.00	8.00	10.00	8.00	20.00	4.00	157.00
yahsp2	14.00	19.00	20.00	15.00	0.00	20.00	0.00	0.00	7.00	20.00	9.00	0.00	8.00	6.00	138.00
yahsp2-mt	15.00	17.00	13.00	19.00	0.00	20.00	0.00	0.00	10.00	20.00	3.00	0.00	12.00	8.00	137.00
cbp2	17.00	5.00	5.00	3.00	20.00	20.00	16.00	18.00	4.00	15.00	0.00	12.00	0.00	0.00	135.00
cbp	17.00	5.00	5.00	1.00	20.00	17.00	10.00	18.00	4.00	15.00	0.00	11.00	0.00	0.00	123.00
daeyahsp	14.00	17.00	16.00	8.00	0.00	20.00	0.00	0.00	10.00	20.00	0.00	0.00	8.00	7.00	120.00
lprpgp	20.00	18.00	7.00	0.00	19.00	0.00	19.00	0.00	8.00	4.00	9.00	10.00	2.00	2.00	118.00
madagascar-p	20.00	18.00	20.00	1.00	0.00	2.00	0.00	10.00	15.00	0.00	0.00	2.00	0.00	0.00	88.00
popf2	9.00	18.00	16.00	3.00	0.00	0.00	11.00	0.00	9.00	4.00	5.00	5.00	0.00	1.00	81.00
madagascar	17.00	11.00	20.00	1.00	0.00	0.00	0.00	1.00	17.00	0.00	0.00	0.00	0.00	0.00	67.00
cpt4	1.00	3.00	14.00	19.00	0.00	0.00	0.00	0.00	15.00	0.00	0.00	0.00	0.00	0.00	52.00
sharaabi	19.00	0.00	6.00	0.00	7.00	0.00	1.00	0.00	0.00	0.00	0.00	0.00	0.00	0.00	33.00
satplanlm-c	6.00	7.00	16.00	0.00	0.00	0.00	0.00	0.00	3.00	0.00	0.00	0.00	0.00	0.00	32.00
acoplan2	18.00	0.00	0.00	0.00	0.00	0.00	0.00	0.00	0.00	2.00	0.00	0.00	0.00	0.00	20.00
acoplan	18.00	0.00	0.00	0.00	0.00	0.00	0.00	0.00	0.00	2.00	0.00	0.00	0.00	0.00	20.00
total	456.00	391.00	324.00	300.00	300.00	291.00	279.00	266.00	250.00	247.00	245.00	238.00	187.00	88.00	

Table 5.4: Number of problems solved in IPC-7

Part III

Structure

Chapter 6

Width

> Hubo una vez un Rayo que cayó dos veces en el mismo sitio; pero encontró que ya la primera había hecho suficiente daño, que ya no era necesario, y se deprimió mucho.

> Once there was a Flash of Lightning that struck in the same place twice. But it found that it had done enough damage the first time round and was no longer necessary, and it got very depressed.

> *El Rayo que cayó dos veces en el mismo sitio.*
> Augusto Monterroso

Various approaches have been developed for explaining the gap between the complexity of planning (Bylander, 1994), and the ability of current planners to solve most existing benchmarks in a few seconds (Hoffmann and Nebel, 2001; Richter and Westphal, 2010). Existing proposals, however, do not appear to explain the apparent simplicity of the standard domains. In this Chapter, we introduce a new type of width parameter for planning that bounds the complexity of a planning domain in terms of the *goal structure* of the problem. This offers a new approach for understanding the complexity of classical domains. In order to define the new notion of width $w(\Pi)$, we first define a new parametric graph $\mathcal{G}^i$ of problem Π, and then prove the width of the most known benchmark domains, provided that goals are restricted to single atoms.

6.1 Tuple Graph

Many graphs have been introduced in classical planning to reason about the structure of a problem. For instance, *planning graph* was introduced to reason about possible valid plans allowing interfering actions to appear at the same time-step, and then searching for valid plans in the graph through conflict analysis among mutually exclusive actions (Blum and Furst, 1995). Planning graphs are also related to the computation of delete relaxation based heuristics and the extraction of helpful actions. Another example is the *causal graph*. In multivalued domain representations, this graph captures the dependencies of variables through action conditions and effects. The *domain transition graph* instead studies the dependencies between the values of each multivalued variable (Helmert, 2004). Both have been widely used in classical planning for deriving new heuristics (Helmert and Geffner, 2008; Helmert, 2004) and new complexity results (Katz and Domshlak, 2008).

The tuple graph belongs to the same family of graphs that encode the structural features of a problem. More precisely, the *tuple graph* encodes reachability relations over tuples t that represent conjunctions of atoms.

For simplicity we assume that *action costs* are all 1. Thus, plan cost is equal to plan length, and the *optimal* plans are the *shortest* ones. We write $\Pi(t)$ to denote the planning problem that is like Π but with goal t. In order to define the tuple graph, the key question is when a tuple t' can be regarded as a 'successor' of a tuple t in Π. We will define indeed that t' is a successor of t if *every optimal plan* for t can be extended into an *optimal plan* for t' by adding just one action [1]. Note that the 'side-effects' of the optimal plans for t can be used to achieve t' optimally from t. We refer to the side-effects of t as the set of atoms that will be true in every optimal plan that achieves t.

This is formalized below in terms of *tuple graphs* $\mathcal{G}^i$, where T^i stands for the collection of tuples from Π with a size no greater than a given positive integer i:

Definition 6.1. *For* $\Pi = \langle F, I, O, G \rangle$ *,* $\mathcal{G}^i$ *is the* graph *with vertices from* T^i *defined inductively as follows:*

1. *t is a root vertex in $\mathcal{G}^I$ iff t is true in I,*

2. *$t \to t'$ is a directed edge in $\mathcal{G}^i$ iff t is in $\mathcal{G}^i$ and for every optimal plan π for $\Pi(t)$ there is an action $a \in O$ such that π followed by a is an optimal plan for $\Pi(t')$.*

Definition 6.2. *A path $t_0, t_1, \ldots, t_n$ is in $\mathcal{G}^i$ when t_0 is true in the initial situation and any optimal plan for t_k can be extended by means of a single action into an optimal plan for $t_{k+1}, 0 \le k < n$.*

In other words, the presence of the tuple t' of at most i atoms in the graph $\mathcal{G}^i$, indicates that either t' is true in I or that there is another tuple t of at most i atoms in $\mathcal{G}^i$ such that *all* the optimal plans π for t yield optimal plans for t', once a suitable action a is appended to π.

The directed graph $\mathcal{G}^i$ is acyclic because an edge $t \to t'$ implies that the optimal cost for achieving t' is the optimal cost of achieving t plus 1. Since we are associating plan cost with plan length, this means also that a tuple at depth k in the graph has optimal cost k.

As an illustration of this definition, consider a problem $\Pi = \langle F, I, O, G \rangle$ with the following actions, where the expression $a : X \to Y$ denotes an action a with preconditions X and postconditions Y (negated if they are deleted):

---

[1] If this is taken to represent the presence of an action a in Π such that the *regression* of t' through a is in t, the reachability relation on tuples ends up being too weak.

$$a : p_1 \rightarrow p_2 \; ; \; b : p_2 \rightarrow p_3 \; ; \; c : q_1 \rightarrow q_2 \; ; \; d : p_2, q_2 \rightarrow q_3 \; .$$

If $I = \{p_1, q_1\}$ and F comprises all of these fluents, the graph $\mathcal{G}^i$ for $i = 1$ is defined over vertices drawn from T^1, the tuples that contain a single atom from F. If we denote such tuples by the single atom that they contain, then the graph will feature the atoms p_1 and q_1 as roots, along with the edges $p_1 \rightarrow p_2$, $p_2 \rightarrow p_3$, and $q_1 \rightarrow q_2$. The roots are true in the initial situation, while all optimal plans for p_1 can be extended with a single action (a) into optimal plans for p_2, all optimal plans for p_2 can be extended with a single action (b) into optimal plans for p_3, and finally all optimal plans for q_1 (the empty plan) can be extended with a single action (c) into optimal plans for q_2.

Note that the tuple corresponding to the atom q_3 does not make it into the graph $\mathcal{G}^1$. This is because there is no tuple t of size 1 in the graph such that the optimal plans for t can be extended by means of a single action into optimal plans for $t' = \{q_3\}$. Indeed, q_2 is false in the optimal plans for p_2, and p_2 is false in the optimal plans for q_2. The tuple q_3, however, makes it into the graph $\mathcal{G}^2$. This is because the tuple $t = \{p_2, q_2\}$ that belongs to T^2 makes it into the graph $\mathcal{G}^2$, as the optimal plans for either $t'' = \{p_2\}$ or $t''' = \{q_2\}$ can be extended by means of a single action into optimal plans for t, and likewise, the optimal plans for $t = \{p_2, q_2\}$ can be extended by a single action into optimal plans for $t' = \{q_3\}$.

Below we will show that if an atom appears in the graph $\mathcal{G}^i$ for a low value of i, then the atom will be easy to achieve, and moreover, that in most benchmark domains, *all of the atoms* appear in $\mathcal{G}^i$ for low values of i.

The reasons for bringing in optimality considerations, and moreover, for requiring *all* optimal plans for t to be extensible by means of a single action into optimal plans for t' for adding the edge $t \rightarrow t'$ in the graph, will become apparent below. Indeed, in this setting, we will see why optimality requirements make things easier, not harder.

6.2 Width Definition

Let us say now that a goal formula G_1 *optimally implies* goal formula G_2 *in a problem* Π, if all of the *optimal plans* for G_1 are also *optimal plans* for G_2.

Definition 6.3 (Optimal Implication, $\models^*$). *A goal formula G_1 optimally implies a goal formula G_2 in a problem Π, denoted as $G_1 \models^* G_2$, if all optimal plans for G_1 are also optimal plans for G_2.*

Note that this is not the standard logical implication that requires G_2 to be true in all reachable states where G_1 is true, and hence to be an invariant. The Optimal Implication $G_1 \models^* G_2$ uses implicitly the information in the initial situation and the actions of Π, that is, the set of atoms that will be true in every optimal plan that achieves G_1. For example, in the Blocks World domain if $on(b, a)$ is true in the initial situation (regardless of whether other blocks are initially on b), the goal $G_1 = \{ontable(b)\}$ does not logically imply the conjunctive goal $G_2 = \{clear(a), handfree\}$. Yet, $G_1 \models^* G_2$ in Π. In such a case, the last two actions for optimally achieving $ontable(b)$ are $unstack(b, a)$ and $putdown(b)$. The result is that both $clear(a)$ and $handfree$ will hold in the resulting state, and moreover, that there is no cheaper way to get both atoms from such an initial situation. Note, however, that $G_1 = \{ontable(b)\}$ does not imply the single atom $G_2 = \{clear(a)\}$ in Π, as the cost of $clear(a)$ is the cost of G_1 minus one; namely, $unstack(b, a)$ already achieves $clear(a)$, and while the action $putdown(b)$ is needed for achieving G_1, it is not needed for achieving G_2. Consider another simple example where $G_1 = \{clear(a)\}$ and $G_2 = \{holding(b)\}$. In that case $G_1 \models^* G_2$, yet is not an invariant either. The examples show that the focus on optimality allows us to capture inferences that go beyond the purely logical inferences that are warranted in the domain.

Provided with the notion of goal optimal implication, we define the *width* of a planning problem Π and, more generally, the *width* of an arbitrary goal formula ϕ relative to Π, as follows:

Definition 6.4 (Width of formula ϕ). *For a formula ϕ over the fluents in Π that is not true in the initial situation I, the* width $w(\phi)$ *of ϕ relative to Π is the min w such that $\mathcal{G}^w$ contains a tuple $t \in \mathcal{G}^w$ that optimally implies $t \models^* \phi$. If ϕ is true in I, its width is 0.*

Definition 6.5 (Width of problem Π). *The* width *of a planning problem Π, $w(\Pi)$, is the* width *of its goal G relative to Π.*

As in the case of graphical models, the width of a problem will give us a bound on the complexity of solving the problem:

Theorem 6.6. *Given a problem Π, if $w(\Pi) = i$, Π can be solved optimally in time that is exponential in i.*

This result establishes a bound on the complexity of a planning problem in terms of its goal structure. We later describe an algorithm that achieves this bound and runs in time exponential in the width of the problem.

Of course, the crucial question is whether or not there are interesting planning problems that have a bounded, and hopefully small width. The answer is that indeed, *most domain benchmarks appear to have a small width independent of the size of the problems, provided that the problem goal G is restricted to a single atom.* Of course, this result does not settle the complexity of the existing benchmark instances, where goals are *not* single atoms. As far as we know, however, it is the first formal result that places the complexity of these benchmarks squarely in terms of the *goal structure*, and not on the *domain structure*.

6.3 Low Width Benchmarks

Some of the classical benchmarks are easily provable to have a low constant bounded width k for atomic goals G. Most of the proofs show that a chain $t_0, t_1, \ldots, t_n$ that optimally implies every possible atomic goal, independent of the initial state, exists in the tuple graph $\mathcal{G}^k$ for $k = 1, 2$. A chain exists in $\mathcal{G}^k$ if the maximum size of a tuple t_i in the chain is $|t_i| \leq k$, and optimally implies a goal G if the last tuple optimally implies the goal $t_n \models^* G$.

Theorem 6.7. *The domains Blocks World, Logistics, Gripper, and N-puzzle have a bounded width of* 2 *independent of the problem size and initial situation, as long as the goals are restricted to single atoms.*

Proof. (The width of single atoms in the Blocks World domain is at most 2) Given a goal G, we will prove $w(G) \leq 2$ for single atoms ($|G| = 1$) in Blocks World, first by showing that the width of goals like $clear(b)$ and $ontable(b)$ is 1, while the max width for an atomic goal is 2, which results in formulas such as $on(a, b)$. Let us prove first $w(G) = 1$ for $G = ontable(b)$. Clearly, if G is true in the initial situation, then the tuple G will belong to the graph $\mathcal{G}^i$ for $i = 1$. Thus, assume that G is not true initially, and let $b_1, \ldots, b_{n-1}$ be the blocks on top of b, starting from the top, and let $b = b_n$. According to Definition 6.2, in order to prove $w(G) = 1$ we need to show that a path which optimally implies G, such as

$$clear(b_1), hold(b_1), ontable(b_1), hold(b_2), \ldots, ontable(b_n)$$

makes it into $\mathcal{G}^1$.

This is trivial in this case. First, the only optimal plan for $clear(b_1)$, the empty plan, can be extended into an optimal plan for $hold(b_1)$ by means of the single action $unstack(b_1, b_2)$. Then, optimal plans for $hold(b_i)$ can always be extended with the action $putdown(b_i)$ into optimal plans for $ontable(b_i)$, while the *optimal plans* for $ontable(b_i)$ from the above situation can all be extended with the action $unstack(b_{i+1}, b_{i+2})$ into *optimal plans* for $hold(b_{i+1})$, for $i = 1, \ldots, n - 1$. Finally, the last $hold(b_n)$ can be extended into an optimal plan for $ontable(b_n)$ with the action $putdown(b_n)$. Thus, the path exists in $\mathcal{G}^1$ and $w(ontable(b)) = 1$.

The same path proves that $w(clear(b)) = 1$, as explained in Definition 6.3, $hold(b_{n-1})$ optimally implies $clear(b)$, where all optimal plans for $hold(b_{n-1})$ are optimal plans for $clear(b)$.

To complete the proof for Blocks, consider the achievement of a goal $G = on(a, b)$ from an arbitrary initial situation where the goal is false. We should consider three possible cases:

- blocks $a_1, \ldots, a_n$ above a, and blocks $b_1, \ldots, b_m$ above b

- block c_n above a and b above c_1 for $c_1, \ldots, c_n$

- block c_n above b and a above c_1 for $c_1, \ldots, c_n$

In all three cases, there is no tuple in $\mathcal{G}^1$ that implies G. For the first setting, the reason that $w(on(a, b))$ is not 1 is that some optimal plan for $ontable(b_m)$ cannot be extended by means of a single action into optimal plans for $hold(a)$, as the former do not imply preconditions that are required such as $clear(a)$. Indeed, in all the optimal plans for $ontable(b_m)$ in such settings, $on(a_n, a)$ remains true from the initial situation. In the second setting, some optimal plan for $hold(a)$ cannot be extended to $on(a, b)$, as some blocks c_i might be on top of b. In the last setting, all optimal plans for $hold(a)$ imply that $c_1, \ldots, c_n$ are on top of b. By considering pairs, this problem is removed.

We will prove that $w(G)$ is not 1 but actually 2. In the first setting, a path to consider in the graph $\mathcal{G}^2$ is that which starts with any tuple t_0 true in I, e.g., $clear(b_1)$, and then has the sequence of $2n$ pairs (tuples of two atoms)

$$(hold(a_1), clear(b_1)), (ontable(a_1), clear(b_1)), \ldots$$
$$\ldots, (hold(a_n), clear(b_1)); (ontable(a_n), clear(b_1))$$

followed by the sequence of $2m$ pairs

$$(ontable(a_n), hold(b_1)), (ontable(a_n), ontable(b_1)), \ldots$$
$$\ldots (ontable(a_n), hold(b_m)); (ontable(a_n), ontable(b_m))$$

completed by a pair and a singleton tuple

$$(hold(a), clear(b)), (on(a, b)) \ .$$

We need to check that for any edge $t_i \to t_{i+1}$ in this path $t_0, \ldots, t_k$, $k = 2 + 2n + 2m$, $i < k$, all the optimal plans for t_i can be extended by means of a single action into optimal plans for t_{+1}. For the first sequence, optimal plans for $(hold(a_i), clear(b_1))$ can be extended into optimal plans for $(ontable(a_i), clear(b_1))$ with $putdown(a_i)$, while optimal plans for $(ontable(a_i), clear(b_1))$ can be extended with $unstack(a_{i+1}, a_{i+2})$ into optimal plans for $(hold(a_{i+1}), clear(b_1))$. The optimal plans for the last tuple of the first sequence can be extended into optimal plans for the first tuple $(ontable(a_n), hold(b_1))$ with $unstack(b_i, b_{i+1}), i = 1$, which can be extended with action $putdown(b_i)$ for tuples $(ontable(a_n), ontable(b_i))$. Finally, optimal plans for $(ontable(a_n), ontable(b_m))$ can be extended with $pickup(a)$ for $(hold(a), clear(b))$, and then be extended with $stack(a, b)$ for the last tuple $on(a, b)$. Thus, $w(G) = 2$ for the first setting.

In the second setting, a path to consider in the graph $\mathcal{G}^2$ is that which starts with tuple $clear(b)$ followed by the sequence of singleton tuples

$$(hold(b)), (ontable(b))$$

then followed by the sequence of $2n$ pairs (tuples of two atoms)

$$(hold(c_1), clear(b)), (ontable(c_1), clear(b) \ldots$$
$$\ldots, (hold(c_n), clear(b)); (ontable(c_n), clear(b))$$

completed by a pair and a singleton tuple

$$(hold(a), clear(b)), (on(a, b))$$

For the first sequence, optimal plans for $(clear(b))$ can be extended into optimal plans for $((hold(b))$ with only $unstack(b, c_1)$, while optimal plans for $(hold(b))$ can be extended with only $putdown(b)$ into optimal plans for $(ontable(b))$. The optimal plans for the last tuple of the first sequence can be extended into optimal plans for the first tuple $(hold(c_1), clear(b))$ with action $unstack(c_1, c_2)$. Then, optimal plans for $(hold(c_i), clear(b))$ can be extended into optimal plans for $(ontable(c_i), clear(b))$ with $putdown(c_i)$, while optimal plans for $(ontable(c_i), clear(b))$ can be extended with $unstack(c_{i+1}, c_{i+2})$ into optimal plans for $(hold(c_{i+1}), clear(b))$. Finally, optimal plans for $(ontable(c_n), clear(b))$ can be extended with $pickup(a)$ for $(hold(a), clear(b))$, and then can be extended with $stack(a, b)$ for the last tuple $on(a, b)$. Thus, $w(G) = 2$ for the second setting as well.

In the last setting, a path to consider in the graph $\mathcal{G}^2$ is that which starts with tuple $clear(a)$ followed by the sequence of singleton tuples

$$(hold(a_1)), (ontable(a))$$

then followed by the sequence of $2n$ pairs

$$(ontable(a), hold(c_1)), (ontable(a), ontable(c_1)), \ldots$$
$$\ldots (ontable(a), hold(c_n)); (ontable(a), ontable(c_n))$$

completed by a pair and a singleton tuple

$$(hold(a), clear(b)), (on(a, b)) .$$

For the first sequence, optimal plans for $(clear(a))$ can be extended into optimal plans for $((hold(a))$ with only $unstack(a, c_1)$, while optimal plans for $(hold(a))$ can be extended with only $putdown(a)$ into optimal plans for $(ontable(a))$. The optimal plans for the last tuple of the first sequence can be extended into optimal plans for the first tuple $(ontable(a), hold(c_1))$ with action $unstack(c_1, c_2)$. Then, optimal plans for $(ontable(a), hold(c_i))$ can be extended into optimal plans for $(ontable(a), ontable(c_i))$ with $putdown(c_i)$, while optimal plans for $(ontable(a), ontable(c_i))$ can be extended with $unstack(c_{i+1}, c_{i+2})$ into optimal plans for $(ontable(a), hold(c_{i+1}))$. Finally, optimal plans for $(ontable(a), ontable(c_n))$ can be extended with $pickup(a)$ for $(hold(a), clear(b))$, and then can be extended with $stack(a, b)$ for the last tuple $on(a, b)$. Thus, $w(G) = 2$ for the last setting as well.

It is important to notice that without the restriction to *optimal plans* this reasoning would not get through. *Optimality is key for predicting what will be true when a subgoal is achieved*, and this capability is central for decomposing plans into subplans, which is what tuple graphs do.

□

Recall that in general, in order to prove that the width of a domain is bounded by a constant k for a goal G, one needs to show that a graph $\mathcal{G}^i$ for some $i \leq k$ contains a path $t_0, \ldots, t_n$ such that all optimal plans for t_n are optimal plans for G. Often it is not necessary to fully specify the tuples t_i in such paths.

Proof. (The width of single atoms in the N-puzzle domain is at most 2) To show that the width of the singleton goals $at(tile, pos)$ in the sliding puzzles is 2, we take the tuples t_i to be the pairs $(at(tile, pos), at(blank, pos))$ encoding the position of *tile* and *blank* at time i in some optimal plan π for $at(tile, pos)$. We show that *any* optimal plan π_i for t_i can be extended into an optimal plan π_{i+1} for t_{i+1} by appending one action a. Clearly, the physical action that mapped t_i into t_{i+1} in π, is the action that moved the blank from its position in t_i to its position in t_{i+1}, and this is indeed the physical action that is needed to transform π_i into π_{i+1}. Now, the name or identity of action a in STRIPS will depend on: the position p_i of the blank in t_i, the position p_{i+1} of the blank in t_{i+1}, and the name of the tile that is sitting in p_{i+1} after π_i. Yet, we know that such an action exists, and this is all that is needed in order to prove that $w(at(tile, pos))$ is bounded by 2. $\qquad\square$

Proof. (The width of single atoms in the Logistics domain is at most 2) The task in the logistics domain is to transport several packages from their initial location to their desired destinations. Packages can be moved by trucks among locations in the same city, and by planes among airports located in different cities. In order to load a package into a truck (or plane), the package has to be located at the same position as the truck (or plane). Then the truck (or plane) can move and unload a package at its destination.

The width of goals like $at(Truck, Loc)$ and $at(Plane, airport)$ is 1, while the max width is 2 for the atomic goal $at(Pkg, Loc)$. Let us prove first $w(G) = 1$ for $G = at(Truck, Loc)$. We assume that G is not true in the initial situation, as the tuple G would belong to the graph $\mathcal{G}^i$ for $i = 0$. Assume that a location path $L_1, \ldots, L_n$ is the shortest trajectory from the initial location of the $Truck$ and the final location $L_n = Loc$. We can show that the path

$$at(Truck, L_1), at(Truck, L_2), \ldots, at(Truck, L_n)$$

makes it into $\mathcal{G}^1$, as the optimal plans for $at(Truck, L_i)$ can be extended with the action $Move(Truck, L_i, L_{i+1})$ into optimal plans for $at(Truck, L_{i+1})$. The proof for $G = at(Plane, airport)$ follows from the same path that makes it into $\mathcal{G}^1$, where instead of $Truck$ we have $Plane$.

To complete the proof, consider the achievement of a goal $G = at(Pkg, L_g)$ from an arbitrary initial state where truck location $at(Truck, Loc_t)$ and package location $at(Pkg, L_p)$ are all different $L_t \neq L_p \neq L_g$. For simplicity we consider just one truck, but the same reasoning holds for many trucks, selecting the closest one to the package as the only truck, used in the proof. In this case, there is no tuple in $\mathcal{G}^1$ that implies G. If the problem is solvable, there is a path $L_1, \ldots, L_n$ where L_1 and L_n are the initial truck L_t and package L_p locations respectively connecting the truck and the package, and a path $L'_1, \ldots, L'_m$ where L'_1 and L'_m are the initial L_p and goal L_g package locations. We consider paths in the graph $\mathcal{G}^2$ that start with a tuple that is true in I and then has the sequence of n pairs (tuples of two atoms)

$$(at(Trk, L_1), at(Pkg, L_n)), (at(Trk, L_2), at(Pkg, L_n)), \ldots$$
$$\ldots, (at(Trk, L_n), at(Pkg, L_n))$$

followed by the sequence of m pairs and 2 singletons

$$(at(Pkg, Trk)), (at(Trk, L'_2), at(Pkg, Trk)), \ldots$$
$$\ldots, (at(Trk, L'_m), at(Pkg, Trk)), (at(Pkg, L'_m))$$

For the first sequence, optimal plans for $(at(Trk, L_i), at(Pkg, L_n))$ can be extended into optimal plans for $(at(Trk, L_{i+1}), at(Pkg, L_n))$ with the action $Move($

$Truck, L_i, L_{i+1}$). The optimal plans for the last tuple can be extended into an optimal plan for the first tuple of the second sequence by applying action $load(Pkg, Trk)$. Then applying $Move(Truck, L'_i, L'_{i+1})$ extend the optimal plans for the following tuples until $(at(Trk, L'_m), at(Pkg, Trk))$. Finally, an optimal plan for $(at(Pkg, L'_m))$ can be achieved by extending the last optimal plan with the action $unload(Pkg, Trk)$.

In the case of having the package goal location L_g in a different city than the initial location L_p, we need the use of an airplane. For this case, a path leading to G also exists in $\mathcal{G}^2$. Assuming that the airport location of the city that contains location L_p is L'_m (the same location of the last tuple from the previous sequence, where a plane is $at(Plane, L'_m)$, and the airport of the goal location is at L''), we extend the previous path with the tuple sequence

$$(at(Plane, L'_m), at(Pkg, Plane)), (at(Plane, L''), at(Pkg, Plane)), ((at(Pkg, L''))$$

that can be extended optimally for each tuple with the actions $Load(Pkg, Plane)$, $fly(Plane, L'_m, L'')$, and $unload(Pkq, Plane)$ respectively. Moving the package from L'' to the goal location with a truck can be achieved with a similar sequence that we have shown to be in $\mathcal{G}^2$. If the plane is in a different location than the initial airport, we have to interleave the last two sequences with a path that moves the plane to the right location, similar to moving a truck from one location to the other.

$\square$

Proof. (The width of single atoms in the Gripper domain is at most 2) We prove $w(G) \leq 2$ for single atoms in Gripper by showing that the width of goals like $atRobot(l)$ is 1, while the width of $atBall(l)$ is at most 2. Let us prove first $w(G) = 1$ for $G = atRobot(l)$. Assume that G is not true initially and that the robot is located in room l_I, such that $atRobot(l_I)$ is different from the goal $atRobot(l_G)$. Recall that all the locations are connected by a single action *move*. According to Definition 6.2 any path

$$atRobot(x), atRobot(y)$$

makes it into $\mathcal{G}^1$ as all locations can be achieved optimally by a single action. Thus, $w(atRobot(l)) = 1$ for any l.

To complete the proof, we show that $w(G) \leq 2$ for $G = atBall(l_G)$. Consider the achievement of G from an arbitrary initial situation where the goal is false and the initial location of the robot l_R is different from the ball l_B. There is no tuple in $\mathcal{G}^1$ that implies G. The reason is that all optimal plans for a robot at location l_G do not imply the other required precondition $CarryBall$ for achieving G. We will prove that $w(G)$ is not 1, but 2. A path in the graph $\mathcal{G}^2$ that optimally implies G can be one that starts with the tuple $atRobot(l_R)$ and then has the sequence of pairs and a singleton tuple

$$(atRobot(l_B), atBall(l_B)), (atRobot(l_B), CarryBall),$$
$$(atRobot(l_G), CarryBall), (atBall(l_G))$$

Optimal plans for $(atRobot(l_R))$ can be extended into optimal plans for $(atRobot(l_B),$ $atBall(l_B))$ with only $move(l_R, l_B)$, and then extended to optimal plans for $(atRobot(l_B),$ $CarryBall)$ with action $pickBall(l_B)$. Optimal plans again can be extended from $(atRobot(l_B), CarryBall)$ to optimal plans for $(atRobot(l_G), CarryBall)$ with $move$ (l_B, l_G) to finally extend it with $putBall(l_G)$ into an optimal plan for $(atBall(l_G))$. Thus, $w(G) = 2$ for $G = atBall(l)$. The setting where the ball and the robot are initially in the same location follows the same proof where the first tuple is $(atRobot(l_B), atBall(l_B))$ instead of $atRobot(l_B)$. $\square$

Chapter 7

Iterated Width

> Salomon saith, There is no new thing upon the earth. So that as Plato had an imagination, that all knowledge was but remembrance; so Salomon giveth his sentence, that all novelty is but oblivion.

Francis Bacon

In this chapter we prove experimentally that many standard domain benchmarks have low width, provided that goals are restricted to single atoms. We present a blind search algorithm that runs in both time and space exponentially on the problem width. We also show that the algorithm can be used to approximate a lower bound on the real width of the problem, and give experimental results of the approximated width of all standard domains.

7.1 Iterated Width Algorithm

We turn now to the planning algorithm that achieves the complexity bounds expressed by Theorem 6.6. The algorithm, called *Iterated Width* search (*IW*), consists of a sequence of calls *IW(i)* for $i = 0, 1, 2, \ldots$ over a problem Π until the problem is solved. Each iteration *IW(i)* is an i-width search that is complete for problems whose width is bounded by i, and its complexity is $O(n^i)$, where n is the number of problem variables. If Π is solvable and its width is w, *IW* will solve Π in at most $w + 1$ iterations with a complexity $O(n^w)$. *IW(i)* is *a plain forward-state breadth-first search* with just one change: right after a state s is generated, the state is pruned if it does not pass a simple *novelty test* that depends on i.

Definition 7.1 (novelty). *A newly generated state s produces a new tuple of atoms t iff s is the first state generated in the search that makes t true. The size of the smallest new tuple of atoms produced by s is called the* novelty *of s. When s does not generate a new tuple, its novelty is set to $n+1$ where n is the number of problem variables.*

In other words, if s is the first state generated in the search that makes an atom p true, its novelty is 1. If s does not generate a new atom, but instead generates a new pair (p, q), its novelty is 2, and so on. Likewise, if s does not generate a new tuple at all because the same state has been generated before, then its novelty is set to $n + 1$. The higher the novelty measure, the less novel the state. The iterations $IW(i)$ are plain *breadth-first searches* that treat newly generated states with a novelty measure greater than i as if they were 'duplicate' states:

Definition 7.2. *$IW(i)$ is a breadth-first search that prunes newly generated states when their novelty measure is greater than i.*

Notice that $IW(n)$, when n is the number of atoms in the problem, prunes only truly duplicate states and it is therefore complete. On the other hand, $IW(i)$ for lower i values prunes many states and is not complete. Indeed, the number of states *not* pruned in $IW(1)$ is $O(n)$ and similarly, the number of states not pruned in $IW(i)$ is $O(n^i)$. Likewise, since the novelty of a state is never 0, $IW(0)$ prunes all of the child states of the initial state s_0, and thus $IW(0)$ solves Π iff the goal is true in the initial situation. The resulting planning algorithm IW is a series of i-width searches $IW(i)$, for increasing values of i:

Definition 7.3. *Iterated Width (IW) calls $IW(i)$ sequentially for $i = 0, 1, 2, \ldots$ until the problem is solved or i exceeds the number of problem variables.*

Iterated Width (*IW*) is thus a *blind-search algorithm* similar to Iterative Deepening (*ID*) except for two differences. First, each iteration is a pruned *depth-first* search in *ID*, and a pruned *breadth-first* search in *IW*. Second, each iteration increases pruning depth in *ID*, and pruning width or novelty in *IW*.

We have only considered planning problems where actions have uniform costs. However, the algorithm presented so far extends naturally to non-uniform costs provided that the breadth-first search in *IW* is replaced by a uniform-cost search, (e.g. Dijkstra).

From the considerations above it is straightforward to show that *IW* like *ID* is *sound* and *complete*. On the other hand, while $IW(w)$ is *optimal* for a problem Π of width w, *IW* is not necessarily so. The reason is that *IW* may solve Π in an iteration $IW(i)$ for i smaller than w.

As an illustration, consider the following problem, where the goal G of width 2 is achieved non-optimally by $IW(1)$ when $I = \{p_1, q_1\}$ and the actions are $a_i : p_i \to p_{i+1}$ and $b_i : q_i \to q_{i+1}$ for $i = 1, \ldots, 5$, along with $b : p_6 \to G$ and $c : p_3, q_3 \to G$. Indeed, $IW(2)$ achieves G optimally at cost 5 using the action c, yet this action is never applied in $IW(1)$, where states that result from applying the actions a_i when q_j is true for $j > 1$ are pruned, and states that result from applying the actions b_i when p_j is true for $j > 1$ are pruned also. As a result, $IW(1)$ prunes the states with pairs such as (p_3, q_2) and (p_2, q_3), and does not generate states with the pair (p_3, q_3), which are required for reaching G optimally. $IW(1)$, however, reaches G at the non-optimal cost 7 using the action b.

Nonetheless, the completeness and optimality of $IW(w)$ for problems with width w provides the right complexity bound for *IW*:

Theorem 7.4. *For solvable problems* Π*, the time and space complexity of IW are exponential in* $w(P)$*.*

It is important to realize that this bound is achieved without knowing the actual width of Π. This follows from the result below:

Theorem 7.5. *For a solvable problem* Π *with width* w*, IW(w) solves* Π *optimally in time exponential in* w*.*

Proof. The time bound is direct, as the number of states generated in $IW(w)$ is bounded by $b \cdot n^w$, where b is the branching factor of the problem and n is the number of atoms. The number of states generated in $IW(w)$ that are *not* pruned is bounded in turn by n^w.

For the optimality part, note that if the width of Π is w, there must be a rooted path $t_0, t_1, \ldots, t_n$ in the graph $\mathcal{G}^w$ such that t_n implies the goal G of Π. It then suffices to show that the call $IW(w)$ will achieve each tuple t_i in such a path optimally, and therefore G as well. It is worth working this out in detail, as the proof illustrates why edges $t \to t'$ in the graph $\mathcal{G}^i$ require that *all* optimal plans for t be extendable into optimal plans for t' by means of a single action.

From the construction of the graph, the optimal cost of achieving the tuple t_i in the chain $t_0, t_1, \ldots, t_n$ must be i. We need to show that there is an unpruned state s_i in the call $IW(w)$ that generates t_i, and moreover, that the cost of s_i is i. We prove this inductively. This is clearly true for $i = 0$ as t_0 is true in the initial situation. Let us assume then that this is true for all $k = 0, \ldots, i-1$, and prove that this must be true for $k = i$. From the inductive hypothesis, it follows that $IW(w)$ achieves t_{i-1} optimally, resulting in the state s_{i-1} with cost equal to $i-1$. Likewise, from the edge $t_{i-1} \to t_i$ in the graph $\mathcal{G}^w$, any optimal plan for t_{i-1} must extend into an optimal plan for t_i by means of an action. In particular, since we know from the inductive hypothesis that the state s_{i-1} must be the result of an optimal plan π_{i-1} for t_{i-1}, there must be an action a so that π_{i-1} followed by a is an optimal plan for t_i that results in the state s_i. Since the state s_{i-1} was generated and not pruned in $IW(w)$, the state s_i that follows from the application of the action a in s_{i-1} must be generated in $IW(w)$. Now, let s_i' be the first state that generated the tuple t_i. From the argument above it follows that there must be one such state, and moreover, that such a state cannot have been pruned in $IW(w)$ since the size of t_i is less than w, and hence the novelty of such a state in $IW(w)$ cannot be greater than w. Moreover, whether or not s_i is the first state that generates t_i, the cost of achieving t_i in $IW(w)$ is the optimal cost i. Indeed, this is the cost of the plan that results in s_i, and if s_i is pruned, it is because another state s_i' generated t_i before at no more cost, as states in the breadth-first search are generated in non-decreasing costs.

$\square$

The algorithm $IW(w)$ is guaranteed to solve Π if $w(\Pi) = w$, yet as discussed above, the algorithm IW does not assume that this width is known and thus makes the $IW(i)$ calls in order, starting from $i = 0$. We will refer to the min value of i for which $IW(i)$ solves P as the *effective width* of P:

Definition 7.6. *The* effective width *of* Π*,* $w_e(\Pi)$*, is the min i for which IW(i) solves* Π*.*

Clearly, from the results above it follows that:

Theorem 7.7. *The effective width is bounded by the actual width:* $w_e(\Pi) \leq w(\Pi)$.

The notion of effective width has virtues and shortcomings that are orthogonal to those of the actual width: unlike the width, the effective width is not well-defined, while on the other hand, it can be computed in time that is exponential in $w_e(\Pi)$ by running *IW* until a solution is found.

7.2 Experimental Results

The effective width $w_e(\Pi)$ provides an approximation of the actual width $w(\Pi)$. While proving formally that most benchmark domains have a bounded width *for single atom goals* is tedious, we have run the algorithm *IW* to compute the *effective width* of such goals. All experiments discussed below were run on Xeon Woodcrest computers with clock speeds of 2.33 GHz, using a 2GB memory limit. We were using a time cutoff of 2 hours only for Table 7.1, while no time cutoff was needed for Table 7.2.

The results are shown in Table 7.1. We tested domains from previous IPCs. For each instance with N goal atoms, we created N instances with a single goal, and ran *IW* over each one of them. The total number of instances is 37921. For each domain we show the total number of single goal instances, and the percentage of instances that have effective widths w_e equal to 1, 2, or greater than 2. The last row in the table shows the average percentage over all domains: 37% with $w_e = 1$, 51% with $w_e = 2$, and less than 12% with $w_e > 2$. *That is, on average, less than 12% of the instances have an effective width greater than 2.* Actually, in most domains *all* the instances have effective an width of at most 2, and in four domains, all the instances have an effective width of 1. The instances with a majority of atomic goals with an effective width greater than 2, are from the domains Barman, Openstacks, and Tidybot (the first and last from the 2011 IPC).

Iterated Width (*IW*) is a complete blind-search algorithm like Iterative Deepening (*ID*) and Breadth-First Search (*BrFS*). We have also tested the three algorithms over the set of 37921 single goal instances above. While *ID* and *BrFS* guarantee optimality and *IW* does not, in most of the instances they all returned the same result. We are not aware of other suboptimal blind search algorithms wit which to compare. The results are shown in Table 7.2. *ID* and *BrFS* solve less than 25% of the instances, while *IW* solves more than 94%, which is even more than a Greedy Best-First Search guided by the additive heuristic (also shown in the Table). The result suggests that *IW* manages to exploit the low width of these problems much better than the other blind-search algorithms. We will see in the next chapter that a simple extension suffices to make *IW* competitive with a *heuristic* planner over the standard benchmark instances that feature *joint goals*.

7.3 Conclusion

We have proven both theoretically and experimentally that most domain benchmarks have a low width, provided that goals are restricted to single atoms. We

Domain	I	$w_e = 1$	$w_e = 2$	$w_e > 2$
8puzzle	400	55%	45%	0%
Barman	232	9%	0%	91%
Blocks World	598	26%	74%	0%
Cybersecure	86	65%	0%	35%
Depots	189	11%	66%	23%
Driver	259	45%	55%	0%
Elevators	510	0%	100%	0%
Ferry	650	36%	64%	0%
Floortile	538	96%	4%	0%
Freecell	76	8%	92%	0%
Grid	19	5%	84%	11%
Gripper	1275	0%	100%	0%
Logistics	249	18%	82%	0%
Miconic	650	0%	100%	0%
Mprime	43	5%	95%	0%
Mystery	30	7%	93%	0%
NoMystery	210	0%	100%	0%
OpenStacks	630	0%	0%	100%
OpenStacksIPC6	1230	5%	16%	79%
ParcPrinter	975	85%	15%	0%
Parking	540	77%	23%	0%
Pegsol	964	92%	8%	0%
Pipes-NonTan	259	44%	56%	0%
Pipes-Tan	369	59%	37%	3%
PSRsmall	316	92%	0%	8%
Rovers	488	47%	53%	0%
Satellite	308	11%	89%	0%
Scanalyzer	624	100%	0%	0%
Sokoban	153	37%	36%	27%
Storage	240	100%	0%	0%
Tidybot	84	12%	39%	49%
Tpp	315	0%	92%	8%
Transport	330	0%	100%	0%
Trucks	345	0%	100%	0%
Visitall	21859	100%	0%	0%
Woodworking	1659	100%	0%	0%
Zeno	219	21%	79%	0%
Summary	37921	37.0%	51.3%	11.7%

Table 7.1: Effective width of single goal instances obtained from existing bench-marks by splitting problems with N atomic goals into N problems with single goals. I is number of resulting instances. The other columns show the percentage of instances with effective width 1, 2, or greater.

# Instances	*IW*	*ID*	*BrFS*	*GBFS* + h_{add}
37921	35918	9010	8762	34849

Table 7.2: Blind-search algorithm *IW* compared with two other blind-search algorithms: Iterative Deepening (*ID*) and Breadth-First Search (*BrFS*). Numbers report coverage over benchmark domains with single atomic goals. Also included for comparison is the figure for heuristic Greedy Best-First Search (*GBFS*) with h_{add}.

proposed a simple *novelty* pruning rule which, along an iterative blind search algorithm (*IW*), runs in time and space exponential in $w(\Pi)$. The first iteration of this procedure that solves the problem Π gives a lower bound on the actual width of Π. The algorithm *IW*, without looking at the goal, competes with a standard heuristic search planner over instances with single goals, outperforming other common blind search procedures greatly. The major performance gap between *IW* and other blind search algorithms suggests that exploiting problems' low width is as powerful as the use of heuristics for informed search algorithms.

Chapter 8

Serialized Iterated Width

> Ring the bells that still can ring
> Forget your perfect offering
> There is a crack in everything
> That's how the light gets in.

Selected Poems 1956-1968.
Leonard Cohen

In this chapter we extend the Iterated Width procedure to deal with problems that feature conjunctive goals, by introducing a simple form of decomposition. We present first the definition of the width induced by a given *serialization* of the goals, then present an algorithm that generates the serialization at the same time that it solves the subproblems by exploiting their width. Finally we give an experimental evaluation of the resulting algorithm.

8.1 Serialized Width

The fact that single goal atoms can be achieved quite effectively in most benchmark domains by a pruned breadth-first search that does not look at the goal in any way, suggests that the complexity of benchmarks comes from conjunctive goals. Indeed, this has been the intuition in the field of planning since its beginnings, where goal decomposition was deemed to be a crucial and characteristic technique. Previous Chapter analysis formalizes this intuition by showing that the effective width of single atom goals in existing benchmarks is low. This older intuition also suggests that the power of planners that can handle single goals efficiently can be exploited for conjunctive goals through some form of decomposition.

While the notion of decomposition had all but disappeared from previous state-of-the-art planners, it has made a recent comeback in the form of *landmarks* (Hoffmann et al., 2004) and in particular *landmark heuristics* such as that used in the state-of-the-art planner LAMA (Richter and Westphal, 2010). In a way, by treating landmarks as *subgoals* and ordering states by the *number of subgoals achieved*, LAMA serializes the problem without committing to a single serialization. Likewise, the planner PROBE, that came in second right after LAMA in the last 2011 IPC when the first plans were considered [1], uses explicit subgoal serializations in the probes (Lipovetzky and Geffner, 2011b). Thus, since the width of benchmark problems when conjunctive goals are considered is not bounded in general, we focus on the width of those problems *provided a serialization.*

A *serialization* d for a problem Π with goal G refers to a sequence of formulas $G^1, \ldots, G^m$ such that $G^m = G$. In *simple serializations*, G^1 contains one atom from G, G^2 extends G^1 with an additional atom from G, and so on, with m being the number of atoms in G. Other types of serializations are common too; e.g., using landmarks of the problem or other formulas, as in the serialization for Blocks where all blocks are placed on the table in order, and then towers are assembled in order as well.

If we consider the optimal solution to the subproblems, any serialization d for Π defines a family of *sets* of planning problems $\mathcal{P}_d = \mathcal{P}_1, \ldots, \mathcal{P}_m$, such that $\mathcal{P}_1$ contains the problem P_1 that is like Π but with goal G^1, while $\mathcal{P}_i$ for $i > 1$ contains the problems P_i that are like Π but with goal G^i, and initial states s_i that correspond to the states resulting from solving the problems in $\mathcal{P}_{i-1}$ optimally. The width of Π under an arbitrary serialization d can then be defined as follows:

Definition 8.1. *The width of a problem Π given a serialization d, written $w(\Pi, d)$, is the max width over the subproblems in $\mathcal{P}_d$.*

It is clear that the width of a problem given a serialization can be much lower than the width of a problem without it. For instance, in Tower, a version of Blocks where n blocks need to be moved from the table into a given tower $on(b_{i+1}, b_i)$, $i = 1, \ldots, n - 1$, the width grows with n, while the width that follows from the simple serialization d where G^i adds the atom $on(b_{i+1}, b_i)$ for $i = 1, \ldots, n - 1$, is bounded and equal to 1.

Of course, even if there exists a serialization d that yields a low width $w(\Pi, d)$, the question remains: how hard is to find it?. This is a difficult problem that we do not intend to address here; rather, we focus on a simple extension of the iterated width search procedure *IW* that uses *IW* for two purposes: for constructing a simple serialization and for solving the subproblems. This extension will allow us to test the value of *IW* over the actual planning benchmarks, which feature multiple goals. Notice that *IW* can be applied to such problems without introducing a serialization, yet both the width and effective width of such problems are too large. By decomposing a problem into subproblems, a serialization can reduce both of them.

8.2   Serialized Iterated Width Algorithm

Serialized Iterated Width (SIW) is a search algorithm that uses the iterated width (*IW*) searches both for constructing a serialization of the problem $\Pi = \langle F, I, O, G \rangle$ and for solving the resulting subproblems. While *IW* is a sequence of i-width

---

[1] http://www.plg.inf.uc3m.es/ipc2011-deterministic/results

searches $IW(i)$, $i = 0, 1, \ldots$ over the same problem Π, *SIW* is a sequence of *IW* calls over $|G|$ subproblems Π_k, $k = 1, \ldots, |G|$. The definition of *SIW* takes advantage of the fact that *IW* is a blind-search procedure that does not need to know the goals of the problem in advance; it just needs to recognize them in order to stop. Thanks to this feature *IW* is used both for decomposing Π into the sequence of subproblems Π_k, and for solving each one of them. The plan for Π is the concatenation of the plans obtained for the subproblems.

Definition 8.2. *Serialized Iterated Width (SIW) over* $\Pi = \langle F, I, O, G \rangle$ *consists of a sequence of calls to IW over the problems* $\Pi_k = \langle F, I_k, O, G_k \rangle$, $k = 1, \ldots, |G|$, *where*

1. $I_1 = I$,

2. G_k *is the first consistent set of atoms achieved from* I_k *such that* $G_{k-1} \subset G_k \subseteq G$ *and* $|G_k| = k$; $G_0 = \emptyset$,

3. I_{k+1} *represents the state where* G_k *is achieved,* $1 < k < |G|$.

In other words, the k-th subcall of *SIW* stops when *IW* generates a state s_k that consistently achieves k goals from G: those achieved in the previous subcall and a new goal from G. The same is required from the next subcall that starts at s_k. The state s_k *consistently* achieves $G_k \subseteq G$ if s_k achieves G_k, and G_k does not need to be undone in order to achieve G. This last condition is checked by testing whether $h_{max}(s_k) = \infty$ is true in Π once the actions that delete atoms from G_k are excluded (Bonet and Geffner, 2001). Notice that *SIW* does not use heuristic estimators to the goal, and does not even know what goal G_k is when *IW* is invoked on subproblem Π_k. It finds this out when *IW* generates a set of atoms G' such that $G_{k-1} \subset G' \subseteq G$ and $|G'| = k$. It then sets G_k to G'. This is how *SIW* manages to use *IW* for both constructing the serialization and solving the subproblems.

The *SIW* algorithm is sound and the solution to Π can be obtained by concatenating the solutions to the problems $\Pi_1, \ldots, \Pi_m$, where $m = |G|$. Like *IW*, however, *SIW* does not guarantee optimality. Likewise, while the *IW* algorithm is complete, *SIW* is not. The reason is that the subgoal mechanism implicit in *SIW* commits to intermediate states from which the goal may not be reachable. Of course, if there are no dead-ends in the problem, *SIW* is complete.

Last, the benefit of *SIW* over *IW* is that *SIW* runs *IW* over subproblems which, as we will see, often have a low effective width even if the effective width of the original problem is high (recall that the effective width refers to the min value of i for which $IW(i)$ solves the problem). On the other hand, while in *IW*, the effective width of a problem $w_e(\Pi)$ is bounded by its actual width $w(\Pi)$, while in *SIW*, there are no similar guarantees. To express this more precisely, let us define the effective width of a problem under *SIW*:

Definition 8.3. *The* effective width *of a problem* Π *under SIW, written* $w_s(\Pi)$, *is the max effective width* $w_e(\Pi_k)$ *of the subproblems* Π_k, $k = 1, \ldots, |G|$ *induced by SIW.*

Then, while $w_e(\Pi) \leq w_s(\Pi)$ and $w_e(\Pi_k) < w(\Pi_k)$ are both true, it is *not* necessarily the case that $w_s(\Pi) \leq w(\Pi, d)$ is true for the goal serialization $d = G_1, \ldots, G_m$

computed by *SIW*. The reason is that the serialized width $w(\Pi, d)$ is defined using the *optimal solutions* to the subproblems that arise from d, while *SIW* uses *IW* to solve the subproblems. Since *IW* is not necessarily optimal, *SIW* may end up generating subproblems Π_k that are not in $\mathcal{P}_d$ and which may thus have a higher width and effective width. Nonetheless, even if a low serialized width $w(\Pi, d)$ does not ensure a low effective width $w_s(\Pi)$, the experiments below reveal that $w_s(\Pi)$ tends to be quite low over most benchmarks.

8.3 Experimental Results

We have compared experimentally the blind-search algorithm *SIW* to a baseline heuristic search planner using a Greedy Best-First Search (GBFS) and the additive heuristic (Bonet and Geffner, 2001). Neither planner is state-of-the-art, since neither uses key techniques such as helpful actions or landmarks (Hoffmann and Nebel, 2001; Richter and Westphal, 2010). However, the comparison shows that the non-goal oriented form of pruning in *IW* and the simple form of decomposition in *SIW* are quite powerful; as powerful indeed, as the best heuristic estimators. [1]

SIW and GBFS are both written in C++ and use Metric-FF as an *ADL* to *Propositional* STRIPS compiler (Hoffmann, 2003). The experiments were conducted on a dual-processor running at 2.33 GHz and 2 GB of RAM. Processes time or memory out after 30 minutes or 2 GB. The results are summarized in Table 8.1. Out of 1150 instances, *SIW* solves 30 problems more than GBFS, and *SIW* is usually faster and produces shorter solutions.

In terms of coverage, *SIW* performs the best on *Parking*, *Pipesworld-Non-Tankage*, *Visitall*, *Depots* and *Elevator*, while GBFS is the best on *PSRsmall*, *ParcPrinter*, *OpenstacksIPC6*, *Pegsol* and *Sokoban*. The difference in coverage is considerable if we drop domains that feature dead-ends, as this causes both algorithms to be complete. By dropping mainly two domains, *Pegsol* and *Sokoban*, where GBFS solves 53 of the 60 instances and *SIW* solves only 9, the gap in performance jumps from 2.6% to 6.8%.

Regarding plan times and lengths, the averages shown in the bottom row show that *SIW* is 33% faster overall than GBFS. In part, the speed up is due to the computation of the heuristic in GBFS that is avoided in 'blind' *SIW*. The differences are larger concerning plan length where *SIW* plans are three times shorter on average. If the domain *Visitall* is excluded, where *SIW* plans are 13 times shorter, *SIW* still produces plans that are half as long on average. Other large differences in plan length occur in *Pipesworld-Non-Tankage* and *Grid* where *SIW* plans are 4 and 5 times shorter on average respectively. Overall, *SIW* produces better plans in 25 domains, while GBFS produces better plans in 5 domains by a small margin.

Focusing now on the inner workings of *SIW*, Table 8.2 shows the average number of nodes pruned overall in the calls to *IW* per domain (P), the average number of nodes generated but not pruned (NP), and the selectivity ratio: NP

---

[1] The results for GBFS with h_{add} are similar to those that can be obtained with the back-end planner of FF that uses the relaxed planning heuristic instead (Hoffmann and Nebel, 2001) or the use of LAMA with a single queue driven by FF heuristic h_{FF} (Richter and Westphal, 2010).

Domain	I	Serialized *IW* (*SIW*)			GBFS + h_{add}		
		S	Q	T	S	Q	T
8puzzle	50	50	**42.34**	0.64	50	55.94	**0.07**
Barman	20	1	–		–	–	–
Blocks World	50	50	**48.32**	5.05	50	122.96	**3.50**
Cybersecure	30	–	–		–	–	–
Depots	22	**21**	**34.55**	**22.32**	11	104.55	121.24
Driver	20	**16**	28.21	2.76	14	**26.86**	**0.30**
Elevators	30	**27**	**55.00**	**13.90**	16	101.50	210.50
Ferry	50	50	**27.40**	**0.02**	50	32.88	0.03
Floortile	20	–	–		–	–	–
Freecell	20	**19**	**47.50**	**7.53**	17	62.88	68.25
Grid	5	**5**	**36.00**	**22.66**	3	195.67	320.65
Gripper	50	50	101.00	3.03	50	**99.04**	**0.36**
Logistics	28	28	**54.25**	2.61	28	56.25	**0.33**
Miconic	50	50	42.44	0.08	50	42.72	**0.01**
Mprime	35	27	**6.65**	**84.80**	28	17.92	204.76
Mystery	30	27	**6.47**	42.89	28	7.60	**15.44**
NoMystery	20	–		–	**6**		
OpenStacks	30	**13**	105.23	**0.53**	7	112.42	6.49
OpenStacksIPC6	30	26	**29.43**	108.27	**30**	32.14	**23.86**
ParcPrinter	30	9	16.00	0.06	**30**	**15.67**	**0.01**
Parking	20	17	**39.50**	**38.84**	2	68.00	686.72
Pegsol	30	6	**16.00**	1.71	**30**	16.17	**0.06**
Pipes-NonTan	50	**45**	**26.36**	**3.23**	25	113.84	68.42
Pipes-Tan	50	**35**	**26.00**	205.21	14	33.57	**134.21**
PSRsmall	50	25	**13.79**	28.37	**44**	18.04	**4.99**
Rovers	40	**27**	**38.47**	**108.59**	20	67.63	148.34
Satellite	20	19	38.63	216.69	20	**34.11**	**8.44**
Scanalyzer	30	26	**26.81**	**33.96**	28	28.50	129.42
Sokoban	30	3	**80.67**	**7.83**	**23**	166.67	14.30
Storage	30	**25**	**12.62**	**0.06**	16	29.56	8.52
Tidybot	20	7	**42.00**	532.27	**16**	70.29	**184.77**
Tpp	30	24	**82.95**	**68.32**	23	116.45	199.51
Transport	30	**21**	**54.53**	94.61	17	70.82	**70.05**
Trucks	30	2	**31.00**	**4.58**	**8**	34.50	14.08
Visitall	20	**19**	199.00	**0.91**	3	2485.00	174.87
Woodworking	30	**30**	21.50	**6.26**	12	42.50	81.02
Zeno	20	19	**34.89**	166.84	20	35.11	**101.06**
Summary	1150	819	**44.4**	**55.01**	789	137.0	91.05

Table 8.1: Blind-Search *SIW* vs. Heuristic GBFS over real benchmarks (with joint goals). *I* is the number of instances, *S* is the number of solved instances, *Q* is the average plan length, *T* is the average time in seconds. Shown in bold are the numbers *S*, *Q*, or *T* that one planner improves over the other by more than 10%.

over NP + P. On average, 74% of the nodes are pruned right away after they are generated. In 15 domains, more than 90% of the nodes are pruned, and in *Satellite* and *Mprime*, this number reaches 99%.

Table 8.2 shows also the highest and average effective width of the subproblems that result from the serializations generated by *SIW*. The effective width gives an insight about how hard is to achieve joint goals sequentially. Indeed, problems from the *Visitall* domain feature an average effective width of 1, as all of the goals can be achieved one at a time with no disruption at all. On the other hand, the maximal effective width is 4, which occurs in two domains: *8puzzle* and *PSRsmall*. On average, however, the effective width is between 1 and 2, except for five domains with effective widths between 2 and 3: *Sokoban* (2.58), *Barman* (2.56) *PSRsmall* (2.27), *Grid* (2.12), and *TPP* (2.03).

8.4 Conclusion

We have introduced the notion of width $w(\Pi, d)$ induced by a serialization d, over the goals G of a problem Π. While most benchmark domains appear to have a bounded and small width provided that goals are restricted to single atoms, they have large widths for arbitrary joint goals. We have shown, nonetheless, that the algorithm derived for exploiting the structure of planning problems with low width, *IW*, also pays off over benchmarks with joint goals once the same algorithm is used for decomposing the problems into subproblems. Actually, the resulting blind-search algorithm *SIW* is competitive with a baseline planner based on a Greedy Best-First Search and the additive heuristic, suggesting that the two ideas underlying *SIW*, novelty-based pruning and goal decomposition, are quite powerful.

Domain	I	Serialized IW (SIW)				
		Generated	Pruned	% Novel States	Max w_e	Avg. w_e
8puzzle	50	10,006	3,523	74%	4	1.75
Barman	20	–	–	–	3	2.56
Blocks World	50	14,980	53,366	22%	3	1.22
Cybersecure	30	–	–	–	–	–
Depots	22	46,288	845,864	5%	3	1.74
Driver	20	40,449	138,222	23%	3	1.31
Elevators	30	156,309	3,880,408	4%	2	2.00
Ferry	50	1,459	390	79%	2	1.98
Floortile	20	–	–	–	–	–
Freecell	20	6,663	32,781	17%	2	1.62
Grid	5	87,494	47,321	65%	3	2.12
Gripper	50	54,120	101,330	35%	2	2.00
Logistics	28	18,306	288,981	6%	2	2.00
Miconic	50	3,010	9,356	24%	2	2.00
Mprime	35	14,879	1,433,257	1%	2	2.00
Mystery	30	15,303	307,611	5%	2	1.19
NoMystery	20	–	–			–
OpenStacks	30	855	1,851	32%	3	1.80
OpenStacksIPC6	30	12,089	68,963	15%	4	1.48
ParcPrinter	30	510	1,030	33%	3	1.28
Parking	20	198,010	1,045,164	16%	2	1.14
Pegsol	30	190	47	80%	4	1.09
Pipes-NonTan	50	70,676	833,552	8%	3	1.62
Pipes-Tan	50	37,555	694,304	5%	3	1.63
PSRsmall	50	2,864	8,964	24%	4	2.27
Rovers	40	70,384	1,332,660	5%	2	1.39
Satellite	20	90,036	9,262,413	1%	2	1.29
Scanalyzer	30	27,608	552,240	5%	2	1.16
Sokoban	30	39,890	9,422	81%	3	2.58
Storage	30	13,264	205,295	6%	2	1.48
Tidybot	20	2,322	1,110	68%	3	1.81
Tpp	30	19,750	167,402	11%	3	2.03
transport	30	290,665	3,464,898	8%	2	2.00
Trucks	30	13,216	520,903	2%	2	2.00
VisitAll	20	8,119	0	100%	1	1.00
woodworking	30	16,486	376,906	4%	2	1.07
Zeno	20	147,423	1,626,078	8%	2	1.83
Summary	1150	46,399	827,746	26%	2.56	1.69

Table 8.2: Blind-Search *SIW* inner details is the number of instances, *Generated* is the average nodes generated, *Pruned* is the average generated nodes pruned, % *Novel States* stands for the average of nodes considered to be novel, *Max* w_e and *Avg.* w_e stands for maximum and average effective width per domain.

Chapter 9

Decomposition and Width Revisited

> Todas las teorías son legítimas y ninguna tiene importancia. Lo que importa es lo que se hace con ellas.

> All theories are legitimate and none of them are important. What matters is what one does with them.

> Jorge Luis Borges

In this chapter we show how the key ideas from the blind search algorithm *SIW* presented in Chapter 8, novelty-based pruning and goal decomposition, can be integrated in a standard best-first search algorithm; along with old ideas that have been proven to be crucial for high performance planners. We first explain how a heuristic that counts the number of unachieved goals can be used, not as a heuristic term, but for serializing the problem. We then adapt the novelty Definition 7.1 to take into account the serialization, and show how other important terms used by state-of-the-art planners can be integrated. Finally, we evaluate the resulting best-first search planner and compare it with other high performance planners.

9.1 Introduction

Three ideas that have proven crucial in the performance of state-of-the-art planners are delete-relaxation heuristics (McDermott, 1999; Bonet and Geffner, 2001), helpful actions (Hoffmann and Nebel, 2001), and landmarks (Hoffmann et al., 2004; Richter et al., 2008). The LAMA planner (Richter and Westphal, 2010) uses them all in a search architecture made up of four open lists borrowed from Fast Downward (Helmert, 2006). Half of these lists are ordered according to the delete-relaxation heuristic, and half by the landmark heuristic. In addition, one open list for each heuristic is for the states obtained from the application of actions regarded as helpful, defined slightly differently in each case (Richter and Westphal, 2010). Unlike the delete-relaxation heuristic, the landmark heuristic provides an *implicit serialization* of the problem in which plan prefixes that have achieved more subgoals (landmarks) are preferred. Actually, the second best-performing planner in the 2011 IPC when considering the first plans,[1] was PROBE, which appeals to *explicit subgoal serializations* (Lipovetzky and Geffner, 2011b). Since an incorrect serialization can render a problem unsolvable by driving the search towards a dead-end, LAMA ensures completeness by never committing to any serialization. PROBE on the other hand, commits to a serialization in each of the probes that it throws from the states expanded in a complete best-first search.

The aim of this chapter is to show that these and other relevant ideas can be incorporated one by one into a standard best-first search algorithm by adding suitable terms to a basic evaluation function given by a standard delete-relaxation heuristic. From a practical point of view, the resulting planner seems to perform as well as LAMA. From a conceptual point of view, by using a standard heuristic search algorithm and thus reducing all of the planning know-how to the evaluation function, the formulation sheds light on the nature of the key computational ideas in classical planning, and the relation between planning and search. Indeed, while heuristic search has become the mainstream approach in planning, the algorithms used in planning are not the same as those used in search. This raises the question: is this bound to happen due to the domain-independent and factored representations used in planning? The results in this chapter suggest that this is not strictly necessary, and that while inferences over factored representations are crucial for performance, this does not translate necessarily into changing the search algorithm. Indeed, in the resulting planner, the algorithm is a standard best-first search that does not look into the structure of the states, and all inference about planning is compiled into the evaluation function.

We assume STRIPS problems where the cost of the actions is assumed to be 1 so that plan cost is equal to plan length.

We define the evaluation function one term at a time: *serialization term, novelty, heuristic function,* and *helpful actions.* Most of these ideas are well known except for the interpretation of the landmark heuristic as a serialization term, and for 'novelty' which is borrowed from the *IW* algorithm presented in Chapter 7; where it is used inside a breadth-first search algorithm that solves planning problems in time exponential in their width. Here the search algorithm is a standard, forward-state, best-first search.

9.2 Serialization and Novelty

The algorithm *SIW*, detailed in Section 8.2, decomposes the original goal set G of a problem Π into $|G|$ subsets. Each subset $G_{k-1} \subset G_k$ achieves exactly the goals previously achieved plus a new one, for $k = 1, \ldots, |G|$, where G_0 initially is empty. *SIW* is a form of *hill-climbing* over goal set G committing to every intermediate state that achieves a goal subset G_k. It avoids the combinatorial blowup of possi-

---

[1] http://www.plg.inf.uc3m.es/ipc2011-deterministic/results.

ble decompositions of goal G with the payoff of being incomplete in the presence of dead-ends in problem Π. Thus, It does not search in the space of possible decompositions of goal G, but rather commits to the first decomposition that it finds when a state s achieves some G_k. In order to address this shortcoming, we turn to best-first search, where the evaluation function basically provides a 'reward' when a subgoal is achieved, expressed as:

$$f_1(n) = usg(n)$$

where $usg(n)$ measures the number of subgoals not yet achieved in the path to n. The reward that results from the achievement of a new subgoal while maintaining previous ones, translates into a decrement of $usg(n)$ in the evaluation function, preferring first nodes with a small number of subgoals to go.

We then order only top goals so that a top goal g_i is not counted as achieved if there is a another top goal g_j that cannot be achieved without undoing g_i. More precisely, g_i is ordered after g_j if all the actions that add g_j *e-delete* g_i: either delete g_i or have a precondition that is mutex with G_I[1]. The ordering is computed only once from the initial state.

Notice that the search does not commit to any intermediate state. Intuitively, the evaluation function $f_1(n)$ divides the state space into k subspaces, where k is the maximum value that $usg(n)$ can take. Given a problem $\Pi = \langle F, I, O, G \rangle$, the best first search algorithm driven by $f_1(n) = usg(n)$ divides the original state space $\mathcal{S}$ of problem Π into k state spaces $\mathcal{S}_k$, where $k = 0, \ldots, max_n f_1(n)$, and $\mathcal{S}_k \subseteq \mathcal{S}$. States s where goals G of problem Π are true $G \in s$, belong to state space $\mathcal{S}_0$, while states s that achieve all goals but one, no matter which one, belong to state space $\mathcal{S}_1$, etc.

As an illustration consider a grid of cells $c = 1, \ldots, n$, such that the cells form a single line, where a robot starting at the left most cell $c = 1$ must visit every cell. Each state that has visited i cells so far, belongs to the state space $\mathcal{S}_{n-i}$, no matter the robot's location. For example, states where the robot has visited all but the right most cell $c = n$, and where the robot is located at any other cell $c = 1, \ldots, n-1$, belong to the same state space $\mathcal{S}_1$.

The key aspect that we need to address, is how to drive the search in each subspace $\mathcal{S}_k$. Intuitively, the goal of any state s in space $s \in \mathcal{S}_k$ is to achieve any state s' that belongs to any state space $\mathcal{S}_j$ where $j < k$. SIW uses *iterative width* to find a path between every subspace. Analogously, we can use either a heuristic to estimate the distance to the goals, or we can use the *novelty* measure to prune the underlying state space. In Chapter 8 we showed that goal decomposition and novelty based pruning tuns out to be as powerful as the use of a standard delete relaxation heuristic in a best-first search algorithm, and hence we can use the *novelty* term to have a powerful blind search algorithm for finding a path connecting a state from $\mathcal{S}_k$ to a state in $\mathcal{S}_j$, $j < k$.

Roughly, the novelty measure of a state s is 1 if s makes an atom true that was false in all previously generated states; it is 2 if there is no such atom but there is one such pair of atoms, and so on. Here we define a similar measure that takes into account both the serialization implicit in the function $usg(n)$ and the novelty $novel(n)$.

---

[1] A pair of atoms p, q are defined as mutex if $h^2(p, q) = \infty$

We revise the definition of novelty as follows:

Definition 9.1 (*novel(n)*). *In the context of a search algorithm, the novelty measure of a node novel(n) is the size of the smallest tuple t of atoms that is true in n and false in all previously generated nodes n' in the search that belong to the same state space $n, n' \in S_k$.*

Intuitively, the novelty of a node n depends only on previously generated nodes in the search n' with same number of unachieved goals $usg(n') = usg(n)$, which is the main difference from the previous Definition 7.1 of novelty.

The evaluation function f_2 then extends the evaluation function with a term that 'rewards' nodes with low novelty measure, which are actually the ones that the are most 'novel':

$$f_2(n) = novel(n)$$

and *breaking ties according to usg(n)*. As a result, each subspace S_k expands first nodes with novelty 1, then 2, etc. Notice that the number of nodes with the same novelty measure i is normally bounded by the number of atoms $O(F^i)$ in the problem. The order in which nodes are generated can affect the novelty term, but in our experiments the impact of breaking ties randomly does not change the results significantly.

At first glance, f_2 could render similar results as a function f' that considers first $usg(n)$ and then breaking ties by $novel(n)$. The main difference is that the later tries to greedily minimize the number of unachieved goals preferring always states with smaller $usg(n)$, while the former tries first to expand states of novelty 1 from every state space S_k, and then states of novelty 2 from every state space, etc. Thus preferring always states with smaller $novel(n)$ and alternating between states with different $usg(n)$.

9.3 Extensions

We have shown that it is possible to integrate the serialization and novelty term into the evaluation function of BFS. We show now that other techniques common in state-of-the-art planners can be easily integrated as well.

9.3.1 Integration of Landmarks

Landmarks are *necessary* features of any valid solution of a planning problem Π (Hoffmann et al., 2004). These features can be action or fluent formulas, either conjunctive or disjunctive, that must hold in every valid plan. *Disjunctive action landmarks* have been used successfully in optimal planning (Helmert and Domshlak, 2009). *Conjunctive fluent landmarks* have been deemed useful for some benchmark domains (Keyder et al., 2010), while disjunctive and single fluent landmarks have been widely used in satisficing planning (Richter and Westphal, 2010; Lipovetzky and Geffner, 2011b). We focus on the integration of single fluent landmarks.

A fluent landmark L is a formula over the set of fluents F of a planning problem Π, such that any valid plan $\pi = \langle a_1, \ldots, a_n \rangle$ has a prefix $\pi' = \langle a_1, \ldots, a_i \rangle$, possibly of length 0, whose application in the initial state results in a state in which L is true, i.e. $s_0[\pi'] \models L$ (Porteous et al., 2001). All formulas that are true in the initial state I and the goal G of a problem Π, are landmarks by choosing the empty prefix $\pi' = \emptyset$, or the entire plan $\pi' \models G$.

A direct method to account for fluent landmarks in the evaluation function of BFS proposed above, it is to consider the landmarks of the problem as subgoals in the serialization, instead of the original top goals G. The count $usg(n)$ is then similar to the landmark heuristic in LAMA, simplified somewhat: we use only atomic fluent landmarks (no disjunctions) and sound orderings.

Orderings over fluent landmarks state the order in which they must be true. There is a *natural* order between two landmarks $L1 < L_2$ if for every valid plan, L_1 is made true strictly *before* L_2 is made true; there is a *necessary* ordering $L_1 <_n L_2$ if for every valid plan, L_1 is made true strictly *immediately before* L_2 is made true; and a *greedy necessary* ordering $L_1 <_{gn} L_2$ if for every valid plan, L_1 is made true strictly *immediately before* L_2 is made true the first time. Intuitively, the orderings state that L_2 cannot be made true without making L_1 true first. As in LAMA, the count $usg(n)$ is path-dependent, yet this does not compromise the completeness of the algorithm. Fluent landmarks and orderings are derived using a standard polynomial algorithm over the delete-relaxation (Zhu and Givan, 2003; Keyder et al., 2010).

9.3.2 Integration of Delete Relaxation Heuristics

Delete relaxation based heuristics have been widely used by most high performance planners (Bonet and Geffner, 2001; Hoffmann and Nebel, 2001; Richter and Westphal, 2010). A heuristic $h(n)$ estimates the cost from the state encoded in the node n to the problem goal. The most common heuristic estimators used in state-of-the-art planners are h_{add} (Bonet and Geffner, 2001) and h_{FF} (Hoffmann and Nebel, 2001). They have been used within a variety of search techniques, HSP uses h_{add} in WA^*; FF uses h_{FF} first in EHC and then in BFS; and LAMA uses h_{FF} in a dual queue search architecture.

We propose integrating the use of h_{add} to guide the search for a path from a state $s \in S_k$ to a state $s' \in S_j$, $j < k$. Recall that the original state space S is decomposed in several state spaces S_k, where every state in S_k has the same number of unachieved goals $usg(n)$. The only term that contributes to finding such a path is $novel(n)$, but we can further improve the evaluation function to differentiate states with the same number of unachieved goals and *novelty*. Thus, we extend the evaluation function f_2, *breaking ties lexicographically by* $usg(n)$ *and* $h_{add}(n)$. Intuitively, the heuristic term is used only to differentiate states with the same novelty and number of unachieved goals (landmarks). As the heuristic $h_{add}(n)$ estimates the distance to any goal in G, it pushes the search towards states that have fewer unachieved goals, i.e. states with lower values of $usg(n)$, that contribute to finding a path between states in different subspaces S_k and S_{k-1} for $k = 1, \ldots, |G|$, tentatively, closer to sates that satisfy the goal $G \in s \in S_0$.

9.3.3 Integration of Helpful Actions

The term helpful actions [1] was first introduced by FF (Hoffmann and Nebel, 2001). Recall that delete relaxation based heuristics find a solution to the delete free problem Π^+ from a given state. The applicable actions from such a solution are the helpful actions. Various search enhancements have been proposed to take advantage of helpful actions. The approach of FF was initially to consider only states resulting from helpful actions rendering the search incomplete, and then considering all states in case of failure. More recently, planners have taken the approach of alternating the exploration of states resulting from helpful actions and those resulting from all other actions in a multiple queue architecture (Helmert, 2006). Helpful actions thus become a preference rather than a pruning method.

We propose a different approach to integrating helpful actions in the evaluation function of BFS. The novelty term considers actions that produce single new atoms, i.e. ($novel(n) = 1$), as more 'novel' than actions that produce only new pairs, i.e. $novel(n) = 2$. This ranking is useful even if it is not goal oriented. Of course, a new atom generated in the 'direction' of the goal should be preferred to other atoms. We propose capturing this directionality using the notion of helpful actions, as those are the actions that adds a goal or the precondition of an action in a relaxed plan extracted backwards from the goal (Hoffmann and Nebel, 2001).

The notion of helpful actions allows us to make the novelty distinctions finer and goal-directed. The new evaluation function f_3 refines the novelty term in f_2 without adding a new one. The new evaluation function is

$$f_3(n) = novelha(n)$$

breaking ties lexicographically by $usg(n)$ and $h_{add}(n)$, where

$$novelha(n) = 2[novel(n) - 1] + help(n)$$

That is, $novelha(n)$ is 1 if the novelty of n is 1 and the action leading to n is helpful, 2 if the novelty is 1 and the action is not helpful, 3 if the novelty is 2 and the action is helpful, and so on. Basically, novel states (lower $novel(n)$ measure) are preferred to less novel states, and helpful actions are preferred to non-helpful, with the former criterion carrying more weight. Once again this simple criterion follows from performance considerations. Other alternatives can be considered.

9.3.4 Integration of Delayed Evaluation

The largest computational effort made by heuristic search planners is done by the computation of the heuristic estimators. Moreover, many of the nodes generated and placed in the open list (i.e., in the search frontier) do not contribute to the solution, and the heuristic evaluation contributes only by delaying a node from immediate expansion. Delayed evaluation introduced as a search enhancement in FD (Helmert, 2006) and then also used in LAMA, aims at minimizing the impact of this situation by computing the heuristic evaluation only when a

---

[1] A similar concept called preferred operators was introduced in FD (Helmert, 2006).

node is expanded. When a node is generated it uses the heuristic estimate of the parent in the calculation of the evaluation function $f(n)$.

While this results in less informative evaluation functions $f(n)$, the search is able to quickly generate a larger portion of the state space. It usually pays off in problems with very large branching factors, where many more nodes are generated than expanded. In our implementation we use a similar idea, except that we just *delay the evaluation of non-helpful* nodes rather than all generated nodes. This implementation choice has an impact, especially in the largest problems.

9.4 Experimental Results

We compare the best performance configuration with FF, LAMA and PROBE; and finish with a simple ablation study. All configurations are written in C++ and use Metric-FF as an ADL to Propositional STRIPS compiler (Hoffmann, 2003). The experiments discussed below were conducted on a dual-processor Xeon 'Wood-crest' running at 2.33 GHz and 2 GB of RAM. Processes time or memory out after 30 minutes or 2 GB. FF is FF version 2.3, PROBE and LAMA are from IPC 2011. LAMA is executed without plan improvement, reporting the first solution it finds.

Our tests confirm than delaying only non-helpful nodes results in more informative evaluation functions than delaying every node.

In the experiments below, we keep track of three possible values for $novel(n)$: 1 if the size of the smallest tuple added by the node is $= 1$, 2 if the size is 2, and 3 otherwise. We call the best-first search planner with $f_3(n) = novelha(n)$ where ties are broken lexicographically by $usg(n)$ and $h_{add}(n)$, and delayed evaluation, BFS(f). We compare it with three state-of-the-art planners: FF, LAMA, and PROBE(Hoffmann and Nebel, 2001; Richter et al., 2008; Lipovetzky and Geffner, 2011b). Like LAMA, BFS(f) uses delayed evaluation, a technique that is useful for problems with large branching factors (Richter and Helmert, 2009). The $novelha(n)$ measure combines the novelty of n and whether the action leading to n is helpful or not (Hoffmann and Nebel, 2001). The novelty of a node $novel(n)$ is computed approximately, being set to 3 when it is neither 1 nor 2. Similarly, if $help(n)$ is set to 1 or 2 according to whether the action leading to n was helpful or not, then $novelha(n)$ takes six values: 1, 3, and 5, if $novel(n)$ is 1, 2, and 3 respectively, and the action leading to n was *helpful*, and 2, 4, and 6, if $novel(n)$ is 1, 2, and 3 respectively, and the action leading to n was not *helpful*.

Table 9.1 compares the four planners over the 1150 instances. In terms of coverage, BFS(f) solves 5 more problems than LAMA, 18 more than PROBE and 161 more than FF. Significant differences in coverage occur in *Sokoban*, *Parking*, *NoMystery* and *Floortile* where either LAMA or BFS(f) solve 10% more instances than the second best planner. The largest difference is in *NoMystery* where BFS(f) solves 19 instances while LAMA solves 11.

Time and plan quality averages are computed over the instances that are solved by BFS(f), LAMA and PROBE. FF is excluded from these averages because of the large gap in coverage. LAMA and PROBE are the fastest in 16 domains each, and BFS(f) in 5. On the other hand, BFS(f) finds shorter plans in 15 domains, PROBE in 13, and LAMA in 10. The largest differences between BFS(f)

Domain	I	BFS(f)		PROBE		LAMA'11		FF	
		S	T	S	T	S	T	S	T
8puzzle	50	50	0.20	50	**0.09**	49	0.18	49	(0.03)
Barman	20	20	281.28	20	12.93	20	**8.39**	–	(–)
Blocks World	50	50	2.40	50	**0.23**	50	0.41	44	(66.67)
Cybersecure	30	28	70.14	24	69.22	30	576.69	4	(0.73)
Depots	22	22	56.93	22	**5.46**	21	46.66	22	(32.72)
Driver	20	18	57.37	20	1.05	20	**0.94**	16	(14.52)
Elevators	30	30	93.88	30	26.66	30	**4.69**	30	(1.00)
Ferry	50	50	0.03	50	**0.02**	50	0.31	50	(0.02)
Floortile	20	**7**	**29.52**	5	71.33	5	95.54	5	(134.29)
Freecell	20	20	**13.00**	20	41.26	19	27.34	20	(22.95)
Grid	5	5	7.70	5	9.64	5	**4.84**	5	(0.27)
Gripper	50	50	0.37	50	**0.06**	50	0.36	50	(0.03)
Logistics	28	28	0.12	28	**0.09**	28	0.35	28	(0.03)
Miconic	50	50	0.01	50	**0.01**	50	0.28	50	(0.03)
Mprime	35	35	19.75	35	28.72	35	**10.98**	34	(14.82)
Mystery	30	27	**0.92**	25	1.08	22	1.70	18	(0.24)
NoMystery	20	**19**	**1.09**	5	5.47	11	2.66	4	(0.23)
OpenStacks	30	29	129.05	30	64.55	30	**3.49**	30	(6.86)
OpenStacksIPC6	30	30	40.19	30	48.89	30	**4.91**	30	(0.38)
ParcPrinter	30	27	6.48	28	0.26	30	0.28	30	(0.06)
Parking	20	17	577.30	17	693.12	**19**	**363.89**	3	(945.86)
Pegsol	30	30	**1.17**	30	8.60	30	2.76	30	(7.61)
Pipes-NonTan	50	47	35.97	45	**3.18**	44	11.10	35	(12.77)
Pipes-Tan	50	40	254.62	43	102.29	41	**58.44**	20	(87.96)
PSRsmall	50	48	2.62	50	**0.08**	50	0.36	42	(63.05)
Rovers	40	40	44.19	40	24.19	40	**17.90**	40	(31.78)
Satellite	20	20	1.26	20	0.84	20	0.78	20	(0.10)
Scanalyzer	30	27	7.40	28	**5.59**	28	8.14	30	(70.74)
Sokoban	30	23	125.12	25	39.63	**28**	58.24	26	(26.61)
Storage	30	20	4.34	21	**0.07**	18	8.15	18	(39.17)
Tidybot	20	18	198.22	**19**	35.33	16	113.00	15	(9.78)
Tpp	30	30	36.51	30	58.98	30	**18.12**	28	(53.23)
Transport	30	30	55.04	30	44.72	30	94.11	29	(167.10)
Trucks	30	15	8.59	8	113.54	16	**0.53**	11	(3.84)
Visitall	20	20	84.67	19	308.42	20	77.80	6	(38.22)
Woodworking	30	30	19.12	30	15.93	30	**12.45**	17	(0.22)
Zeno	20	20	77.56	20	6.18	20	**4.28**	20	(0.17)
Summary	1150	1070	63.36	1052	49.94	1065	44.35	909	(51.50)

Table 9.1: BFS(f) vs. LAMA, FF, and PROBE. I is the number of instances, S is the number of solved instances, T is the average time in seconds. T averages are computed over problems solved by all planners except FF, which is excluded because of the large gap in coverage. Numbers in bold show performance that is at least 10% better than the other planners.

Domain	I	BFS(*f*) Q	PROBE Q	LAMA'11 Q	FF Q
8puzzle	50	**45.45**	61.45	58.24	(52.61)
Barman	20	174.45	169.30	203.85	(–)
Blocks World	50	54.24	**43.88**	88.92	(39.36)
Cybersecure	30	39.23	52.85	37.54	(29.50)
Depots	22	49.68	44.95	61.95	(51.82)
Driver	20	48.06	60.17	46.22	(25.00)
Elevators	30	129.13	107.97	**96.40**	(85.73)
Ferry	50	32.94	29.34	28.18	(27.68)
Floortile	20	43.50	45.25	49.75	(44.20)
Freecell	20	64.39	62.44	68.94	(64.00)
Grid	5	70.60	**58.00**	70.60	(61.00)
Gripper	50	101.00	101.00	**76.00**	(76.00)
Logistics	28	56.71	55.36	**43.32**	(41.43)
Miconic	50	31.46	41.80	**30.84**	(30.38)
Mprime	35	10.74	14.37	**9.09**	(9.53)
Mystery	30	7.07	7.71	7.29	(6.61)
NoMystery	20	24.33	25.17	24.67	(19.75)
OpenStacks	30	141.40	137.90	142.93	(155.67)
OpenStacksIPC6	30	125.89	134.14	130.18	(136.17)
ParcPrinter	30	35.92	36.40	37.72	(42.73)
Parking	20	90.46	146.08	87.23	(88.33)
Pegsol	30	24.20	25.17	25.90	(25.50)
Pipes-NonTan	50	**39.09**	46.73	57.59	(34.34)
Pipes-Tan	50	**40.48**	55.40	48.60	(31.45)
PSRsmall	50	22.15	21.40	**18.31**	(16.71)
Rovers	40	105.08	109.97	108.28	(100.47)
Satellite	20	36.05	37.05	40.75	(37.75)
Scanalyzer	30	29.37	25.15	27.52	(31.87)
Sokoban	30	220.57	233.48	213.00	(213.38)
Storage	30	20.94	**14.56**	24.33	(16.28)
Tidybot	20	62.94	**53.50**	62.31	(63.20)
Tpp	30	112.33	155.63	119.13	(122.29)
Transport	30	107.70	137.17	108.03	(117.41)
Trucks	30	26.50	26.75	24.12	(27.09)
Visitall	20	**947.67**	1185.67	1285.56	(450.67)
Woodworking	30	41.13	41.13	51.57	(32.35)
Zeno	20	37.70	44.90	35.80	(30.60)
Summary	1150	87.93	98.71	98.67	(67.75)

Table 9.2: BFS(*f*) vs. LAMA, FF, and PROBE. *I* is the number of instances, *Q* is the average plan length. *Q* averages are computed over problems solved by all planners except FF, excluded because of the large gap in coverage. Numbers in bold show performance that is at least 10% better than the other planners.

	I	S	% S	Q	T
BFS(f)	1150	1070	93%	82.80	62.89
No Delayed Eval	1150	1020	89%	80.67	65.92
No Heuristic	1150	965	84%	100.47	32.43
No Helpful Actions	1150	964	84%	81.82	64.20
No Novelty	1150	902	78%	86.40	46.11

Table 9.3: Ablation study of BFS(f) when some features are excluded. Delayed evaluation is excluded from the second and subsequent rows, in addition to the feature shown. Columns show the number of instances (I), the number of instances solved (S), % solved (%S), and average plan lengths (Q) and times in seconds (T).

and the other planners are in *8puzzle, Parking, Pipesworld Tankage, Pipesworld Non Tankage,* and *VisitAll* (Table 9.2).

The results show that the performance of BFS(f) is at the level of the best planners. The question that we address next is: what is the contribution of the four different ideas combined in the evaluation function $f(n)$ and in the tie-breakers; namely, the additive heuristic $h_{add}(n)$, the landmark count $usg(n)$, the novelty measure $novel(n)$, or the helpful action distinction $help(n)$? The last two terms are the ones that determine the evaluation function $f(n)$.

Table 9.3 shows the result of a simple ablation study. The first row shows the results for the planner BFS(f) as described above, while the following rows show results for the same planner with one or several features removed: first delayed evaluation, and then the additive heuristic, helpful actions, or novelty. This is achieved by setting $help(n) = 0$, $h_{add}(n) = 0$, and $novel(n) = 1$ respectively in $f(n)$ for all n. The term $novel(n)$ is set to 1 and not to zero because that is the value needed to set the novelty term to 0. In table, the greatest drop in performance arises when the novelty term is dropped; coverage then decreases by 11% from 89%, as opposed to the decreases that result from dropping either helpful actions or the additive heuristic; which are respectively, 6% and 5%. In other words, the novelty measure is no less important in the BFS(f) planner than either the helpful action distinction or the heuristic. Not delaying the evaluation of the heuristic decreases the coverage by 50 problems. Recall that the only nodes delayed are the non-helpful ones. Surprisingly if all nodes are delayed, the coverage drops by 68 problems, even more than not delaying any node. The most important term of all however is the $usg(n)$ that counts the number of unachieved goals, and whose effect is to 'serialize' the best-first search to the goal without giving up completeness (as *SIW*). Moreover, the definition of the novelty measure (9.3.3) uses the $usg(n)$ count to delimit the set of previously generated states that are considered. Yet BFS(f') with the evaluation function $f' = usg(n)$, i.e., without *any* of the other features, solves just 776 instances. On the other hand, with the term $novelha(n)$ added, the number jumps to 965, surpassing FF, which solves 909 problems. This is interesting as BFS(f') then uses no heuristic estimator.

9.5 Conclusion

We have formulated a number of known ideas in planning as suitable terms of an evaluation function which has been used for driving a standard best-first search from the initial state. The resulting planner is competitive with state-of-the-art planners such as LAMA, solving more problems and resulting in slightly better plans. The formulation provides a different angle on these ideas, and on the relation between planning and search. While heuristic search has become a mainstream approach in planning, the algorithms used in state-of-the-art planners are not the ones used in search. Planning algorithms reason about states' structure through search enhancements such as multiple queues for each heuristic estimator, helpful actions pruning, etc. However, these results suggest that this is not strictly necessary, and while inferences over factored representations are crucial for performance, this does not translate necessarily into changes in the search algorithm. Indeed, in the resulting planner, all inference about planning gets compiled into the evaluation function, which is used in a standard best-first search that does not look into the structure of the states. Rather, it uses the evaluation function. Also, by providing a different interpretation of the landmark heuristic as a technique for serialization, we hope to make more visible its limitations and the opportunities for further progress.

Part IV

Conclusions, Related and Future Work

Chapter 10

Conclusions

Estoy como parado en una esquina viendo pasar lo que pienso, pero no pienso lo que veo.

It's like I'm standing on a corner watching the things that I'm thinking go by, but I'm not thinking what I see.

El Perseguidor.
Julio Cortázar

In this chapter we summarize the contributions of the dissertation, present related work, and discuss current and future lines of research based on the work developed so far.

10.1 Contributions

In this section we outline the main contributions of this thesis, and refer to the chapters and publications were they appeared:

1. The notion of *consistent causal chains:* sequences of causal links a_i, p_{i+1}, a_{i+1} starting with an action a_0 applicable in the current state s and finishing in the goal, where p_{i+1} is an effect of action a_i and a precondition of action a_{i+1}. We show that by enforcing the semantics of causal links, it is possible to propagate side effects along such chains and detect that some of these chains cannot be part of any plan. Consistent causal chains can be used to select applicable actions in a given state, in a way analogous to helpful actions, by pruning actions a_0 that cannot start any consistent causal chain (in Chapter 2, and Lipovetzky and Geffner (2009b)).

2. The use of Consistent Causal Chains as *decomposition backbones* and as devices for defining a *heuristic estimate* of the cost of achieving the goal *along such paths*, resulting in a planner that solves most of the benchmarks with

no search at all. A path dependent heuristic is proposed that, while being more demanding computationally, takes deletes into account and expands an order of magnitude fewer nodes than a standard delete-based relaxation heuristic (in Chapter 3, and Lipovetzky and Geffner (2009a,b)).

3. The idea of *probes*: single action sequences computed without search from a given state that can quickly go deep into the state space, terminating either in the goal or in failure. Using a number of existing and new polynomial inference techniques, most of the benchmarks can be solved with a single probe from the initial state, with no search. Moreover, the use of probes as a lookahead mechanism from each expanded state in a standard greedy best first search increases the number of problems solved, and compares well to state-of-the-art planners (in Chapter 4, and Lipovetzky and Geffner (2011b))

4. A new *width notion for planning* domains that is useful, both theoretically and practically. This width bounds the complexity of a planning domain in terms of the *goal structure* of the problem. We prove that many of the existing domains have a bounded and low width when goals are restricted to single atoms (in Chapters 6,7, and Lipovetzky and Geffner (2012)).

5. A simple, *blind-search planning algorithm* (*IW*) that runs in time exponential in the problem width; and a *blind-search planning algorithm* (*SIW*) that uses *IW* for *serializing a problem* into subproblems and for *solving such subproblems*. Both algorithms are competitive with a best-first search planner using state-of-the-art heuristics over atomic and conjunctive goals (in Chapters 7,8, and Lipovetzky and Geffner (2012)).

6. A state-of-the-art planner that *integrates new and old inferences used in planning* in a standard greedy best-first search method. We show how the key notion of *novelty* can be used by heuristic search algorithms (in Chapter 9, and Lipovetzky and Geffner (2012)).

As a result, three high performance planners are presented: c3 (in Chapter 3, and Lipovetzky et al. (2008), PROBE (in Chapter 5, and Lipovetzky and Geffner (2011a)) and BFS(f) (in Chapter 9 and Lipovetzky and Geffner (2012))

10.2 Related Work

In this section we present related work, first to causal chains and probes, and then to the notion of width for classical planning proposed in this thesis.

10.2.1 Inference

Some of the inferences used by probes and causal chains in satisficing state space planning are used in other approaches to planning as well. *Causal links*, used in this thesis in the form of causal commitments and causal chains, are used in partial order planning (Penberthy and Weld, 1992; McAllester and Rosenblitt, 1991), constraint based planning (Vidal and Geffner, 2005), and recently also in a path based admissible heuristic for optimal planning (Karpas and Domshlak, 2012). Probe's serialization of *landmarks* is similar to the subgoaling scheme in Hoffmann et al. (2004), although with very different results, as probes do additional inference to distinguish good serializations from bad ones. Landmark *goal orderings* are similar to the reasonable goal orderings used by the goal agenda of IPP and FF (Koehler and Hoffmann, 2000), while *consistency tests* for subgoals capture orderings similar to the reasonable and obedient-reasonable ones (Hoffmann et al., 2004). The notion of consistency is used in two ways: to distinguish good from bad subgoals in probes, and to distinguish good from bad actions in c3.

The motivation for PROBE and c3 is related to the motivation behind other recent planners such as eCPT (Vidal and Geffner, 2005) that also aim to solve simple, non-puzzle-like domains, with little or no search at all. This requires capturing the right domain independent inferences that render the search superfluous in such domains. This task is non-trivial, but as shown in PROBE, it can pay off even in planners that do search.

In this sense, probes can be understood as a lookahead mechanism. The use of lookahead in search and planning is very old in AI, and appears more recently in the YAHSP planner, that makes an attempt to lookahead by using sequences of actions extracted from the relaxed plan (Vidal, 2004). While PROBE also looks ahead by using sequences of actions, the design and use of these sequences is completely different in the two planners. In particular, while in YAHSP, the action sequences are executable prefixes of the relaxed plan, in PROBE, they are computed from scratch to achieve each one of the remaining subgoals in sequence. The range of domains that are solved by just throwing a single probe from the initial state is then much larger.

The idea of searching with probes has been considered before in Langley (1992) where *random probes* are used. *Limited discrepancy search* can be thought of as a systematic method for searching with probes (Harvey and Ginsberg, 1995), while *Monte Carlo planning*, as a non-systematic method that uses multiple random probes (Nakhost and Müller, 2009). In contrast, we propose the use of single carefully designed probes.

The ideas of goal serialization and problem decomposition have received a lot of attention in search, and in the early days of planning (Korf, 1987). We revisited these ideas equipped with the techniques that have been developed more recently in planning research to explicitly recognize and exploit the structure of problems that are nearly-decomposable, even if they are not perfectly decomposable. Indeed, planning used to be defined originally as being concerned mainly with these problems (Newell and Simon, 1963) and even with non-decomposable ones, where techniques such as macro-operators were successfully used to serialize *non-serializable* problems like Rubik's cube (Korf, 1985).

10.2.2 Structure

In Part III of this thesis, we introduced a new type of width parameter that bounds the complexity of a planning domain. Other approaches have also been proposed for explaining the gap between the complexity of planning (Bylander, 1994), and the ability of current planners to solve most existing benchmarks in a few seconds (Hoffmann and Nebel, 2001; Richter and Westphal, 2010). *Tractable planning* has been devoted to the identification of planning fragments that, due to syntactic or structural restrictions, can be solved in polynomial time; fragments that include, for example, problems with single atom preconditions and goals, among others (Bylander, 1994; Bäckström, 1996). *Factored planning* has appealed instead to mappings of planning problems into Constraint Satisfaction Problems, and the notion of *width* over CSPs (Amir and Engelhardt, 2003; Brafman and Domshlak, 2006). The width of a CSP measures the number of variables that have to be collapsed in order to ensure that the graph underlying the CSP becomes a tree (Freuder, 1982; Dechter, 2003). The complexity of a CSP is exponential in the problem width. A notion of width for classical planning using a form of Hamming distance was introduced in (Chen and Giménez, 2007), where the distance is set to the number of problem variables whose value needs to be changed in order to increase the number of achieved goals.

A related thread of research has aimed at understanding the performance of modern heuristic search planners by analyzing the characteristics of the optimal delete-relaxation heuristic h^+ that planners approximate for guiding the search for plans (Hoffmann, 2005, 2011). For instance, the lack of local minima for h^+ implies that the search for plans (and hence the global minimum of h^+) can be achieved by local search, and this local search is tractable when the distance to the states that decrement h^+ is bounded by a constant. This type of analysis has shed light on the characteristics of existing domains where heuristic search planning is easy, although it does not address explicitly the conditions under which the heuristic h^+ can be computed efficiently, nor whether or not it is the use of this heuristic that makes these domains easy to solve.

Since the notion of width was introduced and used explicitly in graphical models to bound the complexity of a CSP problem, much work has been done to define a useful width-like notion of a range of problems related to automated planning. A recent successful approach to solving conformant planning problems, is to translate them into classical planning problems. The translation depends on a parameter i that determines its size. When i is bigger or equal to the *conformant-width* of the problem, it can be shown that the translation is sound and complete, i.e. it captures all and only the solutions of the original conformant problem. Moreover, the complexity of the complete translation is exponential in the *conformant width* of the problem (Palacios and Geffner, 2007), which for most of the problems is bounded by a constant of 1. Roughly, the conformant width of a problem is the number of variables relevant to a precondition or a goal in the initial state whose values are not known, and need to be tracked in the classical problem in order to get a valid solution.

Analogously, a successful approach to solving contingent problems (problems with uncertainty and sensing), consists of a translation to non-deterministic but fully observable planning problems, which under certain conditions it is sound and complete. The complexity of the translation is exponential in the *contingent width* of the problem (Albore et al., 2009), which for most problems is also bounded by a constant of 1. The intuition behind contingent width is the same as that behind conformant width, capturing the complexity of keeping track of

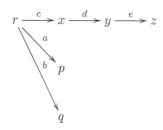

Figure 10.1: Tuple Graph $\mathcal{G}^1$ of problem Π where $I = \{r\}$, goal $G = \{z\}$, and actions $a : r \to p, \neg r$, $b : r \to q, \neg r$, $c : r \to x$, $d : x \to p, q, y$, and $e : p, q \to z$. Labels on top of the rrows are the actions that extend the optimal plans of the tuples.

the uncertainty in the translations, but here extended to capture the availability of sensing, and the information that can be inferred from it.

Tracking the unknown values of fluents is called *belief tracking*. While a bound on the complexity of belief tracking on *deterministic* conformant and contingent planning exists, it is also possible to bound the belief tracking of *non-deterministic* conformant and contingent planning problems. The complexity bound is similar to the one obtained for the deterministic versions, but defined over multivalued variables instead of propositional variables (Bonet and Geffner, 2012).

Recall that the notion of width, introduced in Chapter 6, is defined over graphs $\mathcal{G}^m$ whose vertices are tuples of at most m atoms. This suggests a relation between the width of a problem and the family of admissible h^m heuristics, which are also defined over tuples of at most m atoms (Haslum and Geffner, 2000). A conjecture that we considered is that a width of $w(\Pi) = m$ implies that h^m is equal to the optimal heuristic h^*. The conjecture however is false.

The counterexample is due to Blai Bonet. Consider a problem $\Pi = \langle F, I, O, G \rangle$ where:

- $I = \{r\}$

- $F = \{r, p, q, x, y, z\}$

- $G = \{z\}$

- $O = \langle$

    - $a : r \to p, \neg r$
    - $b : r \to q, \neg r$
    - $c : r \to x$
    - $d : x \to p, q, y$
    - $e : p, q \to z$

  $\rangle$

It can be shown that the problem Π has width $w(\Pi) = 1$, as tuple graph $\mathcal{G}^1$ in Figure 10.1 contains the tuple z that optimally implies goal G. Tuple z is in $\mathcal{G}^1$ as all optimal plans for y can be extended with a single action, i.e. action e, into optimal plans for z. It is important to notice that y is a surrogate of (p, q), as no action in problem Π has y in its preconditions. Notice that if fluent y is removed[1] from problem Π then $w(\Pi) = 2$. There is no other tuple with arity 1 such that all of its optimal plans can be extended with a single action into optimal plans for z, thus $z \notin \mathcal{G}^1$ and there would not be any other tuple $t \in \mathcal{G}^1$ that optimally implies goal G. Tuple z would make it into $\mathcal{G}^2$ through tuple (p, q).

Yet, $h^*(\Pi) = 3$ with optimal plan $\pi = \langle c, d, e \rangle$, while the heuristic h^m for $m = 1$, is h_{max}, which for this problem is 2. Thus, $w(\Pi) = m$ and yet $h^*(\Pi) \neq h^m(\Pi)$.

It turns out that for this correspondence to be true, an additional clause is needed in the definition of the heuristic h^m; namely, for tuples t of any size, $h^m(t)$ should not be lower than $h^m(t')$ when t' is a tuple of at most m atoms that optimally implies t. Yet, checking this implication in general is as hard as optimal planning, and thus intractable.

10.3   Future Work

In this section we describe some future research directions for extending the work developed in this thesis.

10.3.1   Causal Chains

In Chapter 3 we introduced the notion of *causal chains* (paths), sequences of causal links from a given state that start with an applicable action and finish in the goal. By enforcing their semantics we show that some of these chains are not possible in any valid plan. The *consistent* causal chains are those chains that can be mapped into a valid plan from a given state, although determining whether or not there is a consistent chain from a state is NP-complete. As a result, we have restricted our attention to the set of *minimal* causal chains only. Determining whether or not there is a *consistent minimal* chain is in the worst case intractable too, but generally it can be computed sufficiently fast. We then exploit consistent minimal chains: pruning applicable actions, decomposing the problem into subproblems, and introducing a path-based heuristic that takes deletes into account. Most of the benchmark domains that are solved easily by these techniques, correspond to serializable problems with non or few dead-ends. In order to tackle non-serializable problems, such as 15-puzzle, we need to consider chains that are not minimal, that is, where the actions in the chains are not restricted to being the best supporters in a given chain. The challenging aspect is how to get outside of the minimal chains without having to consider the whole set of possible chains in a state.

Also, we want to study *learning* in the context of path-based planning, in the sense that is used in SAT and CSP: where the causes of failures are identified and used to prune the rest of the search. The pruning and decomposition schemes

---

[1] The optimal plan for the original problem does not change, as no action requires y.

with consistent chains use a backtracking algorithm, which in the case of arriving to a state where there are no possible ways to continue the search, backtracks to its immediate predecessor, and continues the search systematically. Ideally, the search should not backtrack to its immediate predecessor, rather it should backtrack non-chronologically up to the culprit state that introduced the conflict that caused the backtrack. This technique is known as back-jumping. In order to back-jump, we have to recognize first which state caused the failure, and then abstract the reasons of the failure. In addition, this information can be added to the search in order to avoid making the same mistakes, and potentially pruning large portions of the search space. This requires first characterizing which information to learn, how to bound the amount of information gained, and then how to take advantage from it (Dechter, 1990; Marques-silva and Sakallah, 1999). We think that the focus on causal chains, as opposed to action or state sequences, may allow for the use of similar techniques.

Another approach to planning, that differs from heuristic search, is to build a hierarchy of abstracted search spaces. Hierarchical planners solve first one level of the abstraction, and then refine the solution in the successive and more detailed levels of the hierarchy (Sacerdoti, 1974). These planners have been used successfully in many industry applications, although typically they are domain-dependent solvers, where the hierarchy is designed by hand. Some attempts have been made to automatically build such abstractions, assuming that successive refinements do not change the structure of previous abstract solutions. That is, once a solution is found by one abstract level, subsequent levels will not need to change, but rather refine previous solutions (Knoblock, 1994). Similarly, C3 finds an abstract solution (a causal chain), and then refines it until the causal chain becomes a plan. Thus, we want to use paths to get a better understanding of hierarchical planning and the conditions under which it pays off.

Finally, the path-based heuristic used for state-based planning may subsume the notion of consistency, provided that inconsistent paths result in infinite heuristic values. The open question remains: how can we improve the path-based heuristic where the minimality requirement on causal chains in the computation of the path heuristic is dropped? This is likely to result in an additional overhead, but may serve in difficult serializable domains like Sokoban, where the restriction to minimal paths renders many problems unsolvable.

10.3.2 Probes

From the success of probes and their computation, in which problems are mapped into a *series of subgoals* that are heuristically computed along with the probes, two conclusions can be drawn. The first is that most of the classical benchmarks admit good serializations of the landmarks, under which the solution of the problems becomes simple. The second is that while not every serialization is good, the mechanisms in a probe and in particular the consistency tests, appear to find good ones.[1]

---

[1] Landmarks are used in a subgoaling scheme in Hoffmann et al. (2004), but the results do not appear to be as good. One possible explanation for this, is that no additional inference is made to distinguish good serializations from bad ones.

These observations raise two questions that we would like to address in the future. The first is: which methods are good for finding good serializations *when they exist?*. PROBE implements one such method, but it is not necessarily the best such method, and moreover, probes are greedy and incomplete. The second question is: which methods are good for finding and exploiting serializations in problems that have *good but no perfect decompositions?*. The 8-puzzle is an example of this situation: one can place the tile 1 in position 1, the tile 2 in position 2, but then one needs to undo this last subgoal, in order to have tiles 2 and 3 at their target positions.

When a probe fails, its nodes are placed in a GBFS that chooses the next best node to launch the next probe. In some ways, GBFS works as a quick method to repair failures. A more principled behavior would be to recognize the cause of failure of the probe, and launch the next probe from the culprit state. Further research needs to be done to characterize the reasons for a probe to fail.

10.3.3 Width

In Part III of this thesis, we introduced a width parameter for planning that bounds the complexity of a planning domain, based on its goal structure. The width is defined over a graph G^i encoding the optimal reachability relations between fluent tuples, whose size is at most i (Definition 6.1). The width $w(\phi)$ of a formula ϕ over the fluents of a problem Π, is the min i for which G^i contains a tuple that optimally implies ϕ. Recall that we say that a tuple optimally implies the formula ϕ if all optimal plans for the tuple, are also optimal plans for ϕ. Note that the size of the tuple is w, but the size of the formula ϕ is not bounded by w. We also mentioned in Section 10.2 that there is a correspondence between the definition of the h^m heuristic and the optimal heuristic h^*, given that an additional clause is added to its definition: if the width $w(\Pi)$ of a problem Π is m, then $h^m = h^*$. The extra clause has to ensure that if a tuple t' of size m optimally implies a tuple t of an arbitrary size, then $h^m(t') = h^m(t)$. Yet, checking this implication is NP-hard, as we have to compute every optimal plan for every tuple of size m. However, certain types of implications may be tractable, and they could be used to boost h^m, while keeping it admissible and polynomial. We then want to address the question: under which circumstances $h^w = h^*$? Is there any syntactical restriction under which the above question holds?

The complexity of the algorithm $IW(1)$ is $O(|F|)$, which is the number of fluents of the problem, as it generates at most $|F|$ states. This complexity is similar to the complexity of delete-based relaxation heuristics. Therefore, we want to investigate whether or not $IW(1)$ can be used to boost heuristic estimators, as the states in $IW(1)$ are not states of the relaxed problem, but are real reachable states. One way of doing so, is to add the extra clause mentioned before for h^m, where the implications are the ones resulting from $IW(1)$.

We have also shown that most of the standard benchmark domains have low width provided that their goals are atomic fluents, and that joint goals are easy to serialize. If we want to generate hard problems, we have to generate non-serializable problems with high atomic fluent width, where the top-level goals are non recursively decomposable. For example, in order to generate a fluent p

with high width, we can add a dummy fluent *Goal*, added by a single *End* action whose preconditions are the original goals G of the problem. The width of the new *Goal* atom will be the width of the conjunctive goal formula G of the problem. In that case, the top-level fluent *Goal* is decomposable, and if the fluents in G are decomposable and easy to serialize, the problem does not become harder. This leads as to the question: how can we generate non-decomposable problems whose fluents have width w? We hope that by understanding how such problems can be generated, we can gain a deeper understanding of the structures that lead to high or low width.

On the other hand, given a problem Π whose width is $w(\Pi)$, can we lower the width of the problem so that algorithms such as $IW(i)$ can solve them with smaller i values? Recall that $IW(i)$ complexity is $O(|F|^i)$. In the counterexample which proves that $h^m \neq h^*$ when $w(\Pi) = m$, presented in Section 10.2, the width of the problem is 1 instead of 2, due to the introduction of the fluent y that acts as a surrogate of a tuple of size 2. We would like to recognize how to introduce tuples that are surrogates of other tuples, which as a consequence, lower the width of the problem.

The size of the state space reachable with $IW(i)$ is $|F|^i$. We have investigated the extraction of *macro operators* from the state space reachable by $IW(i)$, to be used along normal operators. The use of these macros typically would act as a lookahead defined over the state space induced by $IW(i)$. The open question is: how can we define the subset of macro operators to be considered in the branching of the original search space?

Similarly, we have looked into different branching schemes for searching in the space of possible goal serializations. *SIW* greedily commits to a single serialization while solving the subproblems, but is not necessarily the best, especially in the presence of dead-ends, where *SIW* gets trapped.

We also have looked at how to integrate *accumulated costs* in the best-first search that include the novelty term in the evaluation function. Rather than using the term $g(n)$ that counts *all* of the actions done on the way to n from the root node as in A*, we tried to use a local cost term $g_L(n)$ that reflects just the cost of the 'last subproblem' induced by the landmark heuristic (Section 9.2). For this, we count in $g_L(n)$ the number of nodes n' (and hence actions) in the path to n from the root, such that $usg(n) = usg(n')$. That is, nodes are regarded as part of the same 'subproblem' when they have the same number of unachieved subgoals (landmarks), and it is the cost of actions done in the same subproblem that is added up. Indeed, this improves the quality of solutions returned by $BFS(f)$ without degrading the coverage, but we believe that a better characterization of the local accumulated cost is needed.

The width is defined over classical problems, but we are interested in defining a similar width notion over probabilistic or non-deterministic problems. Still, the novelty definition in non-classical problems should be defined differently. The open question remains: can we extend this notion to these models and exploit it in this context?

Intuitively, the notion of novelty can be seen as a method to diversify the search in a systematic way. This can be extremely useful when the goal is not well-defined, and as we show in Table 7.2, *IW* performs much better than other blind search algorithms.

From a different perspective, assume that we are given a plan for a problem Π. It is possible, with $IW(i)$, to build a plan 'skeleton' by dropping actions and assuring that the cost of 'filling the gaps' is a low polynomial. Namely, that each action a_i from the plan skeleton assures that the preconditions of a_{i+1} can be reached with $IW(i)$ with a low i value. The questions that need to be addressed are: (1.) how can we minimize skeleton size, while assuring that filling the missing actions can be solved by $IW(1)$? (2.) What relationships would the plan skeletons have with hierarchical abstractions and decomposition? And (3.) can we learn possible serializations of the problem through the plan skeletons? Note that the actions of the plan skeletons can be completely different from causal links, and may capture possible serializations of non-serializable problems such as the 15-puzzle. Each of these questions pose challenges that we look forward to addressing.

Bibliography

Alexandre Albore, Héctor Palacios, and Héctor Geffner. A translation-based approach to contingent planning. In *Proceedings of the Twenty-First International Joint Conference on Artificial Intelligence (IJCAI 2009)*, pages 1623–1628, 2009. 146

Eyal Amir and Barbara Engelhardt. Factored planning. In *Proceedings of the Eighteenth International Joint Conference on Artificial Intelligence (IJCAI 2003)*, pages 929–935. Morgan Kaufmann, 2003. 146

Fahiem Bacchus. AIPS'00 planning competition. *AI Magazine*, 22(3):47–56, 2001. 5

Christer Bäckström. *Five years of tractable planning*, pages 19–33. IOS Press, 1996. 146

Christer Bäckström and Bernhard Nebel. Complexity results for SAS+ planning. *Computational Intelligence*, 11(4):625–655, 1995. 5

Avrim Blum and Merrick Furst. Fast planning through planning graph analysis. In *Proceedings of the Fourteenth International Joint Conference on Artificial Intelligence (IJCAI 1995)*, pages 1636–1642. Morgan Kaufmann, 1995. 3, 13, 14, 25, 106

Blai Bonet and Hector Geffner. Planning as heuristic search: New results. In *Proceedings Fifth European Conference on Planning (ECP-99)*, pages 359–371, 1999. 8, 16, 17

Blai Bonet and Hector Geffner. Planning as heuristic search. *Artificial Intelligence*, 129:5–33, 2001. 3, 8, 11, 15, 17, 66, 123, 124, 129, 133

Blai Bonet and Héctor Geffner. Width and complexity of belief tracking in non-deterministic conformant and contingent planning. In *Proceedings of the Twenty-Sixth National Conference on Artificial Intelligence (AAAI 2012)*, pages 1756–1762. AAAI Press, 2012. 147

Blai Bonet, Gabor Loerincs, and Hector Geffner. A robust and fast action selection mechanism for planning. In *Proceedings of the Fourteenth National Conference on Artificial Intelligence (AAAI 1997)*, pages 714–719, 1997. ix

Ronen I. Brafman and Carmel Domshlak. Factored planning: How, when, and when not. In *Proceedings of the Twenty-First National Conference on Artificial Intelligence (AAAI 2006)*, pages 809–814, 2006. 146

Daniel Bryce and Oliver Buffet. International planning competition uncertainty part: Benchmarks and results. At http://ippc-2008.loria.fr/wiki/images/0/03/Results.pdf, 2008. 67

Tom Bylander. The computational complexity of STRIPS planning. *Artificial Intelligence*, 69:165–204, 1994. ix, 6, 11, 105, 145, 146

Hubie Chen and Omer Giménez. Act local, think global: Width notions for tractable planning. In *Proceedings of the Seventeenth International Conference on Automated Planning and Scheduling (ICAPS 2007)*. AAAI Press, 2007. 146

Thomas H. Cormen, Charles E. Leiserson, Ronald L. Rivest, and Clifford Stein. *Introduction to Algorithms*. The MIT Press, 2001. 6

Rina Dechter. Enhancement schemes for constraint processing: Backjumping, learning, and cutset decomposition. *Artificial Intelligence*, 41(3):273–312, 1990. 149

Rina Dechter. *Constraint Processing*. Morgan Kaufmann, 2003. 146

Rina Dechter and Judea Pearl. Generalized best-first search strategies and the optimality of A*. *Journal of the ACM*, 32(3):505–536, 1985. 10

Stefan Edelkamp. Planning with pattern databases. In Amedeo Cesta and Daniel Borrajo, editors, *Pre-proceedings of the Sixth European Conference on Planning (ECP 2001)*, 2001. 11

Jörg Hoffmann Emil Keyder and Patrik Haslum. Semi-relaxed plan heuristics. In *Proceedings of the Twenty-Second International Conference on Automated Planning and Scheduling (ICAPS 2012)*, pages 128–136, 2012. 62, 67

Richard Fikes and Nils Nilsson. STRIPS: A new approach to the application of theorem proving to problem solving. *Artificial Intelligence*, 1:27–120, 1971. 5

Maria Fox and Derek Long. The third international planning competition: Results and analysis. *Journal of Artificial Intelligence Research*, 20:1–59, 2003. 5

Eugene C. Freuder. A sufficient condition for backtrack-free search. *Journal of ACM*, 29:24–32, 1982. 146

Michael R. Garey and David S. Johnson. *Computers and Intractability; A Guide to the Theory of NP-Completeness*. W. H. Freeman & Co., 1990. 33

Cenk Gazen and Craig Knoblock. Combining the expressiveness of UCPOP with the efficiency of Graphplan. In *Proceedings of the Fourth European Conference on Planning (ECP 1997)*, pages 221–233, 1997. 42

Alfonso E. Gerevini, Patrik Haslum, Derek Long, Alessandro Saetti, and Yannis Dimopoulos. Deterministic planning in the fifth international planning competition: PDDL3 and experimental evaluation of the planners. *Artificial Intelligence*, 173(5–6):619–668, 2009. 5

Peter E. Hart, Nils Nilsson, and Bertram Raphael. A formal basis for the heuristic determination of minimum cost paths. *IEEE Trans. Syst. Sci. Cybern.*, 4:100–107, 1968. 9

William D. Harvey and Matthew L. Ginsberg. Limited discrepancy search. In *Proceedings of the Fourteenth International Joint Conference on Artificial Intelligence (IJCAI 1995)*, 1995. 145

Patrik Haslum and Héctor Geffner. Admissible heuristics for optimal planning. In *Proceedings of the Fifth International Conference on Artificial Intelligence Planning and Scheduling (AIPS 2000)*, pages 140–149, 2000. 14, 25, 62, 67, 147

Patrik Haslum, Blai Bonet, and Héctor Geffner. New admissible heuristics for optimal planning. In *Proceedings of the Twentieth National Conference on Artificial Intelligence (AAAI 2005)*, 2005. 11

Patrik Haslum, Adi Botea, Malte Helmert, and Blai Bonet. Domain-independent construction of pattern database heuristics for cost-optimal planning. In *Proceedings of the Twenty-Second AAAI Conference on Artificial Intelligence (AAAI 2007)*, 2007. 11

Malte Helmert. A planning heuristic based on causal graph analysis. In *Proceedings of the Fourteenth International Conference on Automated Planning and Scheduling (ICAPS 2004)*, pages 161–170, 2004. 11, 62, 106

Malte Helmert. The Fast Downward planning system. *Journal of Artificial Intelligence Research*, 26:191–246, 2006. 8, 15, 16, 65, 129, 134

Malte Helmert and Carmel Domshlak. Landmarks, critical paths and abstractions: What's the difference anyway? In *Proceedings of the Nineteenth International Conference on Automated Planning and Scheduling (ICAPS 2009)*, 2009. 14, 132

Malte Helmert and Héctor Geffner. Unifying the causal graph and additive heuristics. In *Proceedings of the Eighteenth International Conference on Automated Planning and Scheduling (ICAPS 2008)*, pages 140–147. AAAI Press, 2008. 11, 62, 106

Malte Helmert, Patrik Haslum, and Jörg Hoffmann. Flexible abstraction heuristics for optimal sequential planning. In *Proceedings of the Seventeenth International Conference on Automated Planning and Scheduling (ICAPS 2007)*. AAAI Press, 2007. 11

Malte Helmert, Minh B. Do, and Ioannis Refanidis. Sixth international planning competition. http://ipc.informatik.uni-freiburg.de, 2008. 5

Jörg Hoffmann. The Metric-FF planning system: Translating "ignoring delete lists" to numeric state variables. *Journal of Artificial Intelligence Research*, 20: 291–341, 2003. 40, 55, 91, 98, 124, 135

Jörg Hoffmann. Where 'ignoring delete lists' works: Local search topology in planning benchmarks. *Journal of Artificial Intelligence Research*, 24:685–758, 2005. 146

Jörg Hoffmann. Analyzing search topology without running any search: On the connection between causal graphs and h^+. *Journal of Artificial Intelligence Research*, 41:155–229, 2011. 146

Jörg Hoffmann and Stefan Edelkamp. The fourth international planning competition. *Journal of Artificial Intelligence Research*, 24:519–579, 2005. 5

Jörg Hoffmann and Bernhard Nebel. The FF planning system: Fast plan generation through heuristic search. *Journal of Artificial Intelligence Research*, 14: 253–302, 2001. ix, x, 8, 10, 12, 13, 15, 17, 24, 65, 66, 105, 124, 129, 133, 134, 135, 146

Jörg Hoffmann, Julie Porteous, and Laura Sebastia. Ordered landmarks in planning. *Journal of Artificial Intelligence Research*, 22(1):215–278, 2004. 14, 58, 66, 77, 78, 93, 121, 129, 132, 145, 149

Erez Karpas and Carmel Domshlak. Cost-optimal planning with landmarks. In *Proceedings of the Twenty-First International Joint Conference on Artificial Intelligence (IJCAI 2009)*, pages 1728–1733, 2009. 14

Erez Karpas and Carmel Domshlak. Optimal search with inadmissible heuristics. In *Proceedings of the Twenty-Second International Conference on Automated Planning and Scheduling (ICAPS 2012)*, 2012. 145

Michael Katz and Carmel Domshlak. Structural patterns heuristics via fork decomposition. In *Proceedings of the Eighteenth International Conference on Automated Planning and Scheduling (ICAPS 2008)*. AAAI Press, 2008. 11, 106

Henry Kautz and Bart Selman. Pushing the envelope: Planning, propositional logic, and stochastic search. In *Proceedings of the Thirteenth National Conference on Artificial Intelligence (AAAI 1996)*, pages 1194–1201. AAAI Press, 1996. 3

Emil Keyder. *New Heuristics For Classical Planning With Action Costs*. PhD thesis, Universitat Pompeu Fabra, 2010. 13, 40, 98

Emil Keyder and Héctor Geffner. Heuristics for planning with action costs revisited. In *Proceedings of the 18th European Conference on Artificial Intelligence (ECAI 2008)*, pages 588–592, 2008. 40, 50, 73, 77

Emil Keyder, Silvia Richter, and Malte Helmert. Sound and complete landmarks for and/or graphs. In *Proceedings of the Nineteenth European Conference on Artificial Intelligence (ECAI 2010)*, pages 335–340, 2010. 14, 77, 132, 133

Craig A. Knoblock. Automatically generating abstractions for planning. *Artificial Intelligence*, 68(2):243–302, 1994. 41, 149

Jana Koehler and Jörg Hoffmann. On reasonable and forced goal orderings and their use in an agenda-driven planning algorithm. *Journal of Artificial Intelligence Research*, 12(1):339–386, 2000. 46, 145

Richard E. Korf. *Learning to solve problems by searching for macro-operators.* Pitman Publishing, Inc., 1985. 145

Richard E. Korf. Planning as search: A quantitative approach. *Artificial Intelligence*, 33(1):65–88, 1987. 96, 145

Pat Langley. Systematic and non-systematic search strategies. In *Proceedings of the First International Conference on Artificial Intelligence Planning Systems (AIPS 1992)*, pages 145–152. AAAI Press, 1992. 145

Nir Lipovetzky and Héctor Geffner. Path-based heuristic (preliminary version). In *ICAPS 2009 Workshop on Heuristics for Domain-Independent Planning*, 2009a. 144

Nir Lipovetzky and Héctor Geffner. Inference and decomposition in planning using causal consistent chains. In *Proceedings of the Nineteenth International Conference on Automated Planning and Scheduling (ICAPS 2009)*, pages 217–224, 2009b. 143, 144

Nir Lipovetzky and Héctor Geffner. Searching with probes: The classical planner probe. In *Proceedings International Planning Competition (IPC-7)*, 2011a. 144

Nir Lipovetzky and Héctor Geffner. Searching for plans with carefully designed probes. In *Proceedings of the Twenty-First International Conference on Automated Planning and Scheduling (ICAPS 2011)*, pages 154–161, 2011b. 122, 130, 132, 135, 144

Nir Lipovetzky and Héctor Geffner. Width and serialization of classical planning problems. In *Proceedings of the Twentieth European Conference on Artificial Intelligence (ECAI 2012)*, pages 540–545, 2012. 144

Nir Lipovetzky, Miquel Ramirez, and Héctor Geffner. C3: Planning with consistent causal chains. In *Proceedings International Planning Competition (IPC-6)*, 2008. 40, 144

JoaÃd'o P. Marques-silva and Karem A. Sakallah. Grasp: A search algorithm for propositional satisfiability. *IEEE Transactions on Computers*, 48:506–521, 1999. 149

David McAllester and David Rosenblitt. Systematic nonlinear planning. In *Proceedings of the Ninth National Conference on Artificial Intelligence (AAAI 1991)*, pages 634–639, Anaheim, CA, 1991. AAAI Press. x, 18, 25, 31, 57, 67, 70, 72, 144

Drew McDermott. A heuristic estimator for means-ends analysis in planning. In *Proceedings of the Third International Conference on Artificial Intelligence Planning Systems (AIPS-96)*, 1996. ix, 66

Drew McDermott. Using regression-match graphs to control search in planning. *Artificial Intelligence*, 109:111–159, 1999. 129

Drew McDermott. The 1998 AI planning systems competition. *AI Magazine*, 21: 35–55, 2000. 5

Drew McDermott, Malik Ghallab, Adele Howe, Craig Knoblock, Ashwin Ram, Manuela Veloso, Daniel Weld, and David Wilkins. PDDL – the planning domain definition language. Technical Report CVC TR-98-003. http://ftp.cs.yale.edu/pub/mcdermott, 1998. 5

Hootan Nakhost and Martin Müller. Monte-Carlo exploration for deterministic planning. In *Proceedings of the Twenty-First International Joint Conference on Artificial Intelligence (IJCAI 2009)*, 2009. 145

Dana S. Nau. SHOP2: An HTN planning system. *Artificial Intelligence*, 20:379–404, 2003. 41

Bernhard Nebel, Yannis Dimopoulos, and Jana Koehler. Ignoring irrelevant facts and operators in plan generation. In *Proceedings of the Fourth European Conference on Planning (ECP 1997)*, pages 338–350, 1997. 26, 44

Allen Newell and Herbert A. Simon. GPS: a program that simulates human thought. In E. Feigenbaum and J. Feldman, editors, *Computers and Thought*, pages 279–293. McGraw Hill, 1963. 96, 145

Xuan Long Nguyen and Subbarao Kambhampati. Reviving partial order planning. In Bernhard Nebel, editor, *Proceedings of the 17th International Joint Conference on Artificial Intelligence (IJCAI 2001)*. Morgan Kaufmann, 2001. 25, 57

Angel Olaya, Sergio Jimenez, and Carlos Linares. Seventh international planning competition. http://www.plg.inf.uc3m.es/ipc2011-deterministic, 2011. 5

Hector Palacios and Héctor Geffner. From conformant into classical planning: Efficient translations that may be complete too. In *Proceedings of the Seventeenth International Conference on Automated Planning and Scheduling (ICAPS-2007)*, pages 264–271, 2007. 146

Judea Pearl. *Heuristics*. Addison Wesley, 1983. 9, 11

J. Scott Penberthy and Daniel S. Weld. UCPOP: A sound, complete, partiall order planner for adl. In *Proceedings of the 3rd International Conference on Principles of Knowledge Representation and Reasoning (KR'92)*, pages 103–114, 1992. 144

Ira Pohl. Heuristic search viewed as path finding in a graph. *Artificial Intelligence*, 1(3):193–204, 1970. 10

J. Porteous and S. Cresswell. Extending landmarks analysis to reason about resources and repetition. In *Proceedings of the Planning and Scheduling Special Interest Group (PLANSIG-02)*, 2002. 89

Julie Porteous, Laura Sebastia, and Jörg Hoffmann. On the extraction, ordering, and usage of landmarks in planning. In Amedeo Cesta and Daniel Borrajo, editors, *Pre-proceedings of the Sixth European Conference on Planning (ECP 2001)*, pages 37–48, 2001. 14, 133

Silvia Richter and Malte Helmert. Preferred operators and deferred evaluation in satisficing planning. In *Proceedings of the Nineteenth International Conference on Automated Planning and Scheduling (ICAPS 2009)*, 2009. 17, 135

Silvia Richter and Matthias Westphal. The LAMA planner: Guiding cost-based anytime planning with landmarks. *Journal of Artificial Intelligence Research*, 39:122–177, 2010. ix, 8, 18, 65, 71, 105, 121, 124, 129, 130, 132, 133, 146

Silvia Richter, Malte Helmert, and Matthias Westphal. Landmarks revisited. In *Proceedings of the Twenty-Third AAAI Conference on Artificial Intelligence (AAAI 2008)*, pages 975–982, 2008. 14, 24, 66, 129, 135

Silvia Richter, Jordan Tyler Thayer, and Wheeler Ruml. The joy of forgetting: Faster anytime search via restarting. In *Proceedings of the Twentieth International Conference on Automated Planning and Scheduling (ICAPS 2010)*, 2010. 10

Earl D. Sacerdoti. Planning in a hierarchy of abstraction spaces. *Artificial intelligence*, 5(2):115–135, 1974. 149

John K. Slaney and Sylvie Thiébaux. Blocks world revisited. *Journal of Artificial Intelligence*, 125(1-2):119–153, 2001. 6

Austin Tate. Generating project networks. In Raj Reddy, editor, *Proceedings of the Fifth International Joint Conference on Artificial Intelligence (IJCAI 1977)*, pages 888–893. William Kaufmann, 1977. x, 18, 24, 25, 31, 67, 70, 72

V. Vidal and Héctor Geffner. Solving simple planning problems with more inference and no search. In *Proc. CP-05*, 2005. 24, 25, 26, 144, 145

Vincent Vidal. A lookahead strategy for heuristic search planning. In *Proceedings of the Fourteenth International Conference on Automated Planning and Scheduling (ICAPS 2004)*, pages 150–159, 2004. 145

Vincent Vidal and Héctor Geffner. Branching and pruning: An optimal temporal POCL planner based on constraint programming. *Artificial Intelligence*, 170(3): 298–335, 2006. 25, 57

Daniel S. Weld. An introduction to least commitment planning. *AI Magazine*, 15 (4):27–61, 1994. 25

Hakan L. S. Younes and Reid G. Simmons. VHPOP: Versatile heuristic partial order planner. *Journal of Artificial Intelligence Research*, 20:405–430, 2003. 57

Lin Zhu and Robert Givan. Landmark extraction via planning graph propagation. In *ICAPS 2003 Doctoral Consortium*, pages 156–160, 2003. 133

Index

www.ingramcontent.com/pod-product-compliance
Lightning Source LLC
Chambersburg PA
CBHW080415060326
40689CB00019B/4254

9 781312 466210